Human and Environmental Security

An Agenda for Change

Edited by
Felix Dodds
and
Tim Pippard

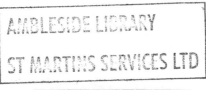

EARTHSCAN

London • Sterling, VA

First published by Earthscan in the UK and USA in 2005

Copyright © Stakeholder Forum for Our Common Future

ISBN: 1-84407-214-2 paperback
　　　 1-84407-213-4 hardback

Typesetting by JS Typesetting Ltd, Porthcawl, Mid Glamorgan
Printed and bound in the UK by Cromwell Press, Trowbridge
The cover for this book was designed and produced by John Mould, an artist, graphic
designer and writer

Cover photograph: Nelson Syozi

For a full list of publications please contact:

Earthscan
8–12 Camden High Street
London, NW1 0JH, UK
Tel: +44 (0)20 7387 8558
Fax: +44 (0)20 7387 8998
Email: earthinfo@earthscan.co.uk
Web: **www.earthscan.co.uk**

22883 Quicksilver Drive, Sterling, VA 20166-2012, USA

Earthscan is an imprint of James and James (Science Publishers) Ltd and publishes
in association with the International Institute for Environment and Development

A catalogue record for this book is available from the British Library

Library of Congress Cataloging-in-Publication Data
Human and environmental security: an agenda for change / edited by Felix Dodds
and Tim Pippard.
　　　 p. cm.
　　Includes bibliographical references and index.
　　ISBN 1-84407-214-2 — ISBN 1-84407-213-4
　 1. Security, International. I. Dodds, Felix. II. Pippard, Tim.
　　JZ5588.H848 2005
　　327.1'72—dc22

　　　　　　　　　　　　　　　　　　　　　　　　　　　　　　2005014879

Printed on elemental chlorine-free paper

Contents

List of Figures and Boxes

Figures

Boxes

List of Contributors

Celso Amorim is the Brazilian Minister of Foreign Relations, a post he has held since 2003. This is the second time he has occupied the position, having first served in the office from 1993–1994. He has worked as a diplomat for nearly 40 years, and among other posts abroad he was Brazil's permanent representative to the United Nations (UN) and the World Trade Organization (WTO) in Geneva from 1999 to 2001 and Brazil's permanent representative to the UN in New York from 1995 to 1999, as well as occupying positions in the Organization of American States (OAS) in Washington, DC from 1973 to 1974. He taught political science and international relations at the University of Brasília (UnB) from 1977 to 1979. After graduating from the Itamaraty's Rio Branco Institute (IRBr), he completed a master's degree in international relations at the Diplomatic Academy of Vienna in 1967, and has a doctorate in political science from the London School of Economics. Amorim was born in Santos (SP) in 1942, is married and has four children.

Hilary Benn has been the UK Secretary of State for International Development since October 2003. He joined the Department for International Development (DFID) in 2001 as Parliamentary Under-Secretary of State, moved to the Home Office as Parliamentary Under-Secretary of State for Community and Custodial Provision in May 2002, before returning to DFID as Minister of State in March 2003. He was elected as Member of Parliament for Leeds Central in June 1999 and was a member of the Environment, Transport and the Regions Select Committee and Vice-Chair of the Backbench Education Committee of Labour MPs. In 1997 he was appointed as special adviser to the Rt Hon David Blunkett, then Secretary of State for Education and Employment. In 1993, he was appointed as Head of Research at Manufacturing, Science, Finance, and was promoted to Head of Policy and Communications in 1996. He was elected to Ealing Borough Council in 1979, where he served as Deputy Leader of the Labour Group from 1985–1994, and as Deputy Leader of the Council and Chair of Education from 1986–1990. He was educated at Holland Park Comprehensive School, London and the University of Sussex. He is married with three sons and one daughter.

Henrique B. Cavalcanti was born in Rio de Janeiro, studied at the Naval Academy, graduated in civil engineering from McGill University in Montreal,

Canada, and holds a diploma in Nuclear Science and Engineering from Pennsylvania State University and the ISNSE at Argonne National Laboratory, Illinois, US. He lectured at the Catholic University and the Federal School of Engineering, was field engineer and managing director of electric power utilities in Southern Brazil, a director of ECOTEC Consultants, chairman and CEO of the Brazilian Steel Corporation (SIDERBRÁS) and managing director of the International Environmental Bureau in Geneva, Switzerland. Later he became senior adviser for the Global Environment Facility (GEF), Chairman of the UN Commission on Sustainable Development (CSD), Brazilian Commissioner to the World Exhibition on Oceans in Lisbon, and President of the Intergovernmental Forum on Chemical Safety (IFCS). An adviser to the Brazilian Ministry of Environment, he is now president of Fundação Pró Natureza, FUNATURA, a board member of IBAM (the Brazilian Municipal Management Institute) and member of the Pan American Academy of Engineering, having formerly served as trustee of the LASPAU Program at Harvard University, the Iwokrama Project in Guyana and the Marine Stewardship Council in London, UK, and as member of the Brazilian Independent Commission on Oceans, and the Commission on Sustainable Consumption at Oxford University. A former Deputy Minister of Mines and Energy and Deputy Minister of Interior, from 1967 to 1975, Henrique Cavalcanti was Federal Minister of Environment and the Amazon in 1994.

Felix Dodds is executive director of Stakeholder Forum for a Sustainable Future, a position he has held since 1993. From 1997 to 2001 he was co-chair of the NGO Coalition working at the United Nations Commission on Sustainable Development. He has facilitated NGO global lobbying for the UN Habitat Conference (1996), UN Rio+5 (1997) and a number of UN Commissions on Sustainable Development meetings. He has been a member of the Commission on Globalization and the International Advisory Boards for Global Forum 1994, Bonn Freshwater Conference (2001) and the Hilltops to Oceans Conference (2004). He was one of the co-developers of the multistakeholder dialogues at the UN Commission on Sustainable Development. His other books are *Into the Twenty First Century – An Agenda for Political Realignment* (editor, 1986, Greenprint), *The Way Forward Beyond Agenda 21* (editor, 1997, Earthscan), *Earth Summit 2002 A New Deal* (edited with Toby Middleton, 2000 and 2002, Earthscan), *How to Lobby at Intergovernmental Meetings: Mine is a Café Latte* (with Michael Strauss, 2004, Earthscan). He lives in San Sebastian in Spain.

Christine K. Durbak, PhD, a psychoanalyst in private practice and stress management consultant to corporations, formed the non-profit organization World Information Transfer (WIT), Inc, in 1987, which she currently chairs. She has served as president of the National Association for the Advancement of Psychoanalysis (NAAP), vice-chair of the NGO Executive Committee, chair of the NGO Health Communication Committee and is currently chair and CEO of Physicians Weekly, LLC. Durbak received her PhD from Fordham University and her BA from New York University.

Anna-Karin Eneström is minister for political affairs at the Permanent Mission of Sweden to the United Nations in New York. Prior to her move to New York she was head of the humanitarian division at the Ministry for Foreign Affairs in Stockholm. Anna Karin Eneström has previously been posted to Nairobi and Strasbourg. She has a master of law from Uppsala University.

Jason Franks recently completed his PhD in the School of International Relations at the University of St Andrews. His study *Rethinking the Roots of Terrorism* (Palgrave, forthcoming 2005) seeks to examine how the roots of terrorism can be understood. It involves a critique of the orthodox understanding of terrorism and suggests a re-thinking of the causes via multi-level and multi-dimensional approaches.

Jim Garrison is president of the State of the World Forum, a San Francisco-based non-profit institution dedicated to discerning and implementing those principles, values, and actions necessary to guide humanity towards a more sustainable global civilization. Prior to founding the Forum in 1992, at the behest of Mikhail Gorbachev, Garrison founded and became president of the Gorbachev Foundation/US. In 1991, he founded the International Foreign Policy Association in collaboration with Georgian President Edward Shevardnadze and former US Secretary of State George Schultz. From 1986 to 1990, Garrison served as executive director of the Esalen Institute Soviet American exchange programme, which engaged in private sector diplomacy with Russian counterparts. He is the author of *The Plutonium Culture* (SCM); *The Darkness of God:Theology After Hiroshima* (SCM, 1982); *The Russian Threat: Myths and Realities* (Gateway Books, 1983); *The New Diplomats* (Resurgence Press, 1984); *Civilisation and the Transformation of Power* (Paraview Press, 2000), and *America as Empire: Global Leader or Rogue Power?* (Berrett-Koehler Publishers, 2004). He holds a PhD in Philosophical Theology from Cambridge University, and a BA magna cum laude in World History from Santa Clara University.

Hannah Griffiths is Corporates Campaigner at Friends of the Earth (FOE), where she has been working since 1999 on issues related to corporate globalization. Prior to this, she worked at the British Council on education, employment and women's projects. She is a director of The Ilisu Dam Campaign – a coalition of environmental and human rights groups that successfully opposed British involvement in the controversial Ilisu Dam in the Kurdish region of Turkey – and coordinated FOE's input into the campaign. More recently, she has been working to improve the quality and quantity of activism on corporate globalization. She coordinated FOE's input into the European Social Forum held in London in late 2004 and is involved in the World Social Forum. She is a founding member of The Refugee Project, a coalition of NGOs and community groups looking at how corporate globalization contributes to forced migration. She coordinates FOE's campaign on Shell, with a focus on environmental justice. She graduated from Imperial College London in 1998 with an

MSc in Global Environmental Change and Policy. Hannah Griffiths would like to thank the following people from Friends of the Earth for their help with Chapter 17: Craig Bennett, Helen Burley, Eve Mitchell and Blathin Wong.

Devyani Gupta has worked on sustainable development, humanitarian aid, refugees and migration with a number of organizations including the European Commission, the United Nations High Commissioner for Refugees (UNHCR), Stakeholder Forum for a Sustainable Future and the International Institute for Environment and Development. She is fluent in Hindi and holds an MA (University of Chicago) in International Relations. Currently she is working on health and social care delivery for vulnerable adults in England at the UK Department of Health.

David Hannay served for 35 years as a member of the British Diplomatic Service. After postings in Tehran, Kabul, Brussels and Washington, he was the UK Permanent Representative to the European Union (1985–1990) and then UK Permanent Representative to the United Nations (1990–1995). Following his retirement from the Diplomatic Service, he served as the British government's Special Representative for Cyprus (1996–2003); and in 2003–2004 as a member of the UN Secretary-General's High Level Panel on Threats, Challenges and Change. He has been an independent member of the House of Lords since 2001, and is a member of its European Union Select Committee. He is pro-chancellor of the University of Birmingham. He was educated at Winchester College and New College, Oxford.

Noeleen Heyzer is Executive Director of the United Nations Development Fund for Women (UNIFEM), the leading operational agency within the UN to promote women's empowerment and gender equality. Since joining UNIFEM, Dr Heyzer has worked on strengthening women's economic security and rights; promoting women's leadership in conflict resolution, peacebuilding and reconstruction; ending violence against women; and combating HIV/AIDS from a gender perspective. Before joining UNIFEM, Dr Heyzer was a policy adviser to several Asian governments on gender issues, playing a key role in the formulation of national development policies, strategies and programmes from a gender perspective. Heyzer has been a founding member of numerous regional and international women's networks and has published extensively on gender and development issues. Born in Singapore, she received a BA and MA from the University of Singapore and a doctorate in social sciences from Cambridge University in the UK. She has received several awards for leadership, including the Dag Hammarksjöld medal in 2004 and the National Council for Research on Women (NCRW) 'Women Who Make a Difference' Award in 2005.

Marian Hobbs is New Zealand Minister for the Environment, for Urban Affairs, for Disarmament and Arms Control, and for the National Library and Archives. As Associate Minister of Foreign Affairs she is also responsible for

Official Development Assistance. She became Minister Responsible for the Law Commission and Associate Minister of Justice in December 2004. Before entering Parliament in 1996, she had a lengthy involvement in education and social service. She has operated at every level of education, was a member of Canterbury University Council from 1994–1996 and was Principal of Avonside Girls' High School, Christchurch, from 1989–1996. She has also worked for the National Council of Churches' aid agency, Christian World Service, and chaired Presbyterian Support Services for the Canterbury region. She is a familiar commentator on public issues on New Zealand's two radio networks. She is a passionate cricket fan, sailor and supporter of the New Zealand arts community with a particular love for choral music. She has two children.

Sabin Intxaurraga is the Basque Minister for Land Use Planning and the Environment, a position he has held since September 2001. Since that time he has also been serving as the president of the Urdaibai Biosphere Reserve Board of Trustees and the president of the public environmental enterprise IHOBE, South Africa. He has previously held the positions of Basque Minister for Education, Universities and Research from July to September 2001 and Basque Minister for Justice, Employment and Social Security from July 1998 to June 2001. He was also Mayor of Zeanuri on two occasions from 1979–1983 and again from 1987–1995. He holds two master's degrees, in marketing from EHU-UPV (Basque Public University), and in leisure management from the University of Deusto. Born in December 1949, Intxaurraga is married with three children.

Melinda Kimble is senior vice president at the UN Foundation in Washington DC, overseeing programme areas concerning health, population, the environment and peace/human rights. Prior to joining the Foundation in May 2000, she served as a State Department Foreign Service Officer, attaining the rank of Minister-Counselor. She served in policy-level positions in the Bureau of Economic and Business Affairs, overseeing multilateral development issues and debt policy; in the Bureau of Oceans, International Environment and Scientific Affairs (OES), leading environmental negotiations (e.g. Climate Change Conference, Kyoto, Japan, 1997). Her assignments abroad include Côte d'Ivoire, Egypt and Tunisia. She speaks French and Arabic and holds two masters degrees: Economics (University of Denver) and MPA (Harvard's Kennedy School of Government).

Serge Lepeltier served as the French Minister of Environment and Sustainable Development from April 2004 until June 2005. He began his career in industry, as the general manager of Cave des Vignerons de Rasteau, a wine producing company, from 1980 to1986, and then as general manager of the Groupe Sablières du Berry, a sand and gravel producing company, from 1986–1990. Since 1989, Lepeltier has held several political offices, including the Mayor of Bourges (1995–2004) and Chairman of the local municipalities' community of Bourges (from 2002). He has also held a number of posts in political parties and foundations, most notably Vice Secretary-General of Union pour un Mouvement Populaire (UMP) from 2002–2004, and Vice President of the Club Nouvelle Republique since 2003. He is the author of numerous reports and books, his most recent being *France and French people in Front of the Heat Wave: Lessons of a Crisis* (2004). Lepeltier was born in October 1953, and graduated in commercial studies at HEC, a leading French high-level commercial studies school.

Anders Lidén is Sweden's permanent representative to the United Nations in New York. He has previously been posted at the UN, as special assistant to Ambassador Jan Eliasson, in his assignment as UN-mediator in the Iran-Iraq conflict 1988–1991, and most recently as deputy representative of Sweden on the Security Council from 1997–1998. Ambassador Lidén has been director general for political affairs at the Swedish Ministry for Foreign Affairs, and has served as a diplomat in Lebanon, Jordan and Israel. He holds a PhD in political science from the University of Lund, Sweden.

Jeffrey A. McNeely was appointed International Union for the Conservation of Nature and Natural Resources (IUCN) Chief Scientist in 1996. He has been at IUCN since 1980, when he was appointed Executive Officer of the Commission on National Parks and Protected Areas. He served as Director of the Programme Division from 1983 to 1987, when he became Deputy Director General (Conservation). He was named Chief Conservation Officer in 1988, a position which was converted to Chief Biodiversity Officer in 1992. He has published over 300 technical and popular articles on a wide range of conservation issues, seeking to link conservation of natural resources to the maintenance of cultural diversity and to economically sustainable ways of life. He serves on the editorial advisory board of seven biodiversity-related journals.

Tim Pippard is Content Editor for *Jane's Sentinel Security Assessments* at Jane's Information Group in London. Prior to joining Jane's in November 2004, he was research associate at the United Nations Association-UK, where he focused on peacekeeping operations, UN reform, post-conflict justice and the future of transitional administrations. He has also served as Human and Environmental Security Coordinator for Stakeholder Forum for a Sustainable Future and as an editorial consultant to the convenor of the Middle East Policy Initiative Forum. He holds an MA in International Peace and Security from King's College, University of London and a BA (Hons) in Comparative American Studies from the University of Warwick.

Jan Pronk is Special Representative of the UN Secretary-General for the Sudan, an appointment made effective on 18 June 2004. Pronk has led a distinguished career, both as a prominent European politician and as a senior United Nations official. Prior to his current appointment, Pronk served as the Secretary-General's Special Envoy for the World Summit on Sustainable Development

held in Johannesburg in 2002, and was formerly Deputy Secretary-General of
the United Nations Conference on Trade and Development (UNCTAD) from
1980 to 1985, and Assistant Secretary-General of the United Nations from
1985 to 1986. Pronk has played a prominent role in promoting sustainable
economic and environmental development, serving three times as Minister for
Development Cooperation in the Government of the Netherlands and, more
recently, as Minister of the Environment. He was President of the United
Nations Conference of Parties of the Convention on Climate Change (CoP 6)
held in The Hague in November 2000 and Bonn in July 2001. In November
2002 he became the Chair of the International Institute for Environment and
Development (IIED) and, in December 2003, he became Chair of the Geneva-
based Water Supply and Sanitation Collaborative Council (WSSCC). He has
also been Treasurer of the Brandt Commission. He is currently Professor in
Theory and Practice of International Development at the Institute of Social
Studies, The Hague. Pronk was born on 16 March 1940, is married and has a
son and a daughter.

Oliver Richmond is a reader in the School of International Relations, University of St. Andrews, UK. He has written on various aspects of peace and
conflict theory, on ethnic conflict, sovereignty, and on various post-Cold War
peacebuilding processes. His most recent study was The Transformation of
Peace (Palgrave, forthcoming 2005), which examined the evolution of the concept of the liberal peace as it has been theorised in peace and conflict theory,
and practised in international interventions and peacebuilding since the end
of the Cold War.

Claudia M. Strauss, Ed. D., Professor of Education, is Director of World
Information Transfer's UN Programme, managing editor of the *World Ecology
Report* (WIT), has written on the history of women's education and is trained
in psychoanalytic psychotherapy. She has served as co-chair of the NGO
Committee on Sustainable Development, vice-chair of the Committee on the
Status of Women, Board member of UNA-USA's Council of Organizations
and served as a member of the US Delegation to the UN Commission on
Sustainable Development. Claudia Strauss received her Ed. D. from Columbia
University and her BA from George Washington University.

Anna Tibaijuka joined UN Habitat as Executive Director in September
2000, currently making her the highest ranking African woman in the UN
system. During her first two years in office, she oversaw major reforms
that led the UN General Assembly to upgrade the UN Centre for Human
Settlements to a fully fledged UN programme, now called UN-Habitat – the
UN Human Settlements Programme. Her appointment as executive director
was confirmed at the Under-Secretary-General level, and she was elected by
the General Assembly to her first four-year term in July 2002. Prior to joining
UN Habitat, Tibaijuka was the special coordinator for Least Developed
Countries (LDCs), Landlocked and Small Island Developing Countries at

the UN Conference on Trade and Development (UNCTAD) responsible for strengthening the capacity of LDCs in trade negotiations with the World Trade Organization. From 1993 to 1998, when she joined UNCTAD, she was associate professor of economics at the University of Dar-es-Salaam. During this period she was also a member of the Tanzanian Government delegation to several United Nations Summits including the United Nations Conference on Human Settlements (Istanbul, 1996); the World Food Summit (Rome 1996); the Fourth World Conference on Women (Beijing, 1995) and the World Summit for Social Development (Copenhagen, 1995). Tibaijuka has also been a Board Member of UNESCO's International Scientific Advisory Board since November 1997. A Tanzanian national, she holds a doctorate of science in Agricultural Economics from the Swedish University of Agricultural Sciences in Uppsala, and was awarded an honorary doctorate of science degree in 2003 for her work by the University College London. She speaks English, Swahili, Haya, Swedish and some French, and has published five books and many articles.

Klaus Toepfer is executive director of the United Nations Environment Programme (UNEP) and director-general of the United Nations Office at Nairobi (UNON). He was also appointed acting executive director of the United Nations Centre for Human Settlements (formerly UNCHS/Habitat, now UN Habitat) from July 1998 to August 2000. Before joining the UN, Toepfer held several posts in the Federal Government of Germany. He was federal minister of Regional Planning, Building and Urban Development as well as coordinator of the Transfer of Parliament and Federal Government to Berlin from 1994 to 1998. He held office as federal minister of the Environment, Nature Conservation and Nuclear Safety from 1987–1994. Prior to becoming a member of the German Federal Cabinet he was State Minister of Environment and Health of the Federal State of Rhineland-Palatinate (1985–1987) and State Secretary at the Ministry of Social Affairs, Health and Environment for the same state (1978–1985). Before his political career as a member of the Christian Democratic Union (CDU) began, Toepfer was full professor at the University of Hannover where he directed the Institute of Regional Research and Development (1978–1979). He was head of the Department of Planning and Information in the State Chancellery of the Federal State of Saarland (1971–1978) and head of the Economics Department of the Central Institute for Regional Planning of the University of Münster (1970–1971). He holds a doctorate in Philosophy and a degree in Economics.

Patricia Wouters, director of the International Water Law Research Institute, University of Dundee, Scotland (BA, LLB, University of Ottawa, Canada; LLM, Berkeley, California; DES, PhD, Graduate Institute of International Studies/University of Geneva, Switzerland, guest research fellow, Max-Planck Institute for Public International and Comparative Law, Heidelberg, Germany), teaches international and national water law and policy. She researches in these areas of law and has lectured and worked around the world, providing

legal advice to the public and private sector (including projects for the World
Bank, UNECE, UNEP, UNESCO, GTZ, DFID, SIDA) on issues related to
water resources management. Dr Wouters is series editor of the Kluwer Book
Series, 'International and National Water Law' and the International Water
Association Book Series, 'Water Law and Policy'.

Foreword

Klaus Toepfer

The award of the 2004 Nobel Prize for Peace to the Kenyan environmental activist Wangari Maathai was the clearest sign yet of the increasing acceptance by the international community that environmental security and human security are inextricably linked. That process has been evolving for some time, marked by milestones such as the 1972 United Nations Conference on the Human Environment, which gave birth to the United Nations Environment Programme (UNEP), the 1992 Earth Summit, the Millennium Summit and the 2002 World Summit on Sustainable Development (WSSD).

These conferences have helped to raise the profile of the environment on the international development agenda, as well as in the minds of the public. They have also given rise to a growing body of important environmental agreements and commitments. Nevertheless, as the environment ministers of France, Germany and Spain pointed out in a forceful communiqué in May 2005, despite all these efforts we are driving the planet towards an ecological catastrophe. It would appear that we do not yet give environmental considerations the weight they deserve. The price will be paid by generations to come.

I therefore welcome the publication of *Human and Environmental Security: An Agenda for Change* in time for the 2005 World Summit being held at United Nations (UN) headquarters in New York in September. At this Summit, governments will debate essential reforms to the UN and review progress towards the achievement of the Millennium Development Goals (MDGs). These eight time-bound and realizable objectives are a set of minimum targets for human development. Achieving them is essential if we are to fulfil the pledges made 60 years ago by the founding members of the UN to save succeeding generations from the scourge of war, and promote social progress and better standards of life in larger freedom.

This phrase, 'in larger freedom', which appears in both the UN Charter and the Universal Declaration of Human Rights, has become especially prominent this year because of 'In Larger Freedom: Towards development, security and human rights for all', the Secretary-General's report for the 2005 World Summit. In his report, Kofi Annan notes that 'humanity will not enjoy security without development, it will not enjoy development without security, and it will not enjoy either without respect for human rights'. He also explicitly links success in achieving these objectives with the sustainable use of the Earth's environmental resources: 'All our efforts to defeat poverty and pursue sustainable development will be in vain if environmental degradation and natural resource depletion continue unabated.'

In March 2005, the Millennium Ecosystem Assessment (MEA) revealed that 60 per cent of the world's ecosystems are in decline or even degraded to an extent that we can no longer rely on their services. These services include climate regulation, clean air and water, fertile land and productive fisheries. They are the services that help to keep disease and pests in check and that provide valuable new medicines and protect communities from natural disasters. The statistics are frightening: a third of all amphibians, over a fifth of mammals and a quarter of the world's coniferous trees are threatened with extinction; global fish stocks are down by 90 per cent since the dawn of industrialized fishing.

It is tempting to say that these services are invaluable, for indeed they are. For example, forests not only provide fuelwood, medicinal plants and food to as many as 1.6 billion people, their destruction releases up to 20 per cent of the greenhouse gases that contribute to global warming. They also harbour countless species of plants and animals, many that we have not yet even catalogued, let alone studied for their potential benefit to humankind. Nevertheless, forests around the world are being felled at a rate of more than 250km² a day – more than 90,000km² a year, an area approximately the size of Portugal or Jordan.

Nonetheless, it is also possible to give a very real economic value to the ecosystem services that we so blithely destroy. By some estimates, the Earth's atmosphere, wildlife, soils, water bodies and other natural resources are worth US$33 trillion. For instance, the water purification, flood protection and other services provided by an intact wetland are worth as much as US$6000 a hectare. Once cleared for intensive agriculture, that same wetland is worth just a third of this. Once might imagine, then, that we would prize our wetlands, forests and other resources, and actively conserve them as economically important natural capital. Sadly not: over the past century, around half the world's wetlands have been lost and drained. This outmoded thinking has to go. If wetlands, forests, rivers and the air we breathe were held in the same esteem as our cultural heritage or valued as much as factories, shops or prime real estate, it would be considered gross vandalism to damage them in the way we do.

The economic impact of environmental degradation is also plain to see in the rising annual costs of weather-related disasters. According to Munich Re, one of the world's largest re-insurance companies, 2004 was once again a record-breaking year, with insured losses totalling US$44 billion, mainly due to hurricanes, cyclones and typhoons. And these insured losses are only the tip of the iceberg. When disasters strike, it is invariably the uninsured poor who suffer most, through loss of life and hard-won livelihoods. They have the highest vulnerability to disasters and the least coping capacity. Years of endeavour can be wiped away in a minute. This point was graphically and tragically made in December 2004 when the Indian Ocean tsunami killed more than a quarter of a million people and devastated the lives of countless more. In this case, the world mobilized in an unprecedented show of solidarity to help the victims. Unfortunately, the same cannot be said for the many other silent tsunamis round the globe, many of which are environment related.

Among the lessons coming out of the tragedy of the Indian Ocean tsunami is that, in many instances, a little more environmental care and awareness could have mitigated the effects of the disaster. It is a lesson we see repeatedly, even if we do not seem to learn from it. It is a sad fact of today's world that environment-related tragedies have become all too predictable. Time and again we see ordinary natural phenomena, such as heavy rains or prolonged dry spells, triggering extraordinary and sometimes catastrophic events. Across the globe billions of people are living on the brink of disaster. Global population growth, combined with the effects of climate change, mean that the number of vulnerable people will continue to increase unless governments and the international community truly commit to learning from these events.

Environmental neglect, coupled with poverty, can turn natural hazards into disasters. It is also the anchor that keeps poor people mired in poverty, creating a vicious circle from which, for too many people, there is little hope of escape. This is particularly evident in Africa, the continent that is most obviously lagging behind in terms of achieving the MDGs. The decline of ecosystem services, the threat of climate change and the burden of HIV/AIDS threaten to condemn millions of Africans to continued poverty for generations to come. Thankfully world leaders have woken up to the fact that this is not just a problem for Africa, but for the world, agreeing, for instance, to cancel the debts of the world's most highly indebted countries and generally boost levels of aid.

As the Secretary-General's High Level Panel on Threats, Challenges and Change noted in December 2004, 'today's threats to human security recognize no national boundaries, are connected, and must be addressed at the global and regional as well as the national levels'. I am pleased that the editors of *Human and Environmental Security: An Agenda for Change* asked Lord David Hannay, the UK's representative to the High Level Panel, to contribute the opening chapter, in which he highlights some of the underlying themes that the panel considered.

The panel identified six clusters of threats to human security, included among them the economic and social threats posed by poverty, infectious disease and environmental degradation. Between them they are responsible for millions of preventable deaths each year, presenting a formidable obstacle to sustainable development and threatening global security. It is no coincidence that 90 per cent of current conflicts are found in the poorest 30 per cent of countries. Nor is it a coincidence that the poorest countries have the greatest environmental challenges. Poverty destroys the environment. Environmental degradation breeds poverty. It is also clear that, as global resources come under increasing pressure from soaring production and consumption, and as environmental conditions continue to deteriorate, we will have to be increasingly alert for the warning signs of potential conflict. It is plain to me that protecting and sustainably managing the environment is the peace policy of the future.

What I find increasingly heartening is that this analysis is no longer simply the province of environmental professionals. Colin Powell, until recently the United States Secretary of State, has called sustainable development a 'security imperative'. Poverty, environmental degradation and the despair they breed are 'destroyers of people, of societies, of nations'. They provide the ingredients for the destabilization of countries, even entire regions.

I am also encouraged to see that environmental protection is also being increasingly linked with sound economics. At a recent meeting with G8 ministers, UK Chancellor Gordon Brown – significantly not an environment minister but a finance minister – said: 'If our economies are to flourish, if poverty is to be banished, and if the well-being of the world's people enhanced, not just in this generation but in succeeding generations, we must make sure we take care of the natural environment and resources on which our economic activity depends'.

These are the kinds of voices we need to hear more and more. Our political, economic and physical security all depends to a great extent on how we manage our environment. In today's complex world, everything is interconnected. The contents of this book reflect that complexity. By bringing the elements of peace and security, sustainable development and global governance under one cover, and by emphasizing the centrality of environmental issues to all aspects of human interaction and development, *Human and Environmental Security: An Agenda for Change* provides a considerable contribution to what, I believe, is the great debate of the 21st century.

The 2005 World Summit represents a once in a generation opportunity. As the world's governments prepare to review 60 years of the UN and our progress during this millennium to eradicate poverty and achieve sustainable development, I believe it is truly time for an agenda for change. Business as usual is not an option. We need to capitalize on our pledges and progress, represented by the Millennium Declaration, the Kyoto Protocol and the Monterrey Conference on Financing for Development, and ensure that we maintain and increase the momentum for creating a world in which the wishes of the founders of the UN are truly fulfilled.

Editorial Note and Acknowledgements

Our vision for this publication was always a clear, albeit demanding one: to draw together those elements of security under discussion by the UN Secretary-General's High Level Panel on Threats, Challenges and Change in a way that articulated the links between them and offered solutions as to how best tackle them. Embarking on this project in mid-2004, it should come as no surprise that we encountered the same causes of insecurity that dominated the panel's discussions: the use of force by states; intervention in humanitarian crises; nuclear proliferation; terrorism and non-state actors; global governance and sovereignty; and poverty, development and the environment. All of these factors threw up numerous, challenging questions, to which there are no easy answers, but to which we hope this book attempts to respond.

From our perspective, the broad notion of human security provided the most effective benchmark from which to approach these complex issues. As stated in the Final Report of the Commission on Human Security of May 2003, 'human security complements state security, enhances human rights and strengthens human development. It seeks to protect people against a broad range of threats to individuals and communities and, further, to empower them to act on their own behalf. And it seeks to forge a global alliance to strengthen the institutional policies that link individuals and the state – and the state with a global world.'

That the Secretary-General's own blueprint for change, 'In Larger Freedom: Towards development, security and human rights for all', took as its framework the basic tenets of human security – 'freedom from want', 'freedom from fear' and 'freedom to live in dignity' – confirmed to us the value in adopting this human security approach to the security challenges of the 21st century.

The importance of environmental factors to us in conceptualizing this book should not be understated, however. We were acutely aware, as Klaus Toepfer stresses in the Foreword, that environmental security and human security are inextricably linked, and that such links have evolved steadily over the last three decades, crystallized most notably by the creation of the UN Environment Programme in 1972 to act as a catalyst, advocate, educator and facilitator in the promotion of the wise use and sustainable development of the global environment. We have reached the point where no discussion of current or emerging threats to security can seriously take place in the absence of a focus on human and environmental issues.

So the task we set our authors – that of advancing concrete solutions to today's security threats through the lens of human and environmental security – was by no means a simple one, and it is to their immense credit that they have so skilfully achieved exactly what Celso Amorim encourages in his introduction to this volume: the creation of a new paradigm of international cooperation that takes into account new global challenges and realities. In echoing the conclusions of the report of the High Level Panel, *A More Secure World: Our Shared Responsibility*, the chapters amply demonstrate that today's threat's recognize no national boundaries, are connected, and must be addressed at the global and regional as well as the national levels. Needless to say, as editors it has been a privilege to have worked with such a distinguished group of experts, without whom our vision of this book would not have become a reality.

But of course, putting together this book would not have been possible without the immense amount of behind-the-scenes and all too often unnoticed work done by the production staff, and we are extremely grateful to a range of people in this regard. Firstly, to everyone involved at Earthscan/James and James for their contributions – Rob West, Jonathan Sinclair Wilson and, not least, to Camille Adamson.

Our special thanks and gratitude must be extended to John Mould, the designer of the front cover. John succeeded – in a manner in which the rest of the book attempts to replicate – in capturing the essence of the book, demonstrating graphically the interconnectedness of threats facing today's world in a single, dramatic and eye-catching image.

For ensuring copyright arrangements were in place, our appreciation goes to Kate Piersanti and Kathy Slater at Berrett-Koehler publishers, to Elizabeth Guilaud-Cox at the UN Environment Programme, and to Marie-Louise Gambon and Annet Van Green at the Institute of Social Studies in The Hague.

Special mention must go to Jennifer Cooper and Karen Judd at the United Nations Development Fund for Women, and to Craig Davies at the UK Department for International Development, whose assistance over the past year has been invaluable. In addition, we are indebted to the help we received from Jennifer Macmillan in the office of Hon. Marian Hobbs and Ambassador David Taylor (the New Zealand Ambassador to Korea); from Cecilia Andersson, Jay Moor, Laura Patrella and Rolf Wichmann at UN Habitat; from Eva-Lena Gustafsson and Daniela Estay at the Swedish Mission to the UN; and from Caroline Maloney and Claudia Meulenberg at the UN Foundation. Our thanks also to Helen Burley, Eve Mitchell, Craig Bennett and Blathin Wong at Friends of the Earth, and David Simpson at UNEP, as well as Jeremie Averous, Elena Peresso, Paul Riederman, Everton Vargas, Elisa Peters, Maria Figueroa Kupcu, Derek Osborn and Margaret Brusasco MacKenzie, all of whom played an important role in ensuring the smooth compilation of this publication. Finally to Navid Hanif and Edward Mortimer for their inspiration and wisdom in helping conceive the idea of this book over coffee in the Vienna Café in the UN Basement in New York.

Felix Dodds and Tim Pippard
San Sebastian and London

List of Acronyms and Abbreviations

APEC	Asia Pacific Economic Cooperation group
ASEAN	Association of Southeast Asian Nations
AU	African Union
BNFL	British Nuclear Fuels
BWI	Bretton Woods Institutions
CBD	Convention on Biological Diversity
CBI	Confederation of British Industry
CDM	Clean Development Mechanism
CFS	Committee on Food Security
CIS	Commonwealth of Independent States
CNN	Cable News Network
CO_2	carbon dioxide
CORE	Corporate Responsibility Coalition
CSD	(UN) Commission for Social Development
CSD	(UN) Commission on Sustainable Development
CSI	Containerized Security Initiative
CSR	Corporate Social Responsibility
CWC	Chemical Weapons Convention
DDR	Disarmament, Dembolization and Reintegration
DDT	dichlorodiphenyltrichloroethane
DFID	Department for International Development
DJSI	Dow Jones Sustainability Index
DMZ	Demilitarized Zone
DPKO	(UN) Department of Peacekeeping Operations
DPRK	Democratic Peoples Republic of Korea
DRC	Democratic Republic of Congo
DTI	(UK) Department of Trade and Industry
ECA	Export Credit Agencies
ECOSOC	(UN) Economic and Social Council
ECPS	(UN) Executive Committee on Peace and Security
EIA	Environmental Impact Assessment
EITI	Extractive Industries Transparency Initiative
ELN	Ejército de Liberación Nacional (National Liberation Army, Colombia)
EPA	Environmental Protection Agency

EU	European Union
FAO	(UN) Food and Agricultural Organization
FARC	Fuerzas Armadas Revolucionarias de Colombia (Revolutionary Armed Forces of Colombia)
FDI	foreign direct investment
FOE	Friends of the Earth
FOEI	Friends of the Earth International
FTSE	Financial Times Stock Exchange
GA	(UN) General Assembly
GATT	General Agreement on Trade and Tariffs
GBV	gender-based violence
GCIM	Global Commission on International Migration
GDP	Gross Domestic Product
GEF	Global Environment Facility
GGE	Greenhouse Gas Emissions
GM	genetically modified
GNP	Gross National Product
GWP	Global Water Partnership
G8	group of eight leading industrialized countries
G77	group of developing countries (now over 140)
HDR	Human Development Report
HEU	highly enriched uranium
HIPC	heavily indebted poor countries
HLWG	High Level Working Group
IAEA	International Atomic Energy Agency
IALANA	International Association of Lawyers Against Nuclear Arms
ICBL	International Campaign to Ban Landmines
ICC	International Chamber of Commerce
ICC	International Criminal Court
ICJ	International Court of Justice
ICLEI	International Council for Local Environmental Initiatives
ICRC	International Committee of the Red Cross
IEG	International Environmental Governance
IFI	International Financial Institutions
ILC	International Law Commission
ILO	International Labour Organization
IMF	International Monetary Fund
IMO	International Maritime Organization
IMTF	Integrated Mission Task Force
IOM	International Organization for Migration
IPCC	Intergovernmental Panel on Climate Change
IPPNW	International Physicians for the Prevention of Nuclear War
IUCN	International Union for the Conservation of Nature and Natural Resources
JAM	Joint Assessment Mission
LAM	Legal Assessment Model

LDCs	Least-developed countries
MDA	Multilateral Nuclear Approaches
MDGs	Millennium Development Goals
MEA	Millennium Ecosystem Assessment
MEA	multilateral environmental agreement
MERCOSUR	Mercado Comun del Cono Sur (Southern Cone Common Market)
MINUSTAH	United Nations Stabilization Mission in Haiti
MNA	multilateral nuclear approaches
MONUC	United Nations Observer Mission in the Democratic Republic of the Congo
MSP	multi-stakeholder processes
NATO	North Atlantic Treaty Organization
NEG/ECP	New England Governors/Eastern Canadian Premiers
NEPA	National Environmental Policy Act
NGOs	Non-Governmental Organizations
NHPC	National Hydro Power Cooperation
NPT	Nuclear Non-Proliferation Treaty
nrg4SD	Network of Regional Governments for Sustainable Development
NWS	Nuclear Weapon States
OAS	Organization of American States
ODA	Overseas Development Assistance
OECD	Organisation for Economic Co-operation and Development
OSCE	Organization Security and Cooperation in Europe
PBDE	polybrominated diphenyl ether
PCB	polychlorinated biphenyls
PIC	Prior Informed Consent
POPs	Persistent Organic Pollutants
POTO	Prevention of Terrorism Ordinance
PPM	parts per million
PRS	poverty reduction strategy
PRSP	Poverty Reduction Strategy Papers
PSI	Proliferation Security Initiative
RFTF	results-focused transitional framework
RTA	Regional Trade Agreements
SAARC	South Asian Association for Regional Cooperation
SARS	Severe Acute Respiratory Syndrome
STAR	Secure Trade in the APEC Region
TNC	transnational company
UN	United Nations
UNAIDS	Joint United Nations Programme on HIV/AIDS
UNAMA	United Nations Assistance Mission in Afghanistan
UNCED	United Nations Conference on Environment and Development
UNCTAD	United Nations Conference on Trade and Development

UNDP	United Nations Development Programme
UNEO	United Nations Environment Organization
UNEP	United Nations Environment Programme
UNESCO	United Nations Educational, Scientific and Cultural Organization
UNFCCC	United Nations Framework Convention on Climate Change
UNFPA	United Nations Population Fund
UNHCR	United Nations High Commission for Refugees
UN Habitat	UN Human Settlements Organization
UNIFEM	UN Development Fund for Women
UNMIL	UN Mission in Liberia
UNMIS	UN Mission in Sudan
UNMOVIC	United Nations Monitoring, Verification and Inspection Commission
WEHAB	Water, Energy, Health, Agriculture and Biodiversity
WHO	World Health Organization
WIPO	World Intellectual Property Organization
WMD	Weapons of Mass Destruction
WRI	World Resources Institute
WSSD	World Summit on Social Development
WSSD	World Summit on Sustainable Development
WTO	World Trade Organization
WSSCC	Water Supply and Sanitation Collaborative Council

Introduction

Celso Amorim

The widespread acceptance of the need to promote sustainable development for human well-being reflects how far the international community has come in understanding the profound relationship between the environment and social and economic development. This process did not take place overnight, but rather evolved over time, particularly in the two decades that spanned the convening of the first United Nations Conference on the Human Environment, in Stockholm in 1972, and the United Nations Conference on the Environment and Development (UNCED), in Rio de Janeiro in 1992.

The Rio Conference advanced the concept of sustainable development to the forefront of the international agenda, through the principles enshrined in key documents such as the Rio Declaration and Agenda 21, as well as through the many environmental agreements it spawned. The recognition that states share common but differentiated responsibilities was to transform the nature of the North–South dialogue with regard to the environment. It did so by gradually supplanting simplistic or reductionist approaches to environmental challenges, such as deforestation, biodiversity loss, and climate change, with a broader perspective that encompasses the urgent need to address major problems such as poverty, hunger and social exclusion that afflict the developing world.

The Johannesburg Plan of Action adopted at the World Summit on Sustainable Development (WSSD) in 2002 built on the commitment of the international community to the goal of strengthening the objectives set out in Rio ten years before. The Millennium Summit in the year 2000 had already done the same by setting out the Millennium Development Goals (MDGs). Both signalled the importance of turning words into action, of fully realizing the larger vision those singular earlier moments in international affairs had embodied.

The objective of promoting the conservation and sustainable use of environmental resources for the betterment of mankind will only be achieved through international cooperation on a broad scale. In particular, commitments to make adequate financial resources available and promote the transfer of clean technologies to developing countries need to be fully implemented. An adequate framework for this purpose is already in place in the web of multi-lateral environmental agreements that have been negotiated over the past years. In addition, the United Nations Environment Programme (UNEP) plays an important role and should be strengthened.

Changes in the area of environmental governance are certainly needed, but should be sought by means of objective solutions, such as greater coordination between UNEP, the UN Commission on Sustainable Development (CSD) and the Global Environment Facility (GEF). Greater coherence is also neces-sary between the rules set out in multilateral environmental agreements and action by states or international institutions, particularly financial institutions. This will contribute to overcoming the implementation deficit with regard to multilateral environmental agreements and to enhancing the practice of the concept of sustainable development in its three pillars – the social, the eco-nomic and the environmental.

It was heartening, in this regard, to see issues related to sustainable de-velopment – climate change, to be specific – at the centre of the debate in the G8 Summit in 2005, alongside the discussion of international economic chal-lenges. This was even more important because the discussions involved large developing countries such as Brazil, China, India and South Africa, which have developed important know-how in environmental technologies. Take, for instance, the area of renewable energy, where Brazil has taken the lead in ethanol, biodiesel and flex-fuel engines. At the same time, however, these coun-tries often lack the financial means to promote the use of these technologies through South–South cooperation.

The G8 Gleneagles Summit is, therefore, an example of the partnership that needs to be re-established between the developed and the developing worlds to deal with pressing environmental issues. In this case, it can provide an effective platform for strengthening the climate change regime, particularly the United Nations Framework Convention on Climate Change (UNFCCC), which recognizes that the priority for developing countries must be the economic development of their populations.

The Second South Summit in Doha, in June 2005, also reaffirmed the importance for developing countries of promoting sustainable development and the sustainable use of environmental resources. The Doha Declaration stresses, in this regard, the need for finding innovative financing sources, and recognizes the importance of initiatives such as 'Action on Hunger and Poverty' convened by Brazilian President Luiz Inacio Lula da Silva, which is another example of an effective international partnership.

Reinforcing internal capacities in developing countries, so as to ensure better conditions for the implementation of local policies and measures, and improving the flow of information among different government bodies and levels of government involved in the solution to environmental problems, is key. It will not only lead to benefits in environmental, social and economic terms, contributing to create jobs, income and greater sustainability, but will also promote increased security and a safer, more stable global environment.

But even as we are engaged in this dynamic, multifaceted international process, with a view to the ultimate goal of sustainable development, we are reminded of the results of the Millennium Ecosystem Assessment (MEA) released in early 2005. They point to the degradation of our environment, to the increased risk this brings to human well-being and confront us once again with the need for urgent action.

This publication, *Human and Environmental Security: An Agenda for Change*, is therefore extremely timely. The contributions contained in this volume develop concepts, many of them contained in the Report of the UN Secretary General's High Level Panel on Threats, Challenges and Change, that need to be further discussed. These concepts will also be on the agenda at the World Summit meeting for the 60th Anniversary of the UN in September 2005, which will mark an important moment for reflection at the international level.

The moment is therefore ripe for a discussion of the relationship between environment and security. However, we must be careful to bear in mind that concepts such as human and environmental security raise issues that go well beyond incorporating into the governmental decision-making process considerations regarding conflicts that could arise from the use of environmental resources or from environmental degradation. These notions also beg the far more difficult question of whether environmental reasons can be invoked as a threat to international peace and security. They also have implications for the role of diplomacy.

These are certainly large and complex questions, for which there are no easy answers. The arrival of *Human and Environmental Security: An Agenda for Change* will provide an excellent contribution to the debate, by tackling, through well written and thoughtful essays, issues that range from climate change and biodiversity to food security, trade, migrations, nuclear non-proliferation and the future of global governance.

We have all been painfully reminded of the link between a healthy environment and human well-being by the Indian Ocean tsunami disaster in late 2004. But the underlying factors which aggravated its human and environmental costs were those of poverty and underdevelopment. Therefore, promoting development on a sustainable basis continues to constitute the only permanent and effective instrument for the establishment of peace, security and prosperity for individual countries and the international community as a whole.

As we look ahead we must not lose sight of this reality. Even as we refine our understanding of the questions related to human and environmental security, we should always bear in mind that, in the end, we must go back to the ultimate aim of promoting sustainable development on a global scale. In order to do this, we must create a new paradigm of international cooperation that takes into account the new global challenges and realities. This book will provide much needed food for thought on how best to achieve it.

Part 1
Peace and Security

'A More Secure World: Our Shared Responsibility' – Report of the UN Secretary-General's High Level Panel on Threats, Challenges and Change

David Hannay

Introduction

In November 2003, United Nations (UN) Secretary-General Kofi Annan appointed the High Level Panel on Threats, Challenges and Change (the Panel) to report to him on security threats facing the world in the 21st century and how to respond to them. The background to the commissioning of this report is well known. Throughout the Cold War, the UN remained at least partially paralysed. In most cases, notably any circumstances that involved confrontation between the superpowers, the UN had no prospect of playing a useful or effective role, less still of fulfilling its mandate of ridding the world of the scourge of war.

With the end of the Cold War, however, all that changed. For the UN a whole range of things, previously unthinkable or impossible, suddenly became politically possible: Iraq's invasion of Kuwait was reversed, with full UN authority; and a considerable number of regional and proxy wars were brought to an end through UN peacekeeping operations – in Namibia, Cambodia, El Salvador and Mozambique.

However, no systemic attempt was made to rethink the UN mission or consider what the main threats to international peace and security were in the post-Cold War era. Despite an attempt in 1992 to undertake a serious critique of the way ahead, with former Secretary-General Boutros Boutros Ghali's Agenda for Peace (UN, 1992), the UN's main stakeholders opted for muddling through. Soon this approach brought its own nemesis, and two main weaknesses emerged. One was the lack of execution and effectiveness. Even when the Security Council voted ambitious, if often ambiguous, mandates, it failed to muster the resources or the determination when the going got rough. The proportion of successes to failures dropped sharply, as appalling events such as the Rwandan genocide and the Srebrenica massacre occurred under the noses of UN peacekeepers. The other weakness arose from disputes over the use of force under UN authority: in recent years, the organization became paralysed in deadlock, first in 1999 over Kosovo, and then in 2003 over Iraq, even though Security Council resolutions were being flouted.

Surely then, Kofi Annan was right when he told the General Assembly in September 2003 that the UN had reached a fork in the road, that it could not simply go on as before, that it was time to take a hard look at the threats and challenges that now and prospectively face us, and to see if we could build a new consensus on an effective collective response to them (UN, 2003). That was the task the Secretary-General set the Panel.

The report itself, which we delivered to Kofi Annan in December 2004, is now squarely in the public domain, its 101 recommendations the subject of vibrant and wide-ranging discussion (UN, 2004). The first thought I would like to emphasize is that the Panel, composed as it was of 16 individuals drawn from every region of the world, submitted a report that represents the views of all of us. Of course there were differences of analysis and perspective amongst us – there still are, no doubt – but we were able to reach a broad measure of agreement on what needed to be done if the UN was to become more effective and more able to respond to the demands for peace and security that reach it from so many different quarters.

And we firmly agreed with the Secretary-General that it is the touchstones of effectiveness, efficiency and equity that need to be applied to every aspect of the reform agenda. It was that view that led us to ensure that our approach was a policy-driven one, and not one dominated by institutional tinkering; one that started from an examination of the policies needed to enable the UN to respond to the threats and challenges of the 21st century, and which then moved on to look at the changes in policies and institutions needed to deliver the objectives set out so eloquently in the UN Charter – and as valid today as they were in 1945.

I will not provide a synopsis of the report, which is the outcome of a year's hard work – six three-day sessions of the Panel itself, a large number of regional and other seminars and symposia designed to reach out to national politicians, academics, journalists, commentators on international relations, a mass of written submissions were sent in to us, and briefings from experts in the fields we were studying – firstly because the report has its own synopsis, and secondly, because I would urge that it be read in full and at leisure. It is densely argued and its recommendations are far-reaching – indeed I would venture to suggest that it is the single most far-reaching official review of the UN's role, particularly in the fields of peace and security, since the founding fathers met in San Francisco in 1945 and signed the UN Charter. It takes an overall approach to this enormously complex subject that needs to be looked at in the round, even if the individual recommendations need to be followed up on a number of different tracks. So I will focus on a number of the underlying themes that came to dominate our work and to shape our conclusions; and on some thoughts about the follow-up.

The threat agenda

We began, naturally, with the threats the world faces. Clearly, these have changed quite fundamentally since the end of that long Cold War period when the world lived on the brink of annihilation from a clash between two nuclear-armed superpowers and when many regional wars fought by the proxies of these two superpowers were simply off-limits to the UN. The Panel concluded relatively quickly that the threat agenda we faced was not a narrow one limited to international terrorism and to the proliferation of weapons of mass destruction, real though these threats certainly are; but a much wider one, including also the phenomenon of the failure of states often leading to major regional instability and conflicts, and a whole range of issues that have not traditionally been considered as part of the peace and security nexus at all – poverty, environmental degradation, pandemic diseases and the spread of organized crime, to mention the most prominent.

We reached this conclusion not simply because in many parts of the world – in Africa, in Latin America – these so-called 'soft' threats are often seen as even more menacing and imminent than the 'hard' threats of the narrower agenda, but also because we became increasingly aware of the interconnections and overlap between the different categories of threat that rendered the whole 'hard/soft' categorization misleading and inadequate. After all, the greatest terrorist outrage in recent times was launched from a failed state, Afghanistan, and the greatest genocide in another, Rwanda. Organized crime has frequently undermined international efforts at post-conflict peacebuilding. Pandemic diseases such as HIV/AIDS threaten the stability of many states, in Africa in particular. The correlation between poverty and insecurity leaps at you from the charts in the Panel's report. A third consideration was also prominent: every one of these threats required a collective response if it was to be effectively combated. So only a broad, common agenda provided any hope of mustering such a response.

When we came to examine responses to these threats and challenges we rapidly found ourselves at risk of being drawn into something of an ideological, almost a theological, battle – between those who believed in unilateral responses and those who believed in multilateral ones. I have to say that we found rather more true believers in these two opposing areas among commentators and polemicists than we did amongst practitioners in foreign ministries and defence and interior ministries around the world. The latter category contained few people who seriously thought that any single country, even the world's current single superpower, could on its own mount an adequate response to all the threats it faces; and few too were those in this category who believed that multilateral organizations possessed the philosopher's stone that could cope with them all.

So, while there are clearly genuine and difficult policy choices to be made between the two approaches, it became clear that the crude juxtaposition of them conceals more than it reveals – and that in many cases, the most effective response is a 'both/and' approach, not an 'either/or' one. For instance, in dealing with terrorism or the proliferation of weapons of mass destruction, it is fairly obvious that states, and their intelligence and law-enforcement capabilities, are essential to any effective action and cannot be replaced by multilateral institutions. But it is just as obvious that the normative capacity of international organizations and their scope for organizing cooperation on a wide-ranging basis are essential for dealing with a range of threats and challenges that do not respect national boundaries, and which have often seized on globalization as an ally in the pursuit of their objectives.

From this we concluded that a collective response was needed to every one of these challenges, but that dealing with each effectively would require a judicious blend between the national and the international when it came to action.

The use of force

No issue troubles the international community more (and has divided it twice recently when a decision point was reached – over Kosovo and Iraq) than the use of force, whether that be decided collectively at the UN or unilaterally. We have attempted to chart a way forward, navigating through a minefield of conflicting pressures. We concluded that Article 51 of the UN Charter, which recognizes the legitimacy of the unilateral use of force for self-defence and for pre-emptive action when a threat is genuinely imminent, should be neither expanded nor constrained. But we did not consider that that provision of the Charter extended to preventive coercive action where a threat was not imminent; and we suggested that such action, if it is to achieve legitimacy, needs to be decided collectively in the Security Council.

We set out certain guidelines for reaching such decisions on the use of force – seriousness of threat, proper purpose, last resort, proportional means, balance of consequences – and have proposed that the Security Council and individual states endorse these. They will provide no push-button certainty; decisions will still have to be taken on a case-by-case basis. But they may offer a greater degree of predictability, and, I would add, some deterrent effect, to decision making in this matter. The same may be said of our endorsement of the emerging international norm of the duty to protect individuals from harm or abuse, a duty that falls initially on the state in which they reside but ultimately, if that state is unwilling or unable too provide such protection, on the international community.

We have no illusions that our ideas in this respect will gain easy or instant acceptance. Nor do we harbour the fantasy that endorsement of them will bring certainty to the making of decisions in individual cases. Here, as elsewhere, no doubt, hard cases will continue to make bad law. But we do regard this part of our report as an important plank in the building of a new consensus.

Failing or failed states

The failure of states under stress is a phenomenon with which the world has become all too wearily familiar over the last 15 years. It has affected every continent: from the Solomon Islands in the South Pacific, through Afghanistan and Cambodia in Asia, to a whole raft of countries in Africa – Somalia, Rwanda, Burundi, Liberia, Sierra Leone, Côte d'Ivoire and the Congo, to mention the most prominent – to the former Yugoslavia in Europe and Haiti in the Americas. These failures have facilitated terrorism, made genocide possible, inflicted untold suffering and loss of life on the citizens of the states in question, and created regional instability and mayhem affecting many neighbouring countries. And yet the response of the international community has on the whole been hesitant, tardy and inadequate. One only has to look at Darfur to see that process in being.

We believe it is necessary for the Security Council to treat this phenomenon in future as a single continuum, running the whole way from early warning, which should trigger preventative action, through a whole range of non-military preventative measures, leading only to the use of force when alternative methods have failed and ending in durable and sustained post-conflict peacebuilding.

To assist it in carrying out these complex functions, we recommended the establishment, as a subsidiary organ of the Security Council, of a Peacebuilding Commission. Such a body will, we believe, only be able to work effectively if it reaches out beyond the restricted membership of the Security Council to involve also the International Financial Institutions (IFI) (the International Monetary Fund (IMF) and the World Bank) the UN Economic and Social Council (ECOSOC), the main donors and troop contributors, and relevant regional and subregional organizations.

International terrorism

The members of the Panel never doubted that they would have to address the issue of international terrorism. This was not just because the events of 11 September 2001 had transformed the way we all looked at threats to international peace and security, although the ripples from that appalling disaster are still spreading out across the murky pond of international politics. But 9/11 did change the dimensions of the threat: it revealed the extent to which the threat had become a global one, against which global responses would be needed.

As we analysed the phenomenon of international terrorism, we became aware that a purely coercive response – one based on intelligence and police work, and, in some cases, on military force by a coalition of a limited number of like-minded countries – was not on its own sufficient, essential though it was. It is extremely important to attack the causes as well as the symptoms of terrorism, and they were extremely complex. That led us to the conclusion that the use of military force in this field was likely to be an exception rather than the norm. The circumstances that had occurred in Afghanistan, when the Taliban had given a safe haven and full cooperation to Al-Qaeda, were unlikely to be replicated very often, if only because of the consequences that then befell that regime. It really was a travesty to think that we were faced with a stark choice between a unilateral and a multilateral approach. It made no sense at all to believe that international organizations could, on their own, conduct the fight against terrorism; but equally it made no sense to believe that the kind of global response required could be mustered without the involvement of international organizations, in particular the UN.

So we put forward proposals as to the basis on which that could be done. We recommended a global approach, one that outlaws the targeting of non-combatants wherever it occurs and whatever the plea of extenuating circumstances; that provides assistance to developing countries to build the panoply of prevention needed to ensure that terrorists cannot find safe havens for their money, their weapons or themselves; and one that develops a broad strategy for dealing not only with acts of terrorism, but also with the causes of it that enable terrorists to find support and shelter.

Weapons proliferation

We recognized that the various international regimes to prevent the proliferation of weapons of mass destruction – nuclear, chemical, biological and radiological – were under great strain. A world in which those regimes had further eroded or had even collapsed would be an infinitely more insecure one; and would be closer to the nightmare of such weapons falling into the hands of terrorists who might have no compunction about using them and would be open to no effective deterrent measures.

To avoid such developments, we recommended a range of urgent actions – to encourage acceptance of the International Atomic Energy Agency's (IAEA) Additional Protocol providing for snap inspections, to promote the Proliferation Security Initiative (PSI), to increase cooperation between the IAEA and the Chemical Weapons Convention (CWC) and the Security Council on the basis of regular reports, to resume negotiations on an intrusive regime of inspection for biological installations, to prepare for a biological incident or attack.

While we recognized and firmly endorsed the balance in the nuclear non-proliferation regime, between the need to prevent weapons proliferation and the need to respect the right of states to develop their civil nuclear programmes, we considered that the time had come to renew efforts to avoid the development of new capacity for the enrichment of uranium and the separation of spent fuel to extract plutonium, given the propensity of these two technologies to provide a short cut to a weapons programme.

So we urged the IAEA to negotiate an international system that would enable them to guarantee the provision of enrichment and reprocessing services at market rates and without risk of interruption, to any country in full compliance with their safeguards obligations; and we suggested that, for a limited period, while such a scheme was under negotiation, states should agree to a voluntary moratorium on any new enrichment and reprocessing facilities. In addition to these measures, we believed that the 2005 review of the Non-Proliferation Treaty (NPT) would provide an opportunity that should not be missed for the accepted nuclear weapons states to give more substance to their arms reduction commitments. And we recommended that the Security Council undertake to act in any circumstance where a non-nuclear state was attacked or threatened with attack by nuclear weapons.

Role of regional organizations

The role of regional organizations was prominent in our deliberations and in our recommendations. We recognized that, where they exist – in Europe, in Africa and in the Americas – they have already brought substantial benefits in increased stability and confidence and in conflict prevention. There are many parts of the world where these commodities are in short supply, and where the development of such organizations could be of real value – in the Gulf, South Asia and North East Asia for example – and we encouraged that. But we also recognized that Chapter VIII of the UN Charter, which provides for cooperation between the UN and regional organizations, had been grossly neglected and underutilized. We proposed that that now be remedied. Specifically we suggested the possibility of agreements between the UN and any regional organization that had the capacity to conduct conflict prevention and peace operations, providing for cooperation over early warning, mediation, logistics and training; we proposed a special multi-year commitment to assist capacity building by the African Union (AU); and we recommended that, when the UN authorizes a regional organization to undertake a peace operation, it should be prepared to give it also the backing of financing under the UN system of assessed contributions.

The case for comprehensive collective security

I have so far focused on what, for ease of reference but not for categorization, one might call the harder end of the peace and security agenda. But in so far as the rest of the agenda is concerned – poverty, environmental degradation, pandemic disease – if the Panel's analysis demonstrates anything it is that the twin challenges of development and security are inextricably linked. It is as true to say that you cannot hope to achieve development goals without peace and security as to say you cannot hope to achieve peace and security without development. We need to avoid loose talk of a 'grand bargain' in which the developed world gets peace and security in return for providing more aid, and concentrate rather on building a new consensus around the whole agenda now being tabled for governments to decide.

The Panel was very conscious that we were not alone in this field; nor were we the principal players. Taking the lead in setting the global development agenda for 2005 and beyond was the Millennium Project, a team of 250 researchers headed by Professor Jeffrey Sachs. Its report published in January 2005, 'Investing in Development: A Practical Plan to Achieve the Millennium Development Goals', sets the human security agenda on a breathtaking scale (UN Millennium Project, 2005).

The Secretary-General sent forward separately his definitive views on these issues in his March 2005 report, 'In Larger Freedom: Towards development, security and human rights for all' (UN, 2005).

For our part, we made clear our view that substantially greater financial resources will be needed to fuel development programmes and to counter AIDS and other pandemic diseases; that it is critically important to bring the Doha Development Round of trade negotiations to a conclusion at latest in 2006; and that it is high time to start thinking about and negotiating a post-Kyoto set of arrangements that will bring both the United States and the main developing countries within its ambit and provide a more effective response to global warming than what has been attempted so far.

Institutional reform

So much for the policies: what about the institutions? I have already touched on these when I mentioned the proposal to establish a new Peacebuilding Commission; and also about the strengthening of links between the UN and regional organizations. But we looked systematically at all the main institutions set up under the Charter and one – the Human Rights Commission – outside it. A few we have identified as having outlived their usefulness and being anachronistic. These we have proposed should be abolished. This goes for the Trusteeship Council, for the Military Staff Committee and for the enemy states clauses. The rest we have aimed to strengthen and to make more representative and more effective.

The General Assembly, it seems to us, needs to become more focused and less formulaic in its handling of the burning issues of the hour; we would hope to see it at the centre of the establishment of the new consensus which should take shape in the latter part of 2005. The Security Council needs to be enlarged. We sent forward two models, one involving the admission of new permanent members, albeit ones without a power of veto, the other involving the creation of a new category of longer term, but still non-permanent, members. Both models involve a Security Council of 24 members; both envisage a review in 2020 of whatever arrangement is agreed. ECOSOC will be involved in the new Peacebuilding Commission; but it needs also more leadership from a restricted member group and more capacity to make an effective input to the UN's developmental activities. The Human Rights Commission needs to be rescued from the trap of intergovernmental, tactical diplomatic negotiation into which it has fallen, and helped to be more objective and more professional; we believe heads of delegation should be human rights experts, as was originally intended; and that the Commission should be assisted by an advisory council or panel of individuals, proposed by the Secretary-General and the High Commissioner for Human Rights, who could bring their objectivity and professionalism to bear on the debates. We also proposed making membership of the Commission universal; the present division between members and observers who jockey for influence is not useful or healthy.

Secretariat

Underpinning all this is the need for a stronger, more professional Secretariat, and a Secretary-General with more control over his human resources and more authority to switch them from areas of lesser immediate priority to those that urgently required boosting. We recommended the establishment of a second post of Deputy Secretary-General, the new incumbent being explicitly devoted to the peace and security agenda and the present one freed up to deal more effectively with the development and administrative agenda. We would like to see a considerable re-structuring of the staff of the secretariat with a rationalization of the structure and full advantage taken of forthcoming retirements. We recommended sixty additional posts to give the new Deputy Secretary-General some analytical capability and to staff a Peacebuilding Bureau, in particular with experts having field experience.

Conclusions

This hectic scamper through the Panel's report demonstrates that it touches on most aspects of the UN's activities. There is much in the report that I have not mentioned, and I am sure it will also be suggested that we failed to include in our recommendations ideas that have often been canvassed in the past – abolition of the veto, for example, or the creation of a UN rapid reaction force, or the setting up of a UN Economic and Social Security Council. We did indeed consider all these ideas, and many others, but we concluded they were not within the reach of the practically negotiable, so we decided not to pursue them.

I doubt if the Panel can reasonably be accused of lack of ambition in the nature and scope of the proposals it has made. But we were determined to put forward an action plan that was both realistic and capable of being implemented quite rapidly if the political will is there to reach the necessary decisions. The world needs a strengthened UN here and now, not in 20 or more years' time.

A second point: the issue of membership of the Security Council, resolution of which has proved elusive for more than 10 years, risks dominating if not the agenda, then at least the airwaves. It must not become the cuckoo that expels all the other birds from the nest. It is an extremely important issue that needs to be settled now. But it is not the case that all the other proposals in the report depend for their validity and their viability upon that one question. They need to be considered and decided on their own merits.

Some will question whether any of this is capable of realization if the US remains at best ambivalent in its attitude towards the UN. I am one of those who have always believed that the UN cannot hope to succeed without, or in opposition to, the US, and that the US cannot hope to succeed without the UN – which it, more than any other nation, had the responsibility for creating in 1945. I still believe that. We must now put it to the test, not spend too much time holding up our finger to find out which way the wind is blowing.

Lastly, it is important to remember that no amount of systemic change at the UN will in itself be of much avail if the main protagonists do not re-double their efforts to resolve a number of long-running, still festering disputes. In that context, Palestine, Kashmir and North Korea stand out a mile.

For all the setbacks it has faced in recent years, the UN remains indispensable to the international community it serves. And yet, support for the UN, however broad, is shallow; expectations of it are often excessive, as is the subsequent criticism when it fails to meet these expectations. If support is to become both deeper and better informed about the realities of international life, it is essential that national politicians and the institutions of civil society are drawn into the discussion. There seems to be a new willingness to address all these issues. But will there be the perseverance and the determination in the future to see them through to a conclusion? On the answer to that question the outcome for many parts of the Panel's agenda will depend.

References

UN (1992) 'An Agenda for Peace: Preventive diplomacy, peacemaking and peace-keeping', Report of the Secretary-General, document A/47/277 – S/24111, 17 June, United Nations, New York

UN (2003) 'Secretary-General's address to the General Assembly', document A/58/PV.7, 23 September, United Nations, New York

UN (2004) *A more secure world: Our shared responsibility*, Report of the Secretary-General's High Level Panel on Threats, Challenges and Change, document A/59/565, 2 December, United Nations, New York

UN (2005) *In Larger Freedom: Towards development, security and human rights for all*, Report of the Secretary-General, document A/59/2005, 21 March, United Nations, New York

UN Millennium Project (2005) 'Investing in development: A practical plan to achieve the Millennium Development Goals', United Nations, Sales No 05.III.B.4; www.unmillenniumproject.org

2

The Peacebuilding Commission: Linking Security and Development

Anders Lidén and Anna-Karin Eneström

Introduction

This year – 2005 – could be decisive for the United Nations (UN), and for UN peacebuilding. The UN celebrates its 60th anniversary and has to adjust in order to cope with the challenges of globalization and new threats to our security and well-being. Its Secretary-General, Kofi Annan, has launched an ambitious programme for reform through the report of his High Level Panel on Threats, Challenges and Change (United Nations, 2004) and his own subsequent report, 'In Larger Freedom: Towards development, security and human rights for all', of March 2005 (UN, 2005). He has proposed a package of reforms in the areas of global security, development and human rights, and linked it to the achievement of the Millennium Development Goals (MDGs), adopted in September 2000. For Kofi Annan, as for many others, including the Swedish Government, the link between security and development is obvious.

This link is central to Swedish foreign policy, and so are the visions of the UN Millennium Development Declaration of the year 2000. We believe in an integrated approach when dealing with issues of peace and security, including development and poverty eradication, respect for human rights and the rule of law, protection of civilians, promotion of democracy and good governance, as well as protection of the environment. The late Swedish Foreign Minister Anna Lindh was very clear about stressing human rights and development cooperation as natural, integral parts of a broad security policy:

> *The challenges we face today, such as poverty, HIV/AIDS, ethnic conflicts and terrorism, are all global and interlinked. They can only be met by us together, through multilateral solutions and stronger global partnerships. Global markets*

> *must be balanced by global values such as respect for human rights and international law, democracy, security and sustainable economic and environmental development.*

> *Lindh (2003)*

The Swedish development assistance policy, adopted by the Swedish Parliament in December 2003, makes a development assistance perspective an integral part of all government activities with a common overall objective – to contribute to equitable and sustainable global development (Swedish Government, 2003).

For the past century, domestic peace and stability in Sweden has been built through reforms aiming to overcome the divisions and gaps in society by addressing economic, social and political inequities. It has become natural, in the same manner, for Swedes to see the potential dangers in the global inequities, and thus to agree with the fundamental link between security and development, and to politically support the allocation of resources to development in faraway countries. There is also strong support for development and the eradication of poverty as goals in their own rights.

Reforming the UN

The UN reform process is complicated, sometimes frustrating and tedious. Suspicion and fear, exacerbated by the crisis over Iraq, is still there. Some developing countries believe that reforms will only reflect and even cement the imbalance of power that already exists in the international system. The US, on the other hand, whose participation is so important for an effective multilateralism and a potent UN, fears a UN that would limit its power, tie its hands and prevent it from looking after its own security interests.

European countries can help in bridging those fears and suspicions. We share the view of Kofi Annan that no state is strong enough to meet all threats against its security alone. And we are increasingly aware of the threats caused by economic and social imbalances that globalization has brought closer to our doorsteps. The European Union (EU) Security Strategy acknowledges the mutual interdependence between security and development, and the need to address the root causes of conflict with early and effective preventive measures (European Union, 2003). At the same time, Europeans are strong advocates for the spread of democracy, respect for human rights and the rule of law throughout the world.

The EU takes an uncompromising stand in the struggle against terrorism and wants to see a comprehensive convention against this evil practice. The EU has also adopted a strategy for preventing the proliferation of weapons of mass destruction. Even though we take our own collective measures, we feel strongly committed to the UN and global multilateral cooperation, and we want the UN Secretary-General to succeed in his reform efforts.

By linking development, security and human rights in his March 2005 report, the Secretary-General is bringing together the perspectives of rich western countries and poor developing countries. In the summit meeting at the UN in September 2005, we hope that this link will be recognized, and that the nations of the world will come together in support of much needed reform. The meeting will be chaired jointly by Sweden and Gabon. The Secretary-General's reform proposals have received a particularly positive response from Europe and Africa. A European–African partnership might very well be a key to a successful reform process.

A peacebuilding commission

The Secretary-General's proposal for a Peacebuilding Commission is the most promising idea so far to combine security and development activities in the UN system. It is one of the reform proposals that have been met with immediate and widespread approval among both developed and developing countries. It helps to raise the hope for a successful outcome of the September summit.

The aim of the proposed commission would be to assist countries recover from conflict. It would bring together the UN Security Council and the UN Economic and Social Council (ECOSOC), according to the Secretary-General's suggestion, reporting to them in sequence, depending on the phase of a conflict. It would be open for participation by donor countries, those contributing troops, UN institutions, the Bretton Woods Institutions (BWI) and regional organizations. An overall purpose would be to ensure well-prepared decisions by the UN system on peacebuilding activities. The commission would provide a forum for exchange of information and coordination between relevant actors. It would aim at mobilizing a more focused and sustained international political and financial support for countries in post-conflict situations.

Once a country has been torn by civil strife, it becomes even more evident that there is no sustainable security without development, and no sustainable development without security. Civil wars and conflicts have become one of the most common security threats that we face today. Poverty is a root cause of conflict, and the adverse effects of war or internal violence on development and human security are incontestable. Lack of capacity of a state to uphold sovereign functions and to fulfill its obligations and responsibilities towards its citizens has consequences beyond its borders, and is, in fact, a threat to collective security.

Much emphasis must be put on the need for early action to prevent violent conflict. But in the aftermath of conflict it is equally important to prevent a conflict from reoccurring or a new conflict from emerging by engaging in peacebuilding activities. Building state capacity and viable and democratic institutions are cornerstones in any peacebuilding strategy.

To allow the collapse of a state opens the door to violence and anarchy. Apart from causing intolerable suffering to its inhabitants and refugee flows, so-called failed states have turned into hotbeds of terrorism and organized crime, usually with international ramifications. Investing in building state capacity is thus an investment in the collective security for all. We cannot afford to have states never recovering from conflicts, relapsing into yet another conflict, continued violence or state collapse. We have to find ways of stopping states from degenerating into so-called failed states.

More or less two-thirds of the least-developed countries (LDCs) are either in protracted conflict, have had recent episodes of violent conflicts, or are in post-conflict situations. An estimated 40 per cent of countries emerging from violent conflict – 60 per cent in Africa – relapse into conflict within five years. The success of a transition of those countries to consolidated peace and sustainable development is crucial for the achievement of the MDGs, as well as for the maintenance of international peace and security.

What is the recovery period?

The critical period from the immediate aftermath of a conflict to sustainable development is seen as a transition phase. In a report last year the UN elaborated on the concept of transition and the operational challenges for the UN during transition. The report suggests a definition:

> *For the UN, transition refers to the period in a crisis when external assistance is most crucial in supporting or underpinning still fragile cease-fires or peace processes by helping to create the conditions for political stability, security, justice and social equity.*

We would argue that the post-conflict transition phase should be seen as a much more extended period, not ending until there is consolidated peace, and stable state institutions are in place. The study furthermore confirms that:

> *Transition is not a smooth, sequential process from conflict to peace. On the contrary, transition from conflict to consolidated peace and sustainable development has many facets, existing simultaneously, at varying levels of intensity, susceptible to reversals.*[1]

We must acknowledge that each phase of transition needs to be addressed with different tools and that each state has its own history and its own specific transition.

What is peacebuilding?

By peacebuilding, we mean the assistance to states in creating conditions for restoring security, political stability and reconciliation, building capacity for essential social services, promoting respect for human rights and sustainable democratic as well as economic development. A particularly important aspect of peacebuilding is to establish democratic societies that are based on the rule of law, able to fight corruption and with a strong fiscal management. The training of judges, lawyers, police and even bureaucrats is crucial in this regard. Other central elements in peacebuilding are the so-called DDR processes – 'disarmament, demobilization and reintegration' of combatants into civil society – and security sector reform.

There is also a broad acceptance that peacebuilding must encompass promotion of the respect for human rights, technical assistance for democratic development, as well as incentives for the commencement of economic activities and employment opportunities. Support to private sector activities is important in this respect. Financial investment and sustainable economic growth must be stimulated in order to give young people alternatives to carrying arms or engaging in criminal activities. People need jobs, incentives to lead a productive life, and hope for the future.

In Liberia, in the early stages of post conflict, the UN peacekeeping operation, United Nations Mission in Liberia (UNMIL), disarmed over 100,000 former fighters without any link to rehabilitation and reintegration programs. The UN Development Programme (UNDP) Trust Fund was able to offer reintegration opportunities for a large number of those who were demobilized. However, because of a shortage of funding, tens of thousands are still not reintegrated into society. Without reintegration, they will continue to pose a threat to the entire peace process in their country.

Sweden has initiated a process to enhance a coherent implementation of DDR.[2] The aim is to link the DDR process to the earliest possible stages of peace negotiations, as well as to mandates of peace operations in order to facilitate the stabilization of insecure post-conflict situations during the transition from war to consolidated peace. But the initiative also addresses the issue of adequate funding and an operational mechanism that will allow for demobilization and reintegration to continue beyond the transitional phase.

UN peacekeeping and peacebuilding

The UN has a unique role in addressing the challenges of transition, and already has a broad experience in peacebuilding to draw upon. In Mozambique, El Salvador, Guatemala, Cambodia and East Timor, the UN has been fairly successful in supporting national peacebuilding efforts. Political dialogue has replaced armed violence. We can see sustained peace and promising democratic developments in these countries to which the UN has contributed. Experience shows that the key for successful UN operations in the transition phase has been the availability of financial resources, good donor coordination and non-governmental organization (NGO) involvement (Mozambique), a sustained political and development presence, a comprehensive peace agreement integrating social and economic issues (Guatemala) and the importance of the security dimension of peacebuilding (East Timor).

The UN's comparative advantage lies in its ability to provide international legitimacy to peacebuilding activities, based on international law, including the use of military personnel, its mandate reaching from international security, conflict prevention and peacekeeping to human rights, humanitarian assistance, post-conflict reconstruction and long-term development and its field presence before, during and after a conflict. Assisting states through the transition from violent conflicts to consolidated peace and integration into the world economy is one of the prime challenges for the UN in the 21st century.

But there is a continuous need to improve the UN's performance when it comes to conducting complex, multifaceted peace operations and to engage in effective long-term peacebuilding. If the UN is to succeed in taking on these challenges, coordination is crucial. It has to pull together relevant actors, including the BWI, resources and institutional management on headquarters level, as well as field level for a comprehensive response.

Recent reform initiatives

In 2000, the Report of the Panel on UN Peace Operations ('the Brahimi Report') put forward a set of recommendations to strengthen UN peace operations, among them the need for effective peacekeeping and peacebuilding in complex operations (UN, 2000). As a result of the report, the UN Security Council has adopted decisions on complex, integrated mandates for several peacekeeping missions, notably in the Democratic Republic of Congo (UN Observer Mission in the DRC, MONUC),[3] Liberia (UNMIL),[4] Haiti (UN Stabilization Mission in Haiti, MINUSTAH)[5] and, most recently, Sudan (UN Mission in Sudan, UNMIS).[6] In these missions there are sizable peacebuilding components. The UN Security Council has thus already taken effective decisions to improve its peacebuilding activities within the context of peacekeeping and peacebuilding missions.

The General Assembly special committee on peacekeeping operations followed up on the Brahimi Report in 2005, recognizing the need for the UN Secretariat to plan for peacekeeping missions in such a manner as to facilitate effective peacebuilding and long-term prevention of recurrence of armed conflicts. The committee also stressed the need for strengthened cooperation and coordination among specialized agencies, funds and programmes within the UN system as well as with the BWI, international donors, humanitarian organizations, NGOs and civil society. The aim was to ensure policy coherence on the ground in the post-conflict peacebuilding phase, and a smooth transition to long-term development activities. The special committee, however, has never turned out to be a sufficiently effective intergovernmental structure for dealing with the complex issues of peacebuilding.

ECOSOC, for its part, has also started to focus on peacebuilding. It has established ad hoc advisory groups on countries emerging from conflict, such as Guinea-Bissau, Burundi and Haiti. The groups have been useful for exchange of information between states, including donor countries, on bilateral and multilateral activities, but have failed to generate any political or financial commitments.

Why the need for a peacebuilding commission?

The establishment of a Peacebuilding Commission could help to solve some of the remaining shortcomings of UN peacebuilding, including a so-called 'gap problem', described by Kofi Annan in his March 2005 report:

> *If we are going to prevent conflict we must ensure that peace agreements are implemented in a sustained and sustainable manner. Yet, at this very point, there is a gaping hole in the United Nations institutional machinery: no part of the United Nations system effectively addresses the challenge of helping countries with the transition from war to lasting peace.*

UN (2005)

This gap, in fact, consists of several gaps in dealing with the challenges of effective peacebuilding:

* Until now, there has not existed any intergovernmental body bringing together relevant actors and donors for peacebuilding. The assistance to states in post-conflict situations has been scattered among the Security Council, with its mandate for international peace and security; ECOSOC, with its coordinating powers in the economic and social fields; the boards of the UN funds and programmes; the international financial institutions, where many of the global decisions are made in the economic and financial fields, and bilateral donors. These institutions – ECOSOC in particular – are in dire need of reform; as an intergovernmental body, it has to become a vital organ to also address effectively the links between development and security.

  The Security Council is reasonably effective in its role as a decision-making body, and carries political weight. But to reflect today's realities and to enjoy the necessary legitimacy, it needs to bring in new important players in world politics, including in particular from the developing world.[7] This is important, not least because the overwhelming majority of the countries on the agenda of the Security Council are developing countries. The Security Council already decides today on a range of peacebuilding activities within broader peace operations, but without proper preparation. Major aspects of peacebuilding are related to development, but the Council's decisions are mainly prepared by the peacekeeping department in the UN Secretariat, with much of its focus on military operations. Thus the Security Council lacks a focus on development, and therefore a link to a reformed ECOSOC is desirable

* There has not been any reliable and efficient system for funding peacebuilding activities. Predictability, adequacy and timeliness of resources made available to support states in post-conflict situations have to be enhanced. We believe that the possibility to expand the assessed contributions in support of integrated peacekeeping missions should be further explored.

The assessed contributions should cover at least crucial and initial invest-ments in peacebuilding. This could include efforts to reintegrate and rehabilitate ex-combatants, national dialogue processes, truth and recon-ciliation processes, as well as initial phases of security sector reform. Assessed contributions are the most fair, effective and predictable ways to guarantee funding.

Alternative resources are contributions to UN funds and programmes, and funds pledged at donor conferences. The problem with voluntary con-tributions is that commitments are not always implemented once a conflict has left the media screen. Liberia is just one example, where many of the pledges from the donor conference in February 2004 still have to materialize

*   There has been an urgent need for better inter-agency coordination and support. The UN Department for Peacekeeping (DPKO) has been solely responsible for all UN peacekeeping activities, including the complex, integrated peace missions. There are mechanisms for coordination, like the Executive Committee on Peace and Security (ECPS), and the Integrated Mission Task forces (IMTF). Experience tells us, however, that they have not been as effective as we had hoped. True and effective coordination has been lacking within the UN. For us, it seems particularly important to better involve the UN agencies and the humanitarian organizations in the planning and implementation of UN peace operations. As we have pointed out, many of the tasks within the integrated peace operations have developmental aspects, and the involvement and support of the right actors must be ensured.

A comprehensive peacebuilding strategy

We see the establishment of a Peacebuilding Commission, a peacebuilding support office and a commitment to predictable and adequate funding mech-anisms as necessary and integral parts of a UN peacebuilding strategy. From a Swedish perspective, such a strategy should give attention to the following:

1   The Peacebuilding Commission should be an advisory body. Already at an early stage in a transition period, it should also give advice with regard to long-term post-conflict reconstruction. A key task is to ensure sustained international support and political attention to a country throughout the transition period to consolidated peace. Political attention and financial commitments must continue well past the normal period of a peacekeeping operation

2   Peacebuilding activities must be planned, coordinated and implemented in an integrated manner with peacekeeping. The Peacebuilding Commission should commence its work in parallel with the Security Council's initial deliberations on how to address a conflict or post-conflict situation

3   The reporting by the Peacebuilding Commission in sequence to the Sec-urity Council and the ECOSOC implies a central role for ECOSOC in

the more long-term post-conflict reconstruction efforts. That, however, requires a reformed, strengthened and restructured ECOSOC. ECOSOC should also be required to defer consideration of a country back to the Security Council whenever there is an imminent risk of resurgence of conflict

4   There needs to be a partnership between the UN, bilateral donors and the Bretton Woods Institutions (BWI), respecting their different roles, mandates and governing structures. The active involvement of the BWI is crucial to a successful peacebuilding strategy. In the proposal for a Peacebuilding Commission, the UN departments, funds, programmes and agencies are expected to participate as a single UN delegation. This will hopefully facilitate the BWI's relations to the UN and could forge a more strategic and true partnership for the future.

Conclusion

Peacebuilding has become a real challenge for the UN and the international community. We have to learn from the past. Swift peace operations without a long-term commitment might temporarily help bringing an end to shooting and killing, but if a country is abandoned and left to itself too early, it might turn into a nightmare, not only for its own people, but the international community as well. The examples of Afghanistan, Somalia, Liberia and Haiti are frightening; they should not be repeated.

Fortunately, the link between security and development is becoming increasingly accepted. The link is amply demonstrated in the need for peace-building in post-conflict situations. In its responsibility to uphold international peace and security, the UN has a special role in peacebuilding. Assisting countries in their transition from armed conflict to consolidated peace and development is a huge task, but an important one for the security of all.

Notes

1   Report of the UN Development Group/Economic Committee on Human-itarian Assistance Working Group on Transition Issues, February 2004; www.undg.org/documents/3330–UNDG_ECHA_WG_on_Transition_ Issues__Report__-_Final_Report.doc
2   The Swedish Government website provides more information on the Stockholm Initiative on Disarmament, Demobilization, Reintegration; www.sweden.gov.se/sb/d/4890
3   See Security Council Resolution S/Res/1258, 6 August 1999
4   See Security Council Resolution S/Res/1509, 19 September 2003
5   See Security Council Resolution S/Res/1542 (2004), 30 April 2004
6   See Security Council Resolution S/Res/1590 (2005), 24 March 2005

7   Secretary-General Kofi Annan endorses the position set out in the report of the High Level Panel on Threats, Challenges and Change (UN document A/59/565) concerning reforms of the Security Council; namely: they should increase the involvement in decision making of those who contribute most to the UN financially, militarily and diplomatically; they should bring into the decision-making process countries more representative of the broader membership, especially of the developing world; they should not impair the effectiveness of the Security Council; and they should increase the democratic and accountable nature of the body.

References

European Union (2003) 'A secure Europe in a better world', European Security Strategy, 12 December, EU, Brussels

Lindh, A. (2003) Speech by the Foreign Minister at the Helsinki Conference, 'Searching for global partnerships', 4 December ,2002, Swedish Government, www.regeringen.se/sb/d/1111

Swedish Government (2003) 'Shared responsibility: Sweden's policy for global development', Government Bill 2002/03: 122, 15 May, Swedish Government, Stockholm,

UN (2000) *Report of the Panel on United Nations Peace Operations*, document A/55/305 – S/2000/809, 21 August, United Nations, New York

UN (2004) *A more secure world: Our shared responsibility*, Report of the Secretary-General's High Level Panel on Threats, Challenges and Change, document A/59/565, 2 December, United Nations, New York

UN (2005) *In Larger Freedom: Towards development, security and human rights for all*, Report of the Secretary-General, document A/59/2005, 21 March, United Nations, New York

3

Human Security and the War on Terror

Oliver Richmond and Jason Franks

The civilized world rides out to rescue foreigners from the darkness.

Monbiot, 2005

The claims of human security

Human security debates pit the realist Westphalian state security discourse, typified by the war on terror, against humanitarianism and freedom from fear and want as a right or a need. These new debates have only been explicitly recognized in the last 10 years or so, since the United Nations Development Programme (UNDP) report of 1994 opened up the question of the roots of violence in response to what Hedley Bull might have described as a 'new medievalism' (Bull, 1977, pp264–276). The human security debate (UNDP, 1994; Foong-Khong, 2001; Paris, 2001) has been notable mainly because of its acceptance in some key policy circles (such as within the United Nations [UN] family), and in global civil society. This debate calls for the subjects of security to be redefined from the 'state' to the 'individual'– in other words, from managing inter-state relations to building peace by introducing social, political and economic reforms. Its initial acceptance was mainly because liberal state and international organization objectives shifted from status quo management to multidimensional approaches to peacebuilding in which strategies are applied which aim to transform conflict 'into peaceful non-violent processes of social and political change...' (Ramsbotham et al, 1999).

Former UN Secretary-General Boutros Boutros Ghali's Agenda for Peace (UN, 1992) was an important early post-Cold War attempt to engage with this shift. Agenda for Peace called for the UN to become engaged in addressing the '...deepest causes of social injustice and political oppression...'. This understanding of human security was further reinforced by the publication of Boutros Ghali's subsequent Agenda for Democratization and for Agenda for Development. As one would expect, the more recent Report of the Panel on UN peace operations (the Brahimi Report) retained this version of peace (UN, 2000), as does the Report of the High Level Panel on Threats, Challenges and Change of 2004 (UN, 2004).[1]

Despite these developments, 'security', like 'peace' and 'justice', is an essentially contested concept. The very fundamentals of the concept are open to question: who or what are the objects or referents of security; who provides security; and for whom is security intended: individuals, groups, nations, states, regions, the world – or intangibles such as values? Our answers to these questions have been changing since the end of the Cold War, raising a distinction between 'traditional' and 'new' security. At the very least, most of us would agree that the concept of security is being broadened considerably and continuously, to incorporate military, political, economic, societal and environmental dimensions, and the interlinkages between them. This debate has tackled a number of conceptual questions – for example, regarding the unit of analysis, or object, of security; the tools for achieving security; the relationship between development, human rights, social justice, and security; and the place of ideas such as dignity and equity in security.

In its broadest incarnation human security is 'freedom from want' and 'freedom from fear': positive and negative freedoms and rights. This idea has gained currency in the post-Cold War world as political and intellectual space has opened up. This enabled analysts, progressive officials, and policy makers to move away from the state-centric, power-based model of international politics. The dynamics of globalization broadened the level of analysis included in security thinking, highlighting the often ignored social, economic, human rights, and development insecurities that lie at the root of conflict. Concurrent normative changes in terms of the rights and responsibilities of the international community towards those caught up in conflict have underpinned, and resulted from, these developments. These dynamics have taken on a momentum of their own, which conditions expectations and standards of governance within and between communities, and might be said to have transformed the nature of political community.

The main approach to human security thinking and practice is the broad, development-based, human needs approach, often associated with UNDP, through which basic welfare is seen as the best indicator of security. This model sees individuals as the unit of analysis, claims universality, assumes global interdependence, and argues that prevention is probably the best course of action. A narrower version of human security sees state collapses as a major threat, and encompasses multi-level forms of intervention even if it encroaches upon sovereign prerogatives. Human security has therefore also played an important role in thinking about humanitarian intervention and state building.

It would be quite wrong to suggest that human security is completely new. It is not. In fact it is a re-labelling of older ideas and arguments, including 'comprehensive security' and 'societal security', as well as debates on the nature of war and peace, on social movements, civil society, the democratic peace, and debates over constructing a peaceful international order – from European order to the post-colonial world order. Human security has its roots in the traditions of political liberalism – the idea that the point of politics should be enhancement of the freedom and security of individuals by other actors, such as great powers, regional or international organizations, in the absence of individual agency. Even before the end of the Cold War, the Brandt and Palme Commissions oriented security more towards the individual.

Of course, as recent documentation such as 'The Responsibility to Protect' and 'High Level Panel Report' illustrate, this has created a serious problem. While human security is predicated upon a normative humanism and an ethical responsibility to re-orient security around the individual, the responsibility for its provision inevitably rests with states. Where host states cannot provide, or actively undermine, human security, some international practice suggests that other states may take on the responsibility, and may subcontract this provision to agencies and non-governmental organizations (NGOs). This can be seen to a certain extent in the US's or UK's role in the Balkans or in Sierra Leone, or in the role of the UN system.

States are the guardians of human security for individuals, rather than individuals being the guardian of their own security. States, the UN system, UNDP, Department for International Development (DFID), the World Bank and many international NGOs are responsible for identifying and responding to human security problems. Some commentators, including Fukyama, argue that such behaviour may undermine already existing local capacity (Fukyama, 2004, p53), or that it is part of a form of colonialism. It is true that human security allows a form of deep intervention into the very lives of individuals, formerly protected by the system of state sovereignty.[2]

Furthermore, there have been many cases where intervention has not occurred despite obvious human security issues in contemporary international politics, as in Bosnia from 1992–1995, Rwanda in 1994, Sudan today, or Democratic Republic of Congo (DRC) until 2002, or where it has occurred for other reasons, as in the post-9/11 invasions of Afghanistan and Iraq.

As the above examples illustrate, there is mixed evidence as to whether human security issues present a significant short-term threat to the stability of international order in an empirical sense: there is rather more evidence to show that it presents a normative challenge. Therefore, it should not be surprising that human security considerations played almost no role in the two major interventions of the new decade so far, but rather the focus was on a response to terrorism and the proliferation of weapons of mass destruction in Afghanistan and Iraq, respectively. While there is a much broader understanding that human security issues relating to socioeconomic deprivation, human rights, or AIDS may form the roots of conflict and terrorism and provide fertile ground for both, across liberal states, international and regional organization, international agencies and NGOs, it seems that strategic interests remain a priority.

Furthermore, it is clear that the fact that strategic interests may degrade human security, as can be seen from the Balkans to Middle East, seems not to have presented a major problem to the planners of military response in Bosnia in 1995, Kosovo in 1999, or Afghanistan in 2002 and Iraq in 2003–2004. Strategic interests clearly undermine human security in the short term, even if the indirect argument is made that they may improve human security in the long term. Those that adhere to this mode of thought often critique human security on methodological grounds, for being too broad and all encompassing and unable to differentiate between major and minor security priorities. In response, its proponents make the point that in the globalizing environment, human security issues in any location become a security problem for all.

The war on terror and human [in]security

In the aftermath of 11 September 2001, the US embarked on a war on terror; a perceived global conflict against the perpetrators of the attack on the World Trade Center, aimed at guaranteeing human security in spaces formerly perceived as secure. Up to this point, human insecurity was seen to be a problem of the developing or war-torn world.

Aside from dispensing justice towards the actual perpetrators, the war on terror has provided an agenda for fighting states or regimes that profess support for Al-Qaeda, and seems to include comprehensive political reform of a dysfunctional Arab world that is failing its people and generating hatred of the United States. This agenda, often described as neo-conservative or neo-imperialist, has obvious policy implications. What is more, the US and its allies have clearly shown that conducting a war against terror entails an acceptance of collateral damage, as occurred in the NATO bombing in the Balkans in 1995 and 1999.

Degrading human security as a consequence of the war on terror has been hidden behind the jingoism and militarism of more traditional war discourses. In a new book entitled *An End to Evil: How to Win the War on Terror* Frum and Perle recommend a 'strong' approach to Saudi Arabia, by encouraging secession by the Shias of the oil-rich Eastern Province; aid and encouragement for Iranians to overthrow their government; and to force Syria to withdraw from Lebanon while reforming their economy and politics. They recommend the imposition of a blockade of North Korea and the preparation of a pre-emptive strike on its nuclear plants. They also suggest a revision of the UN charter to make 'pre-emption' easier (Frum and Perle, 2003).

While some of these recommendations are not yet occurring overtly, the wars in Afghanistan (2002) and Iraq (2003) are very real examples of the effects of the war on terror. Because these have been framed as legitimate and just wars, if not strictly legal, human security issues became secondary. It appears that even after the military operation shifted to policing, human security issues remained secondary (partly because of the ongoing resistance across parts of the country).

Far from representing a revolution in US foreign policy, it can be argued that the war on terror is a continuation of the hegemonic state-centric security policy that seeks ideological and economic domination to ensure its own security of interests. US foreign policy seems to be projected in opposition to a threat, and since the end of the Cold War, a number of such threats have replaced that of the Soviet Union. From ethnic primordialism to the clash of civilization, and now the war on terror, this binary can be seen as a new manifestation of an old policy. This produces a dualism whereby state and human security compete, with predictable results within state foreign policy machinery. US President Bush's 'axis of evil' speech has clear similarities with Ronald Regan's view of the Soviet 'evil empire'. This reflects what is often termed US exceptionalism, in which the unspoken rhetorical device at play is the contrast between the evil other and the morally superior US. Yet this superiority seems effectively limited to a myopic concern for internal stability, rather than humanism. The central difference between Reagan and Bush's rhetoric is the nature of the threat. According to realist state-centric understanding, terrorism is seen as a state discourse, is defined in terms of legitimacy and is understood to represent a threat to the state from another state.[3]

Hence, the invasion of Afghanistan and defeat of the Taliban, and the war in Iraq against Saddam Hussein and the Ba'ath regime, are seen ostensibly as state conflicts. However, 'new terrorism', characterized by Al-Qaeda and the Bin Laden network is not state-based. Instead, it is violence perpetrated by unidentified and amorphous non-state groups and/or individuals, who bear no relation to their country of origin and who claim no responsibility for their actions (Laqueur, 2001). It is essentially 'individual terrorism'[4] and needs to be viewed as such by moving away from state discourses and engaging in individual human issues.

How successful, therefore, the invasion of Iraq will be in winning the war on terror, will be an indication of how clearly the *root causes* of terrorism and the individual human perpetrators of it are actually understood. The relegation of human security issues indicates that root causes are not being meaningfully addressed and, indeed, that contrary to the desire to 'do no harm' to innocent civilians, and to build and empower local democratic and economic capacity, such interventions are having a far greater negative impact on human security than has been suggested. If post-conflict peacebuilding in Afghanistan and Iraq follows the pattern after interventions in Bosnia, Kosovo, and East Timor, where under-development, poverty and unemployment are widely experienced despite massive peacebuilding efforts, it may well be that the roots of terrorism are exacerbated rather than addressed by the war on terror.

Reconciling human security and the war on terror

Aside from such criticisms, the war on terror can also be presented as a natural extension of the need for security and freedom, representative of the post-Cold War world and encompassing the need for, and protection of, individual rights represented by the Universal Declaration of Human Rights. Is the war on terror actually a global manifestation of human security, a desire to create a 'safe' world where 'freedom from want' and 'freedom from fear' exist as rights and are protected by law – a natural extension of the Geneva Convention, Wilsonian liberalism, and the UN? This argument locates the war on terror in the humanitarian interventionist debate, suggesting that the war on terror and the invasions of Afghanistan and Iraq are attempts to establish what Duffield calls a 'liberal peace' via preventive war. Even though Duffield is very critical of liberal peace and equates it effectively with a 'civilizing mission' (Duffield, 2001), since the end of the Cold War this liberal rhetoric has become stronger than ever. It is embodied in such international organizations as the UN, institutions such as the World Bank and International Monetary Fund (IMF), agencies such as UNDP and United Nations High Commission for Refugees (UNHCR), and many thousands of different types of NGOs. All have, for various complex reasons linked for the most part to their relationship with their donors, adopted aspects of the liberal agenda.

This Enlightenment-derived process, drawing on the liberal internationalism of the immediate post-World War I world, on the functionalist agendas of post-World War II, and on an uneasy mix of self-determination, liberal democracy, neo-liberal economic reform, human rights, a balancing of state and human security, international legal regimes such as international human rights and humanitarian law, has increasingly become an accepted part of the liberal projection on how world politics now operate.

The conceptualization of the war on terror as it is presented in US excep-tionalist rhetoric is to protect the liberal peace. To know the liberal peace, as most in the West imagine we do, legitimates the use of pre-emptive force to protect it against perceived threats. The problem with this logic is that it has resulted in the marginalization of human security during the use of force for target populations, which itself has implications for the legitimacy of the inter-vention from the point of view of the 'intervened upon'. This then presents major difficulties for the internationals during the post-conflict peacebuilding phase.

Paradoxically, human security can be seen as a central feature in the liberal agenda, practiced by global organizations and NGOs and representing the vanguard of the ideological shift away from state-centric understanding of responsibility towards others. This, we would argue is also true for terrorism, which is embodied far more in the individual than in the state or even non-state group. However, the implication of reconciling the individual approach to human security with individual terrorism[5] is to suggest that the need for human security, common within individuals and propagated by non-state actors, is actually a root cause of terrorism. This is applicable to the war on terror and the realization that failed states or 'hostile' regimes are a breeding ground for terrorism and has been a discourse employed to justify the invasion of Afghanistan and Iraq. Attempting to alleviate these problems therefore means engaging in the human security debate, the implication being that the war on terror is a response to human security problems.

This tautology is also present in human-needs explanations for terrorism. According to Burton, sociobiological human needs require satisfaction on a hierarchical basis, and if they remain unfulfilled, actors will resort to violence (Burton, 1979). Azar suggests that these needs are 'security, identity, representation and equality' (Azar, 1990). This individual human understanding of terrorism can also be seen in the work of Gurr on relative deprivation, in which he suggested that violence develops in society between individuals who perceive a relative imbalance politically, economically and or socially between what they should have and what they actually have (Gurr, 1970).

Human needs, in these terms, become navigation points for policy makers in that they can see where their own actions or those of others, in impinging in such basic areas, may lie at the roots of violence. Human security therefore provides an explanation of the causes of terrorism and a cause of the war on terror. The self-evident truth of both possibilities is that the basic lesson to be learned from human security thinking is that violence, whether terrorism or humanitarian war, begets violence.

While the war on terrorism might purport to be a human security discourse it does in fact exacerbate human security needs. The 'state' understanding of terrorism[6] is defined primarily in terms of state legitimacy, and is largely understood to represent a challenge and threat to state authority that justifies 'legitimate' state violence. Thus the war on terror has not engaged in a roots debate with the causes of terrorism but seeks instead to deal with it in the conventional legal-military, counter-terror and anti-terror manner provided by the state. These function as a method of fighting the manifestation and symptoms of terrorism, and do not necessarily engage its root causes.

Furthermore, the often heavy-handed legal-military state approach, characterized by military assaults, pre-emptive assassinations and 'emergency measures' undermine basic human rights and thus exacerbate the political and socioeconomic problems that potentially created the terrorism in the first instance. This is clearly illustrated in the UN's High Level Panel Report of December 2004. This report suggests that the current war on terrorism has 'in some instances corroded the very values that terrorists target: human rights and the rule of law' (UN, 2004, p45). The panel also 'expressed fear that approaches to terror focusing wholly on police, military and intelligence measures, risk undermining efforts to promote good governance and human rights, alienate large parts of the world's population and thereby weaken collective action against terrorism...' (UN, 2004, p45). There is much empirical evidence to support this. The panel report further recommends a strategy that incorporates addressing the root causes of terrorism, such as 'promoting social and political rights, the rule of law and democratic reform, working to end occupation and address major political grievances, reduce poverty, unemployment and stop state collapse' (UN, 2004, p46). The panel report also seeks to move away from the Manichean approach to terrorism adopted by the war on terror. It seeks instead to engage in defining terrorism by recognizing that 'the state's use of armed force against civilians' should be included; and also that 'people under foreign occupation have a right to resistance and a definition of terrorism should not override this right...' (UN, 2004, p48) Both of these suggestions have obvious implications for the war on terror – particularly the war in Iraq – and perhaps suggest a contradiction between the discourse and practices of human security.

The debates about human security reflect different state and societal security concerns, outlooks, and methodologies in terms of the institutions, actors, and policies that are proposed to promote human security. Human security can be seen as revisionist, requiring adjustments in international trade, development and sovereignty, but it can also be seen as status quo oriented, allowing major states, donors, international organizations and agencies, as well as NGOs, to provide a conduit to intervene in the most intimate aspects of human life, to engage in social engineering, and to propagate the different aspects and norms inherent in the liberal peace. What is clear from the tension between human security and the war on terror is that as a concept, human security tends not to distinguish between the effects of violence applied for just or unjust reasons. As a pure form of humanitarianism it presents victim and aggressor, just war and illegitimate war, as merely contributing to human suffering, and therefore requiring a response. When we factor in the political nature of human security, it may also help us to decide which course of action is right or wrong, and viable both in the short term and the long term.

Like the human-needs approach, human security provides 'navigation points' for policy makers. As a consequence, most of the resistance to human security stems from the fact that it underlines the negative consequences of all forms of violence, both just or unjust, and also places the 'haves' with re- sponsibilities towards the 'have-nots'. Even worse, it enables a representation of a world as it is – without the comforting simplicity of black and white bin- aries through which simple policy decisions can be made (as in the 'war on drugs', 'war on poverty', or the 'war on terror'). Human security presents an analytical picture of a complex world requiring sophisticated responsibility and responses.

Human security: Future trends

What of the future for human security amidst the war on terror? Human security is inextricably connected to political liberalism and, as we have argued, provides a more sophisticated understanding to state-centric approaches in the confusion of the post-Cold War globalizing world. It is also driving the UN, agencies, donors and the multifarious NGOs that are omnipresent in conflict zones. Associating the war on terror with attempts at achieving human security is, as we have argued, distinctly problematic. The UN is keen to distance itself from the war on terror, which is a US foreign policy agenda and a discourse for imposing a western-centric binary (though it is also keen to become engaged in counter-balancing such debates and providing human security). Thus, how far is the human security discourse an attempt by states, willingly aided by internationals; to impose a specific political agenda, associated with the liberal peace, on societies? Is the guise of human security really a Trojan horse for liberal democratization – a covert partner to the less subtle war on terror?

Perhaps even these debates on human security in the post-tsunami world have been superseded and indeed dwarfed by the new environmental consciousness provided by the recent natural disaster in Asia. Certainly, the cost of the war on terror (in financial and human terms) and the effect of international terrorism (in loss of human life) have been questioned in relation to the proportion spent and indeed lost on each. In financial terms alone the US government pledged US\$350 million and the UK £50 million to the victims of the 2004 tsunami. However, the US has spent US\$148 billion and the UK £6 billion so far on the war in Iraq (Monbiot, 2005). This raises obvious questions relating to the motivations behind war and humanitarian aid. It can be argued however that the American and British governments see the Iraq war and the tsunami relief as part of the same civilizing narrative.

The future of human security is perhaps in the reform of the UN, and a need to reconcile universal individual human security issues with the political agendas of states in an insecure and globalizing world. Certainly, the High Level Panel Report suggested some far-reaching and timely changes. In a recent article, Mark Malloch Brown, chief of staff to Kofi Annan, suggested that this is the '…challenge of aligning a too-often sprawling, unfocused UN system around today's priorities. A consequence of globalization that has crept up on all of us is that our security is shared. Poverty in one corner of the world can contribute to terrorism in another. From health pandemics to migration and global warming, today's problems do not respect borders. A new multilateral compact is needed urgently, but it will be effective only if it makes all of us – rich and poor – feel safer' (Malloch Brown, 2005). The concept of human security seems to indicate that pre-emptive war, including the war on terror, may have contradictory effects, easily predictable, but less easily avoided if the international community is indeed embarked upon a course of unilateral uses of forces, even where these are motivated for humanitarian reasons, of against proliferation, terrorism, and associated reasons. There are two possibilities here: either the majority of states who oppose pre-emptive war find more substantial methods of opposition, or the application of such uses of force is far more careful 'to do no harm.' Both seem highly unlikely at present.

Notes

1 See also International Commission on Intervention and State Sovereignty (2001), 'The Responsibility to Protect', International Development Research Centre, Ottawa; www.iciss.ca/report-en.asp. This argued that states should be encouraged to take on more responsibility to protect those in need or in danger, and has also been criticized for effectively suggesting that states alone have this kind of capacity.

2 For more on this, see Richmond, forthcoming 2005, *The Transformation of Peace*, especially Chapter 4.

3   For more on the theoretical debates behind terrorism, see Franks (2004) *Rethinking the Roots of Terrorism: Through the Doors of Perception.*
4   The concept of 'Individual Terrorism' is employed to relate the root causes of terrorism directly to the individual, in contrast to state, structure or group causes (Franks, 2004).
5   The concept of individual terrorism is used to focus the causes of terrorism directly on the individual via theories such as human needs and socio-economic relative deprivation (Franks, 2004).
6   This refers to how terrorism is defined and understood by the state as 'orthodox terrorism theory' (Franks, 2004).

References

Azar, E. (1990) *The Management of Protracted Social Conflict: Theory and Cases,* Dartmouth Publishing Company, Hampshire

Bull, H. (1977) *The Anarchical Society: A Study in Order in World Politics,* Macmillan, London

Burton, J. (1979) *Deviance Terrorism and War,* Martin Robertson, Oxford

Duffield, M. (2001) *Global Governance and the News Wars,* Zed, London

Foong-Khong, Y. (2001) `Human security: A shotgun approach to alleviating human misery?`, *Global Governance,* vol. 7, no 3, July–September

Franks, J. (2004) *Rethinking the Roots of Terrorism: Through the Doors of Perception,* PhD Thesis, University of St Andrews

Frum, D. and Perle, R. (2003) *An End to Evil: How to Win the War on Terror,* Random House, New York

Fukyama, F. (2004) *State Building: Governance and Order in the Twenty First Century,* Profile, London

Gurr, T. (1970) *Why Men Rebel,* Princeton University Press, Princeton, New Jersey

Laqueur, W. (2001) *The New Terrorism,* Phoenix Press, 3rd ed

Malloch Brown, M. (2005) 'Why the UN must reinvent itself of collapse', *The Sunday Times,* 20 February, www.newsint-archive.co.uk/pages/main.asp

Monbiot, G. (2005) 'The victims of the tsunami pay the price of war on Iraq', *The Guardian,* 4 January, www.guardian.co.uk/comment/story/0,,1382857,00.html

Paris, R. (2001) `Human security: Paradigm shift or hot air?`, *International Security,* vol 26, no 2, pp. 87–102

Ramsbotham, O., Woodhouse, T. and Miall, H. (1999) *Contemporary Conflict Resolution,* Polity Press, Oxford

Richmond, O. P. (forthcoming 2005) *The Transformation of Peace,* Palgrave, London

UN (1992) 'An Agenda for Peace: Preventive diplomacy, peacemaking and peacekeeping', Report of the Secretary-General, document A/47/277 – S/24111, 17 June, United Nations, New York

UN (1994) 'An agenda for development', Report of the Secretary-General, UN document A/48/935, 6 May, United Nations, New York

UN (1996) 'An agenda for democratization', Report of the Secretary-General, UN document A/51/761, 20 December, United Nations, New York

UN (2000) Letters from the Secretary-General to the President of the General Assembly and the President of the Security Council, Report of the Panel on UN Peace Operations, document A/55/305– S/2000/809, 21 August

UN (2004) *A more secure world: Our shared responsibility*, Report of the Secretary-General's High Level Panel on Threats, Challenges and Change, document A/59/565, 2 December; www.un.org/secureworld/

UNDP (1994) 'New dimensions of human security', *Development Report*, United Nations, New York, http://hdr.undp.org/reports/global/1994/en/

4

Achieving Nuclear Non-proliferation: A New Zealand Perspective

Marian Hobbs

Weapons that kill large numbers of human beings indiscriminately have no moral or legal justification, regardless of who is holding them. The world will best be able to keep such weapons out of the hands of terrorists only when they and their special weapons materials are in the hands of no one.

Jayanatha Dhanapala, former United Nations Under-Secretary-General for Disarmament Affairs, 2002

Introduction

New Zealand's overriding priority has long been, and will continue to be, the elimination of all weapons of mass destruction (WMD). We are committed to enforcing the international bans on chemical and biological weapons, and we contribute actively to work to ban or control conventional weapons, including anti-personnel landmines, explosive remnants of war and small arms and light weapons.

Our particular focus is on nuclear weapons. More than a decade after the end of the Cold War, thousands of these weapons remain on hair-trigger alert, weapons created out of a wish for security, but which, in fact, constitute the greatest risk to human security in history. Other issues are pressing and important in this regard – for instance, the environment, human health and economic imbalances that exist within and between states.

However, none of these issues, vital as they are, has the potential – quite literally – to destroy our world tomorrow. Our ultimate security will only come from the complete and verifiable elimination of these weapons, and the assurance that they will never be produced again. We do not want existing nuclear weapons states to develop new types of weapons, nor do we want to see more states acquiring nuclear weapons. New Zealand is therefore participating actively both in existing systems and in new initiatives to prevent proliferation.

Overview of present position

The 1970 Treaty on the Non-Proliferation of Nuclear Weapons (NPT) remains the cornerstone of the nuclear disarmament and non-proliferation regime. Under the NPT, five states were recognized as possessing nuclear weapons at that time (the five Security Council permanent members, the United States (US), United Kingdom (UK), France, China, and Russia). The 'grand bargain' of the NPT was that those five states, the nuclear weapons states (NWS), would work towards elimination of their nuclear arsenals, while other treaty members (the non-nuclear weapons states) agreed not to seek nuclear weapons, in return for guaranteed access to the benefits of peaceful nuclear technology.

The International Atomic Energy Agency (IAEA) was given the job of verifying that NPT member states were meeting their commitments, and that nuclear material was not being diverted to weapons programmes. In disarmament jargon, the IAEA is the NPT's 'verification mechanism'.

But the NPT is far from perfect. The path to disarmament was not made verifiable and neither was a timetable stipulated. Some states – most notably India, Pakistan and Israel – did not sign on to the NPT. This meant that they were not constrained by it when they subsequently developed their own nuclear weapons. There is no agreed mechanism to sanction a nation that signs against nuclear weapons but does develop them, such as the Democratic Peoples Republic of Korea (DPRK), and there is no agreement about whether the NWS can develop new forms of nuclear weapons.

All multilateral agreements are necessarily compromises, and we should not discount the treaty because of these imperfections. We must remember that the NPT was negotiated at a time, in the 1960s, when there were predictions that more than 20 countries would have nuclear weapons by the end of the century. That has not happened. Only eight states – the original five NWS, plus India, Pakistan and Israel outside the NPT – are known to have nuclear weapons. And no nuclear weapons have been used for almost 60 years. That is a result of the horror caused by the bombing of Hiroshima and Nagasaki. We must never forget that horror: this is what drives us in our efforts to remove nuclear weapons from the world.

Moreover, the nuclear disarmament provision of the NPT Treaty – Article 6 – is clear, despite the lack of timetable:

> *Each of the Parties to the Treaty undertakes to pursue negotiations in good faith on effective measures relating to cessation of the nuclear arms race at an early date and to nuclear disarmament, and on a treaty on general and complete disarmament under strict and effective international control.*

That is it. That is the basis we have to fall back on in persuading the nuclear weapons states to eliminate their weapons. Adherence to this provision has since been reiterated. The NPT has a major review conference every five years, to consider how to strengthen and advance the treaty. At the 2000 Review Conference, member states agreed to '13 practical steps toward nuclear disarmament', including 'an unequivocal undertaking by the nuclear weapon states to accomplish the total elimination of their nuclear arsenals'. This 'unequivocal undertaking' is vitally important, for it reaffirms the unambiguous intent to which all countries agreed in 1970. Thus the question arises: why is progress towards this goal so painfully slow? The reality is that no state wants to give up its nuclear weapons, and that is why we, those states opposed to WMD, have to keep pushing.

New Zealand, concerned as it has been that nuclear disarmament is being ignored in the rush to prevent proliferation, has worked especially hard through the New Agenda – a group of seven states (Brazil, Egypt, Ireland, New Zealand, Mexico, South Africa, Sweden) formed in 1998 to vigorously pursue nuclear disarmament and work towards a nuclear weapons free world – to ensure that the need for action toward nuclear disarmament is not overlooked. Most of the work is not dramatic. It takes place behind the scenes, as we push incrementally in committees, speeches, conferences, resolutions, to make it clear that the majority of the world wants nuclear disarmament and will not be diverted from that objective. You would think that we would be pushing at an open door. Regrettably, that is not the case: despite all the risks, countries that possess nuclear weapons, most of which also have huge and sophisticated conventional arsenals, remain loathe to part with them.

The group calls for renewed international effort towards nuclear disarmament and outlines a programme to achieve this. The New Agenda countries actively promote the agenda in international fora, and were very influential in forging a successful outcome to the 2000 NPT Review Conference. It runs resolutions on nuclear disarmament at the UN General Assembly. The resolutions have always passed with a large majority, but most North Atlantic Treaty Organization (NATO) members, except Canada, have abstained.

In 2004 we were extremely encouraged when the New Agenda resolution on nuclear disarmament was supported by key NATO states such as Germany, Belgium, Norway, Canada and Turkey, as well as by Japan and South Korea. We must hope that this support will translate into increased pressure on the nuclear weapon states to phase out their nuclear arsenals.

Just before the 2004 UN General Assembly, the foreign ministers of the seven New Agenda countries wrote a joint op-ed piece on nuclear disarmament, published in the *International Herald Tribune* (Amorim et al, 2004). IAEA Director General Mohamed ElBaradei, commented in a subsequent speech:

> *Striving for nuclear disarmament is not an idealistic march towards an unachievable Utopia. Just last month, seven prominent policy makers, the foreign ministers of Brazil, Egypt, Ireland, Mexico, New Zealand, South Africa and*

Sweden spoke out jointly, saying, 'Today, we are more convinced than ever that nuclear disarmament is imperative for international peace and security'. They added, 'Nuclear non-proliferation and disarmament are two sides of the same coin, and both must be energetically pursued'. I could not agree more. It is this type of leadership that is urgently needed.

ElBaradei, 2004

New issues and approaches to WMD

The international security environment did change after the events of 11 September 2001. Suddenly, there was a new awareness by powerful nations that they were vulnerable – to conventional weapons and, even more, to WMD in the hands of non-state actors. The sense of threat was increased by the revelations about the A. Q. Khan network, as the extent of the 'nuclear black market' became clear. The current fear in this world of heightened tensions and increasing technological ability is that the number of states with WMD might grow again, and that non-state actors might get their hands on them. Some 10 countries already can and do enrich uranium.

This threat perception galvanized a series of initiatives over the past two years and especially in 2004 designed to make it more difficult for terrorists to get their hands on WMD or WMD-related materials:

- more stringent controls on exports of strategic goods;
- moves to encourage states to give the IAEA stronger powers of inspection and verification, by acceding to the IAEA's Additional Protocol – in fact there are proposals to make this a condition for supply of nuclear materials;
- the Proliferation Security Initiative (PSI), designed to make it more difficult to transport WMD-related materials;
- the Global Threat Reduction Initiative, designed to help secure vulnerable radioactive sources, associated with ongoing work of the IAEA on security of radioactive sources;
- the G8 Global Partnership Against Proliferation of Weapons of Mass Destruction, designed to secure existing WMD and related materials in the former Soviet Union, and to destroy stockpiles of chemical weapons;
- (and most far reaching), UN Security Council resolution 1540 on non-proliferation, passed in April 2004 (UN, 2004a).

All of these are essentially voluntary, except for Security Council Resolution 1540, which was passed by the UN Security Council under Chapter 7 of the UN Charter. This means that *compliance with it is mandatory for all UN member states*. The provisions are extraordinarily far reaching. States must put effective laws in place to control both domestic production and export of any WMD-related materials, to 'prevent the proliferation of nuclear, chemical, or biological weapons and their means of delivery'.

It seems a pity that the Security Council did not pass a sister resolution to 1540, declaring nuclear disarmament to be mandatory for all member states. However, as the five NPT nuclear weapons states are the five Permanent Security Council members (with the veto), I suppose that is unlikely to happen in the near future.

Challenges and opportunities in 2005

As a cabinet minister, I have an interesting mix of responsibilities: disarmament, international aid and development, and the environment. My work forces me out of single-issue thinking, enabling me to see the integration of different work streams at international and national level. 2005 will be remembered as the year when a number of reports, debates and summits attempted to build towards this integration of effort, all having an impact on disarmament.

Since December 2004, we have been poring over the report of the High Level Panel on Threats, Challenges and Change, appointed by UN Secretary-General Kofi Annan to consider the capability of the UN to respond to security challenges facing the world in the 21st century: challenges from WMD, from unfulfilled development goals and from the ways some parts of the UN system go about their business (UN, 2004b). Progress towards the millennium goals was reviewed in the UN Millennium Project report, *Investing in Development*, released in January 2005 (UN Millennium Project, 2005). The goals for 2015 were set in 2000, and one-third of the way along we needed to measure the progress. How far along are we in meeting the goals set on education, health, provision of clean water and sanitation?

The UN Secretary-General released a further report in March 2005 entitled, 'In Larger Freedom: Towards development, security and human rights for all' (UN, 2005). The Secretary-General's report draws on the work of the High Level Panel and the UN Millennium Project reports to present a reform package that he hopes member states can agree to at the September 2005 World Summit.

The IAEA group of experts report

February 2005 saw the release of the long-awaited report of the IAEA Group of Experts. The group's report – 'Multilateral Approaches to the Nuclear Fuel Cycle' – was commissioned by IAEA Director General Mohamed ElBaradei in June 2004, following his suggestion that wide dissemination of the most proliferation sensitive parts of the nuclear fuel cycle could be the 'Achilles' heel' of the nuclear non-proliferation regime.

The NPT guarantees the right of non-nuclear weapons states to nuclear technology for peaceful purposes. However, if a country develops, for peaceful purposes, a full nuclear fuel cycle including enrichment and reprocessing, then it potentially has access to weapons-grade uranium and plutonium for use in nuclear weapons. How can others be guaranteed that the nuclear programme is for peaceful purposes? This is essentially the dilemma the international community has been facing with Iran's nuclear programme. Should enrichment and reprocessing facilities be placed under multilateral control? The expert group's report attempts to deal with these issues.

The report outlines five approaches to strengthen controls over fuel enrichment, reprocessing, spent fuel repositories and spent fuel storage. They are:

1   Reinforcing existing commercial market mechanisms on a case-by-case basis through long-term contracts and transparent suppliers' arrangements with government backing. Examples would be: fuel leasing and fuel take-back offers, commercial offers to store and dispose of spent fuel, as well as commercial fuel banks
2   Developing and implementing international supply guarantees with IAEA participation. Different models should be investigated, notably with the IAEA as guarantor of service supplies – for example, as administrator of a fuel bank
3   Promoting voluntary conversion of existing facilities to multilateral nuclear approaches (MNA), and pursuing them as confidence-building measures, with the participation of NPT non-nuclear-weapon states and nuclear-weapon states, and non-NPT states
4   Creating, through voluntary agreements and contracts, multinational, and in particular regional, MNAs for new facilities based on joint ownership, drawing rights or co-management for front-end and back-end nuclear facilities, such as uranium enrichment; fuel reprocessing; disposal and storage of spent fuel (and combinations thereof). Integrated nuclear power parks would also serve this objective
5   The scenario of a further expansion of nuclear energy around the world might call for the development of a nuclear fuel cycle with stronger multilateral arrangements – by region or by continent – and for broader cooperation, involving the IAEA and the international community (IAEA, 2005).

Nuclear non-proliferation conference 2005

Heading towards the NPT Review Conference, scheduled in New York from 2 to 27 May 2005, the issues look at this time (April 2005) to be complex, with the NWS (the US in particular) focused strongly on 'horizontal' non-proliferation: that is, no more states to develop nuclear weapons. The prospects for the realization of the NPT Treaty's ultimate objective – the total elimination of nuclear weapons – seem no further advanced than when the NPT Treaty was concluded in 1970.

The challenge lies, as always, between those states with nuclear weapons and their allies who feel protected by that alliance with a nuclear power, and those countries who choose against, or cannot afford, nuclear weapons but who feel threatened by the very existence and therefore possible use of nuclear weapons.

One of the incremental steps could be a focus on verification measures. Such measures, using IAEA, are demanded of the states accessing nuclear energy to ensure that they are not building nuclear weapons. Where do they source their enriched uranium? How enriched is it? But while verification is stringently applied here, it is not applied to the NWS when they assert that they have down-blended highly enriched uranium (HEU) and denatured plutonium. Such assertions need to be verified by an independent body, if only to build trust in the non-proliferation process.

Another option might be to explore vertical proliferation, when nuclear states develop new nuclear weapons or replace older ones. Is such vertical proliferation a transgression against the spirit of the NPT, which was signed by five of the NWS?

Those who favour nuclear disarmament as the solution might consider whether to build on the International Court of Justice's (ICJ) Advisory Opinion in 1996. This noted that there is not, in either customary or conventional law, any specific authorization for, or comprehensive banning of, the threat or use of nuclear weapons. But the court also decided that the threat or use of nuclear weapons would generally be contrary to the rules of international law applicable in armed conflict, and, in particular, the principles and rules of humanitarian law. While it could not conclude definitely whether the threat or use of nuclear weapons would be lawful or unlawful in an extreme circumstance of self-defence, in which the very survival of a state would be at stake, it noted that the threat or use of nuclear weapons should always be compatible with Article 2 (4) of the UN Charter, meet all of the requirements of Article 51 of the Charter, and be compatible with the principles of the international law applicable in armed conflict.

And then there might be a strengthening of the NPT by adding in a time-table, leading step by step to total nuclear disarmament. This is a combination of building on the ICJ Advisory Opinion and strengthening the NPT with a timetable, verification, consideration of vertical proliferation, penalties – all of which could require a Secretariat, and a mechanism for reporting to the Security Council.

New Zealand does not accept that any of these actions can be dismissed as hollow idealism, but whether all this will be achieved at the 2005 NPT Review is debatable. Crucially, significant energy has been building, and while the Review Conference is a focal point, this is a continuing movement towards a world without weapons of mass destruction.

Commission on weapons of mass destruction

The Swedish Government, on the initiative of the late Foreign Minister Anna Lindh, has made the significant contribution of sponsoring an independent Weapons of Mass Destruction Commission, chaired by Hans Blix, formerly head of the UN Monitoring, Verification and Inspection Commission (UNMOVIC). This commission is considering the wider, vexed questions around how to control WMD – such as, what is to be done about those states like India, Pakistan, and Israel that remain outside the nuclear non-proliferation treaty system? The commission will issue a final report in early 2006. Within that report will be a seminar/study on verification issues.

New Zealand has consistently advocated that verification mechanisms for multilateral disarmament agreements should be the strongest possible. We are perfectly willing to accept intrusive inspections at chemical facilities at short notice, as long as the provisions are the same for all. Only strong verification can reassure nations that their neighbours are not arming, and give them enough confidence to disarm themselves.

Trends for the future

In the months following the 2004 Indian Ocean tsunami, a new trend of almost worldwide cooperation has been demonstrated. States have cooperated with each other, regardless of whether they are in the G8 or G77, whether they are large or small, northern or southern, allies or non-aligned. Within most countries there has been strong leadership shown by non-governmental organizations (NGOs) and local communities, and there has been great coordination among state agencies, business corporations, NGOs and local communities. As a trend for the future, this response to the tsunami offers an opportunity to build on for other issues. If such cooperation could be extended to meeting the Millennium Development Goals (MDGS), reducing indebtedness, building fair and transparent trading rules, then the need for WMD could become less credible.

However, to relax into euphoria that peace and justice has arrived is prematurely optimistic, as the trends before the tsunami were far from optimistic. From the perspective of potential nuclear conflict, the Cold War of the last decades of last century was in a way easier to manage. The threat was mostly confined to two power blocs facing off. Although the spectre of thousands of nuclear warheads primed and ready to be deployed was always unsettling, the focus was on those two blocs. And in that myopic focus lie the seeds for some of what we face today. The powers of those blocs ignored civil society, ignored smaller independent states, ignored the developing world, ignored their allies. This has contributed to the diversity of dividing lines that we live with today. International tension is now a lower percentage of threats to peace. Instead, threats come from intra-national conflict, from secessionist groups, from 'non-state actors'. And WMD (nuclear, chemical, biological) are no longer confined by virtue of technical capability to national laboratories funded by state taxes: WMD can be built and delivered by small groups of people. Fragmentation has brought a new raft of issues.

Along with fragmentation has come the reality of Marshall McLuhan's Global Village. True it is a factionalized village, but electronic communication systems have changed how we see ourselves and others in the world. The same technology can have different effects. There is one global village whose information is presented on television, radio, print and internet news/ blogs, all owned by a dwindling number of news corporations. And the other global village (the web) communicates at individual level with speed, eyewitness reports, debate, assertion and rumour. This communication network is monitored, but not yet screened or edited. While for some world citizens the message in corporate media is marketed and packaged, for others there is the open-ended opportunity to search and to report, and to mislead and misunderstand.

Impacts of these trends

For peacebuilding, these trends provide both opportunities and challenges. UN Secretary-General Kofi Annan's March 2005 report, 'In Larger Freedom', makes a valuable contribution to seeing our collective security in interconnected ways. Annan has challenged us all, placing the UN Charter firmly at the centre of our undertakings to ensure that the world can realize 'freedom from want', 'freedom from fear', and 'freedom to live in dignity'. As the UN founders knew 60 years ago, development, security, and human rights and the rule of law, are all crucially interconnected. Achievement of one, such as disarmament and security, will be difficult if not impossible without realizing the others. Reforming the multilateral system to play its part in this endeavour is our central challenge in 2005 and beyond, and New Zealand will join other voices for the creation of an effective Peacebuilding Commission to oversee and coordinate the UN's efforts in this important area.

More opportunities lie in the outreach offered by the internet. We have seen the powerful community response to the tsunami – maybe we can take the nuclear debate out of the committee room to build such a powerful response against WMD that governments cannot ignore it.

It is not a case of devaluing the nation state as having no role to play. Clearly they are still the building blocks of decision making and more importantly the implementation of these decisions. If we use the tsunami experience again, individuals were affected by what they read and saw. Individuals and community groups responded with cash, often collected electronically. NGOs purchased the necessary goods of food, water, medicine. But it was the national defence forces alone that had the transport capacity to move those actual goods from storage to the damaged villages in Aceh and Sri Lanka. The role of the US aircraft carrier Abraham Lincoln, whose off-coast anchorage provided a ready base, was pivotal in those first weeks.

Inclusive decision making

The balance we need to achieve is the inclusion of our communities in the decision-making processes. How many citizens know of the 2005 NPT Review Conference? How many citizens realize the opportunities such a conference can offer to the process of gaining a world without nuclear weapons? That goal of inclusion or even of disarmament may not be welcome by those who own the media corporations, but there is still a people's internet. As a young opposition candidate I knew I could not rely on being reported by the city's newspapers, both owned by the same company. So I ran a campaign based on networks around schools, churches, sports and work. And new communication technologies in the world offer us these opportunities.

We do have a model of community inclusion and power; it is not one to forget. Many have taken up the challenge. The Mayors for Peace, established in 1982 on the initiative of the then-Mayor of Hiroshima, Takeshi Araki, offered cities a way to transcend national borders and work together to press for nuclear abolition. In March 1990, the Mayors' Conference was officially registered as a UN NGO related to the Department of Public Information. In May 1991, it became an NGO in Special Consultative Status registered with the UN's Economic and Social Council. As of 7 December 2004, the Mayors for Peace included the mayors of some 652 cities in 109 countries around the world. They have all expressed their support for a programme to promote the solidarity of cities towards the total abolition of nuclear weapons.

The International Physicians for the Prevention of Nuclear War (IPPNW) is a non-partisan global federation of national medical organizations in 58 countries dedicated to research, education and advocacy relevant to the prevention of nuclear war. The organization seeks to prevent all wars, promote non-violent conflict resolution and minimize the effects of war and preparations for war on health, development and the environment. It works for the abolition of all nuclear weapons, demilitarization of the global economy and an end to the arms trade, re-allocation of resources from military to civilian needs, especially to basic health care and human necessities and sustainable and ecologically sound economic development. Their principal programme areas beyond the core mission of nuclear abolition include projects to end the threats posed by small arms and light weapons, landmines, chemical and biological weapons, and the burden of debt on developing nations.

Lawyers from all over the world have joined together in the International Association of Lawyers Against Nuclear Arms (IALANA), with the common cause of influencing governmental policy toward the total abolition of nuclear weapons and keeping nuclear disarmament a fundamental issue on the international political agenda. They offer legal advice to governments on nuclear disarmament.

And in the disarmament area we do have a successful treaty – the Ottawa Convention on the Prohibition of the Use, Stockpiling, Production, and Transfer of Anti-Personnel Mines and on their Destruction – which was driven by our citizens. The treaty is the most comprehensive international instrument for ridding the world of the scourge of anti-personnel mines. It deals with everything from mine use, production and trade, to victim assistance, mine clearance and stockpile destruction.

But we must remember that governments did not initiate the process. It began, and continued, as a coalition of NGOs and communities affected by landmines. In the early- to mid-1990s a small number of individuals and agencies started to publicize the issue on anti-personnel mines, and in 1991 Human Rights Watch and Physicians for Human Rights published the first detailed study of how landmines were actually being used. The International Campaign to Ban Landmines (ICBL) was founded in 1992 by a half dozen concerned NGOs, with the hope to ban the use, stockpiling, production and transfer of landmines. Within four years the movement had swelled to over 1400 religious, humanitarian and development NGOs and organizations, enjoying the support and endorsement of senior world statesmen, numerous senior military commanders and religious leaders worldwide.

They organized public meetings and used the media creatively and extensively to publicize the horrors of mines, while petitioning politicians and governments to take action to ban landmines. Hundreds of civil society groups flooded to join the movement including major international agencies such as the International Committee of the Red Cross (ICRC) and different UN agencies. And they mobilized people like the Princess of Wales to bring the matter into people's living rooms and on to their TV screens – to such an extent that governments began to seriously consider the idea.

In December 1997, 122 nations signed the Ottawa Convention on the Prohibition of the Use, Stockpiling, Production, and Transfer of Anti-Personnel Mines and on their Destruction Convention. The ICBL, as well as key individuals within the movement, were awarded the 1997 Nobel Peace Prize.

Civil society has continued this active role. For the first time in history, NGOs have, with the *Landmine Monitor*, published annually by the ICBL, come together in a coordinated, systematic and sustained way to monitor a humanitarian law or disarmament treaty, and to regularly document progress and problems. This successfully puts into practice the concept of civil society-based verification.

Suggestions for the future

In the early months of 2005, there were a number of meetings of think-tanks, NGOs and politicians negotiating a way forward for the May NPT Review Conference. The work of initiatives such as the New Agenda Coalition is fundamental in keeping the nuclear disarmament debate alive. We must continue our work, amplifying the disarmament message beyond the 2005 NPT Review Conference. A climate of nuclear disarmament, of the pursuit in good faith of effective measures to that end, is surely more conducive to international peace and security than one in which retention of nuclear weapons (and their possible further development) nurtures grievances, sustains dangerous rivalries and erodes the rule of law.

I know that I wish to advocate for a strengthened treaty, or a new treaty that outlaws nuclear weapons. Nuclear disarmament is still the ultimate goal of New Zealand. Whether we achieve this in three months or three years, we will need a secretariat that serves all the disarmament/arms control treaties and conventions. Cooperation and consolidation is needed within the disarmament enclave in the first instance, and this must link to a strengthened UN. We will need a handful of nations to step up to the microphone, to build a picture of the risks that face us in a world that still has nuclear weapons. New Zealand will be one of these nations.

All this institutional strengthening cannot be done in isolation from the local communities. We must use cleverer ways to reach out and include the different viewpoints – of the Kashmiri community, of the Korean community, of the Middle East communities – of all those threatened by violence, and in particular, nuclear violence. This campaign must not be confined to the seasoned peace activist. Like the anti-mining campaigns, it must include those closest to the threat at community level.

References

Amorim, C., Gheit, A., Cowen, B., Bautista, L.-E., Goff, P., Dlimini-Zuma, N. and Freivalds, L. (2004) 'Seven foreign ministers speak out: Non-proliferation and disarmament go hand in hand', *International Herald Tribune*, 22 September, www.iht.com/articles/2004/09/22/edministers_ed3_.php

Dhanapala, J. (2002) 'The NPT and the future of nuclear weapons', Speech by former United Nations Under-Secretary-General for Disarmament Affairs, Workshop organized by the Monterey Institute for International Studies, France, 14 July, http://cns.miis.edu

ElBaradei, M. (2004) 'Nuclear weapons and the search for security', Statement at the 54th Pugwash Conference on Science and World Affairs by IAEA Director-General, 6 October, www.iaea.org

IAEA (2005) 'Multilateral approaches to the nuclear fuel cycle: Expert Group Report' submitted to the Director-General of the International Atomic Energy Agency, INFCIRC/640, 22 February 2005, www.iaea.org/Publications/Documents/Infcircs/2005/infcirc640.pdf

UN (2004a) Security Council Resolution 1540, UN document S/RES/1540, 28 April

UN (2004b) *A more secure world: Our shared responsibility*, Report of the High Level Panel on Threats, Challenges and Change, UN document A/59/565, 2 December, www.un.org/secureworld/

UN Millennium Project (2005), 'Investing in development: A practical plan for the implementation of the Millennium Development Goals', UN publication, Sales No 05.111.B.4); see www.unmillenniumproject.org

UN (2005) *In Larger Freedom: Towards development, security and human rights for all*, Report of the Secretary-General, document A/59/2005, 21 March, United Nations, New York

5

Women, War and Peace: Mobilizing for Security and Justice in the 21st Century[1]

Noeleen Heyzer

Introduction

Humanity's entry into the 21st century has been both painful and dangerous. In particular, terrorism, and the 'war on terror' that followed, made clear to us that our destinies are linked and our lives intertwined. Now, more than ever, global security is linked with national and human security. The fear and violence that now characterize our world demonstrate, especially after the invasion of Iraq, that no one country, agency or sector of society, however powerful, can alone ensure global peace and human security. The common goals, norms and standards that we develop to guide our interactions with each other – whether as states or local communities, organizations or individuals — are the best, and maybe the only, guarantors of human security.

As shown most clearly by the history of Afghanistan over the last three decades, the intertwining forces of internal and external conflict, and social and gender injustice, undermine the capacity of countries to move towards sustainable peace and development and threaten global peace and security. If we are to find just and equitable responses to the great challenges of this era and increase all forms of human security – economic, political, and social – then those who are most affected by insecurities and injustices must be involved in finding solutions.

Because some of the most entrenched social, economic, political, and cultural injustices are endured by women, half of the world's population, it is necessary to make their voices heard, their perspectives visible, and their solutions legitimate; they must become leaders of communities and institutions, with the power to shape policies and agendas. In an increasingly insecure world, the vision of women who advocate for peace and justice must finally come to the fore as the dominant, rather than the alternative, perspective. Unless we take seriously the theme of the United Nations Women's World Conferences, 'Equality, Development and Peace', we are going to lose out on the possibility of long-term peace and stability.

The roots of conflict and political mobilization

Every major conflict involves an interaction between economic, political, historical, and cultural factors. Some conflicts arise when groups of people feel economically or politically deprived, others when people have their lands or natural resources taken away from them, or their control. Patterns of economic and political governance that perpetuate and reproduce inequalities and exclusion often fuel political mobilization. And in many cases, group mobilization often occurs along lines of ethnic, religious or ideological identity, enhanced by sharp inequalities and various forms of exclusion.

Wars also have an economic dimension, with winners as well as losers. Armed conflicts foster the transnational production and trafficking in arms, drugs, diamonds, as well as human beings. The breakdown of order resulting from conflict creates conditions in which the trafficking of women, children, and men can flourish, often through networks of organized crime. The United Nations (UN) ranks human trafficking as the third largest criminal enterprise worldwide, second only to drugs and arms; it generates an estimated US$9.5 billion each year for the procurers, smugglers, and corrupt public officials who make it possible.[2] In Colombia, for example, the *International Organization for Migration* estimates that 10 women are trafficked out of the country every day, and about 500,000 Colombian women and children are believed to have been trafficked into sexual exploitation or forced labour outside the country.[3]

Where economic opportunities are few and not able to provide for decent livelihoods, the possibilities of enrichment by war are considerable, including recruitment into armed militias, opportunities for looting or misappropriating aid supplies as well as profiteering from shortages of essential goods. For certain people, conflict is more profitable than peace, and violence provides a real alternative for those marginalized under arrangements they perceive as inequitable and unjust. However, it is by no means only disadvantaged or criminal groups that resort to violence to further their cause; privileged groups, including states, also wage brutal campaigns against political adversaries to gain advantage.

In many cases, political mobilization for war is based on lived realities of injustice. In situations where official policies, institutions, and leaders have failed to provide equal security, opportunity, and dignity, a sense of injustice and desperation prevails among certain sections of the population. Under such circumstances, engaging in group mobilization can be a form or process of empowerment, enabling people who feel themselves victims of injustice to become part of a collective movement, with the conviction and hope that they are taking their lives and destinies into their own hands. In conflict societies, where the majority of people are robbed of their capacity to shape the conditions of their lives, political mobilization can be an act of collective self-determination; an attempt by ordinary people to reclaim ownership and direction over their own lives, sometimes even through violent means.

Because inequalities and injustices are often reproduced along the fault lines of social identity, including ethnicity, religion and tribe, political mobilization frequently also takes place in accordance with these political identities, which are often solidified through legal and institutional codification. In many post-colonial countries, racial, ethnic, and religious identities became politically and legally institutionalized through processes of decolonization and nation-building, clearly differentiating populations within bounded categories of identity, as well along binaries of majority and minority, as was seen in the case of Rwanda, where the fall-out from colonial divisions fuelled perceived injustices that fell along ethnic lines, leaving a gruesome legacy.

In many of these countries, group privilege and rights are officially entrenched in the institutions, processes, and practices of the nation state, thereby reproducing multiple disparities among groups who have been classified and administered as distinct and unequal. As a result, group mobilization against real and perceived injustice often takes place along the fault lines of identity. While such mobilization need not employ violent means, in many places it does, particularly when other channels of redress have proven to be ineffective.

Political mobilization along the lines of identity occurs not only horizontally within nation states; it also occurs vertically, such as in cases of state violence against rebel groups, and globally, as we have seen in today's borderless 'war on terror'. Rapidly changing international security policies also produce new political identities. The increased suspicion, monitoring, and profiling of Muslims in the United States (US) following the 11 September 2001 attacks is a clear example of this, as is the current indiscriminate targeting by insurgents in Iraq of anyone perceived as supporting the occupying forces, including Iraqi civilians.

Collective agency

Group mobilization in situations of conflict need not lead to further hostilities between communities, or to embracing violence as a means of achieving their goals. There are forms of collective agency that engage universal principles, norms and standards and promote the protection of rights of all human beings. Women in conflict zones have mobilized within their communities and across borders to demand that the international community put an end to violence, urgently address the impact of war on women and communities and protect the future of their societies. It was mobilization by women, with the support of the UN Development Fund for Women (UNIFEM) that in 2000 led to the adoption of Security Council Resolution 1325 on women, peace and security, under the leadership of the Government of Namibia as president of the Security Council.

With this landmark resolution, women have shown it is possible to redefine international frameworks and policies using their own diverse experiences in conflict areas around the world. They identified women, peace and security as common priorities, requiring an urgent response by various local and international actors, from members of their own communities to member states on the UN Security Council. It was women who pried open the closed doors of the Security Council, availing themselves of a mechanism, known as the Arria Formula, by which those who had actually experienced war and conflict and others outside the formal decision-making process could make their voices and perspectives heard.

It is important for those who represent the international system to identify, support, and respond seriously to people's efforts to mobilize in ways compatible with international values, to make viable non-violent forms of mobilization. It is not simply a question of recognizing people's aspiration to find alternatives to violence; it is a matter of making legitimate people's realities, grievances, and struggles, giving people reason to trust in an international system that protects and defends their rights, empowering local constituencies for reform, and promising people a stake in a common future. This means, among other things, assisting local constituencies in their efforts to address the injustices of the present and the past. The challenge to the international system is an urgent one. Failure to respond in a timely and effective manner could result in an irreversible loss of faith in international norms, as well as in aspirations for an inclusive future that defends the dignity and rights of all people.

Such a loss of faith will only deepen people's sense of betrayal and distrust, and generate the conditions for more hostility and revenge. In short, the challenge to respond effectively is a matter of life and death and demands a rethinking of how we mobilize to create a more secure and just world.

Women, war and peace

Wars are a major source of devastation, human suffering and poverty, affecting all aspects of economic, social and political life. The nature of warfare has changed: it is no longer soldiers who comprise the largest number of casualties, but civilians. In World War I, 14 per cent of the deaths were civilians; today it is estimated that this number has risen to over 75 per cent. The nature of the battlefield has also changed: warfare is no longer fought in remote battlefields between armies, but is fought in our homes, our schools, our communities and, increasingly, on women's bodies.

In this context, it is important to understand the conditions and difficulties of women's lives in times of war and conflict, and to understand how women seek to connect these experiences at the local level to global policy making and action.

Three interrelated dimensions affect women's lives during violent conflict and in the transition to peace: firstly, the specific impact that war has on women's lives, including various forms of violence and the erosion of the economic and social fabric of community; secondly, the importance of women's participation in peace processes; and thirdly, women's role in shaping post-conflict reconstruction processes to ensure their societies are founded on justice, inclusion, and a commitment to the dignity and development of all its members.

In conflicts throughout the world, violence against women has been used as a weapon of war, not just to violate the women, but to humiliate the men of the other side, and to erode the social and moral fabric of entire communities across generations. Women know the cost of violence, extremism and exclusion, the cost of destroyed states and economies, and the cost of accumulated conflicts. They know what it means to have sons, brothers, husbands, and even daughters who have fought and died in conflicts. Many women and girls are forced to hide or flee, lest they be coerced into slavery by militia groups. Others actively join armed movements to seek protection from other armed groups, or seek retribution for the loss of loved ones.

Women know what it means to be displaced, to bear high rates of maternal and child mortality and low rates of access to education and health care. They know what it means to be excluded from public life, and not to be recognized as full citizens. In situations of conflict, women are the first to be affected by infrastructure breakdown, and carry the ever increasing burden of caring and providing for their families, the injured and the wounded, while being forced to adopt survival strategies at the margins of war economies.

Women who have survived wars must find ways to live with the gross injustices that have filled their past and are haunting their present – acts of discrimination and violence committed before, during and even after conflict. In the recovery process, there must be peace with justice and equality. The consolidation of peace cannot be achieved unless there is justice based on the rule of law. This refers to a principle of governance in which all persons, institutions and entities, including the state, are accountable to laws that are consistent with international norms and standards. The charter of the UN itself, together with the four pillars of the international legal system – international human rights law, international humanitarian law, international criminal law, and international refugee law – make up the normative foundation necessary to advancing the rule of law.

The role of the UN

As stated by UN Secretary-General Kofi Annan in his report on the rule of law and transitional justice in conflict and post-conflict societies, helping war-torn societies re-establish the rule of law and come to terms with large-scale abuses is a core mission of the UN. In contexts marked by devastated institutions, exhausted resources, and a traumatized and divided population, this is an overwhelming but urgent task. While the UN has been tailored to respond to the immediate security needs of populations affected by conflict, and to address the grave injustices generated by war, the root causes of conflict have too often been overlooked and insufficiently dealt with. Yet, it is precisely in addressing the causes of conflict and seeking to build societies based on inclusiveness, equality, and rule of law, that the international community can help prevent a return to conflict in the future. Prevention is the first imperative of justice and sustainable peace.

The UN plays an important role in upholding the rule of law by helping countries to strengthen national systems for the administration of justice in accordance with international standards. Increasingly, the UN realizes the importance of adopting a comprehensive approach, by engaging all relevant institutions in the development of national justice systems, and paying attention to various dimensions of this process, including establishing standards of justice, formulating laws that codify them, strengthening institutions that implement them, developing mechanisms to monitor them, and protecting the people who must have access to them.

Most recently, the Joint Assessment Mission (JAM), which the UN fielded in Sudan earlier this year, showed the results of work to UNIFEM and others to ensure that gender concerns were integrated into each of the eight thematic issues reports. Due largely to the participation of gender experts from both the north and the south of Sudan, the JAM provided the basis for women to come together to develop a common agenda to influence the peace process. The JAM recommended urgent priorities and actions for reconstruction, including minimum representation of 30 per cent women in the constitutional review and peace commissions; provisions to prevent gender-based violence (GBV) and to support victims; and capacity building and provisions for gender equality in all relevant institutional development.

While women are often the first victims of armed conflict, they must also be recognized as part of its resolution. Since the adoption of Resolution 1325, there have been some notable achievements. Within its framework, attempts are being made in the UN to develop a more systematic approach to consulting with and involving women in conflict and post-conflict societies, in all stages and at all levels of the peace and reconstruction process. The participation of women in peacemaking, peacekeeping and peacebuilding ensures that their experiences, priorities, and solutions contribute towards stability and inclusive governance. The rebuilding process must address all forms of injustice embedded in conflict and must restore all dimensions of justice – legal, restorative and distributive – from a gender perspective. Impunity for crimes committed against women weakens the foundations of societies emerging from conflict by legitimizing violence and inequality, and exposes women and the larger community to the threat of renewed conflict. During the transition to peace, a unique window of opportunity exists to put in place a gender responsive framework for national reconstruction. The involvement of women in peacebuilding and reconstruction is a key part of the process of inclusion and democracy that can contribute to a lasting peace.

Peace operations are now starting to develop ways of responding to some of the specific concerns of women in conflict zones. The implementation of Resolution 1325, with a strong constituency and broad implications for more than half the world's population is being carefully monitored by women around the world.

Protection in armed conflict

War has become a highly gendered phenomenon. While the vast majority of fighters in armed groups are men, it is increasingly common for women civilians to be targeted through sexual violence, which is increasingly used as a weapon of war against the enemy side. In many places, women and girls are also highly vulnerable to kidnapping, forced labour, and trafficking. In places such as Uganda and the Democratic Republic of Congo (DRC), it is still common for girls to be abducted into armed groups and forced into sexual slavery, with the vast majority becoming infected with sexually transmitted diseases and, increasingly, HIV/AIDS. In addition, women and girls have been forced to trade sex for safe passage, food, and protection, including by members of security forces. Women and girls are seldom protected from these threats; their aggressors are seldom punished.

We also need a better understanding of women's realities not just as victims but also as actors in political conflict. Many women choose to join political movements, including armed groups, in times of conflict. Their roles include civil activists, community workers, combatants, intelligence, nurses, porters, and cooks. Women may join, or even form, these groups because of political conviction or affiliation or to seek protection from enemy forces. In Aceh, for example, many widows and their daughters have joined the guerrilla movement for protection from the Indonesian military and military-backed militia. In such cases, women may be targeted three-fold: as women, as civilians of the opposite side, and as political enemies in armed conflict. Female dependents of combatants are also at high risk of violence and, in many places, have been subjected to gross abuses, including arbitrary detention, kidnapping, torture, and rape.

Justice deficit

Given the nature of contemporary conflicts, it is a political and social necessity to address issues of justice in a multidimensional manner, engaging all institutions of the justice system. Neglect of one inevitably leads to the weakening of the others. If injustices experienced by people during war are not sufficiently attended to, it is unlikely that trust will be established in the rebuilding of peace. Focusing on the way conflict affects women and girls is crucial to re-stitching the social fabric of families and communities after conflict and violence have ripped them apart. Until justice is seriously addressed a sadly ambiguous message is sent to perpetrators of human rights abuse that they are above the law, such as when a perpetrator is promoted to a position of power following conflict. Such perpetrators must be held accountable, and there must be urgent and severe action against this chilling destruction of women and communities.

Women and girls face a massive justice deficit in war-torn societies. By and large, international protection and humanitarian assistance operations are glaring in their neglect of the specific needs of women and girls. Protection and humanitarian assistance for women is glaring in its inadequacy. As the nature of security has changed, blurring the lines between militias and civilians, making it difficult to provide the security needed, we have totally failed to protect women and girls against the multiple forms of violence they are subjected to during conflict. The massacres in Darfur and Sudan, and the mass rapes in Haiti, are the most recent examples.

This is why women stress again and again the need for protection in armed conflict, and an end to impunity for crimes against women. They want accountability for past abuses, the punishment of human wrongs and the protection of human rights. Beyond that, they are no longer willing to be seen only as victims; they want to be recognized as part of the solution in the rebuilding process. They know that no matter which side wins, women will lose unless they are recognized as stakeholders of the future of their societies.

UNIFEM's response

In this area, UNIFEM has supported the development of early warning mechanisms based on the documentation of human rights abuse against women, in countries such as Colombia, the DRC, the Solomon Islands and in Central Asia. We have mobilized UN country teams and peace operations, in partnership with local women's groups, to develop campaigns on ending impunity for violence against women, and put the need to combat trafficking and violence against women on the agenda of rule of law institutions in post-crisis countries, such as the DRC, Kosovo and East Timor. UNIFEM has advocated for the recruitment of women into civilian police and peacekeeping forces, as well as the training of peacekeepers in issues related to violence against women, and in codes of conduct that respect women's human rights. We have supported the work of the gender caucus in the International Criminal Court (ICC) to incorporate sexual violence as a war crime, and to strengthen witness protection and victim support programmes. At the community level we have facilitated consultation on justice reform with women's groups and law enforcement institutions. In Rwanda, for example, UNIFEM trained over one hundred judges of the Gacaca courts on Resolution 1325 and issues of gender justice.

Establishing timely and effective justice is an integral part of any peacebuilding and reconstruction effort, if there is to be a solid foundation for lasting peace and respect for human rights. Failure to address inequalities in the justice system and its discrimination of women jeopardizes the chance of securing sustainable peace and increases the risk of violent conflict, as men and communities that have been humiliated through the violence against their women maintain anger, a sense of injustice, and a desire to seek revenge.

Participation in peace processes

Protection for women during conflict is not enough, however: gender justice and women's rights must be integrated in peace agreements and in the legal and institutional structures supporting post conflict reconstruction. Without women's equal participation and full involvement in peacebuilding, neither justice nor development will be possible in a war-torn society's transition to peace. In many war-torn countries, women assume activist roles while holding together their families and communities. In some cases, they have managed to bring their experiences into formal peacebuilding processes, relating their realities and concerns to official negotiating parties.

When women's voices are heard and heeded, critical priorities that would otherwise be left out of peace processes are often reflected. Such issues include the importance of increasing the presence of women in the civilian, military and police components of peacekeeping operations. Where this has happened, it has led to improved relations with local communities, which is essential to the success of peace interventions. Emphasis is also given to designing disarmament, demobilization and reintegration (DDR) processes to meet the special needs of girls and women who have been abducted into armed groups, women combatants, dependents of combatants, and former soldiers who are trying to return to civilian life. Too frequently, these women are totally excluded from rehabilitation programmes designed to foster reconciliation through support for education, health, access to land, credit, and so on. The needs of women with babies born of rape, or of girls in fighting forces, are seldom incorporated into demobilization and reintegration initiatives. For example, the World Bank reported that in the DDR programme in Mozambique in the mid-nineties, only men were granted resettlement allowances, and only men's clothing was issued, despite the presence of a significant number of female combatants.

In addition, women's peace initiatives, sometimes undertaken across warring sides, involve taking high risk in extreme conflict situations. However, these efforts are insufficiently recognized and supported, both politically and financially. Sustainable peace is, in many ways, contingent on community-based involvement and ownership of the peace process. From the grassroots level to the negotiating table, support for women's participation in peacebuilding contributes to a society's efforts to recover from violent conflict. In war, women are activists, caretakers, providers and survivors. Strengthening women's groups on the ground in conflict areas strengthens the chance that they can provide communities of hope, reaching out across barriers of identity, including clan, ethnicity, religion, and political affiliation and helping people to transcend these. They break the lines along which groups organize and mobilize for war against each other. As we saw clearly in Rwanda, Sierra Leone and elsewhere, when these communities of hope break down, children are much more easily recruited into becoming soldiers, as everyday security and opportunities for social development are eroded.

UNIFEM's response

The international community's support of women's networks and the linking of local initiatives to international systems are crucial to peace processes. From the grassroots level to the peace table, from Afghanistan to Burundi, East Timor to Sudan, UNIFEM is supporting women to influence processes of conflict resolution and post-conflict rebuilding. Our efforts in 2003 to ensure that women's leadership was a high priority in rebuilding Afghanistan yielded promising results. Through supporting the Ministry of Women's Affairs to broaden women's participation in all aspects of reconstruction, reaching out beyond Kabul to women in every province, UNIFEM helped to facilitate the development of a national women's agenda and the engagement of women in the Loya Jirga process.

Up until June 2000, the situation of Burundian women and girls had been completely ignored in negotiations for peace in that country. But in July of that year, UNIFEM succeeded in bringing Burundi's 19 negotiating parties to accept the need for women's involvement in the peace process, leading to the first All Party Burundi Women's Peace Conference. Twenty-three of the Burundi women's recommendations made to the facilitator, Nelson Mandela, were included in the final peace accord. A precedent was set and the entire peace agreement benefited.

However, as we have seen in Burundi, violence and conflict rarely end with formal agreements. Peace is fragile and conflict returns quickly if the post-conflict reconstruction process fails to seriously address both the causes and the consequences of conflict, and put in place policies of inclusion and incentives for future conflict prevention.

Gender justice in post-conflict reconstruction

The term 'post-conflict' is a simplification to describe societies where there has been a termination of hostilities either through negotiations or war, and there has not been a relapse into violence. Their transitional status provides an opportunity to shift agendas towards peace. The term 'gender justice', as used here, refers to the integration of gender perspectives within every dimension of justice, and the role of women in shaping justice frameworks and rule of law institutions in ways that promote their human rights, legal equality and inclusion.

Women have a crucial role to play in the rebuilding of stable societies. International and regional initiatives to link peace with justice not only benefit women, but are also strengthened by them. During the transition to peace, a unique opportunity exists to put in place a gender responsive framework for a country's reconstruction based on the three dimensions of justice: legal justice to address discriminatory laws against women at institutional and policy levels, such as inheritance laws that prevent women from owning property; restorative justice to address violation of human rights and war crimes so that people can move beyond their trauma and begin to construct new lives for themselves; and distributive justice to address structural and systematic injustices such as the political, economic and social inequalities that are frequently the underlying causes of conflict. Although the urgency of each of these three dimensions varies among conflicts and although they are interdependent and mutually reinforcing, the tendency is to focus primarily on restorative justice, addressing past wrongs through tribunals and the criminal justice system. Overlooking any of these dimensions of justice can lead to a recurrence of conflict and weaken the foundations of peace. Using a gender-sensitive approach to all three dimensions can help remove barriers and facilitate the movement of post-conflict countries towards stability, development and inclusive governance. Indeed, gender justice is a critical and integral dimension of any approach to establishing the rule of law and consolidating peace.

There are some essential actions required for sustainable peace which the three dimensions of justice can accelerate. These include the rebuilding of state institutions for inclusive governance; the adoption of a constitution and establishment of legal justice, or rule of law that addresses equality and fairness; the reconstruction of the economic and social infrastructure and destroyed facilities based on distributive justice to address the root causes of the conflict; the healing of the psychosocial trauma of war through truth and reconciliation in order to bring about restorative justice. In the aftermath of conflicts, resources are depleted, infrastructure is destroyed, and social, economic and political relationships are strained. Successful reconstruction depends upon the use of every available resource. Women represent the most precious and underutilized of these resources. Unless a country's constitutional, legal, judicial and electoral frameworks deal with gender equality, then no matter what happens after conflict, or how peaceful a transition, the country will never have a fair chance at development.

UNIFEM's response

UNIFEM has focused on institution-building and the strengthening of women's leadership in post-conflict situations. We have supported women's networks and mechanisms of participation, women parliamentarians, and women's civil society organizations, fostering linkages and partnerships across these as well as other constituencies. Our efforts have proven particularly successful by focusing on substantive issues, such as national development plans, economic security and rights, demobilization and reintegration, and gender equality in the rule of law.

The human security crisis has also, in many places, provided opportunities for positive change. First, in terms of legal justice, the reconstruction process provides the chance for people to reconstruct their national constitutions, their legal systems, their institutions, in ways that build the foundation for linking human security, human rights, and human development. A unique opportunity exists to put in place a gender responsive framework for a country's reconstruction.

Box 5.1 UNIFEM in Afghanistan

Afghanistan is a good example of how UNIFEM is facilitating and supporting women to develop their own vision and agendas. UNIFEM's programme for Afghanistan, based on the Afghan Women's Agenda, focuses on:

* strengthening women's economic security and rights to enjoy secure livelihoods through skills training, employment and access to markets;
* ensuring women's participation in elections and national decision making, and supporting legal and constitutional reforms;
* supporting internally displaced and refugee women to reintegrate into their communities;
* supporting civil society and the media to raise awareness of women's needs;
* supporting the establishment of regional women's centres, in collaboration with the Ministry of Women's Affairs, to train service providers and women's groups in a range of political skills, voter's education, legal and social services.

In Afghanistan, the participation of women in the Constitutional Loya Jirga and the registration process, with the support of the UN Assistance Mission in Afghanistan (UNAMA), UNIFEM and the UN Development Programme (UNDP), were critically important because they recognized women's full citizenship rights and facilitated their ability to exercise these rights. The Loya Jirga adopted the country's first post-Taliban constitution on 4 January 2004, with the majority of the 502 delegates approving a presidential system for the Islamic republic, paving the way for democratic elections later that year. Under this constitution, men and women are deemed to have equal rights and duties before the law.

The work on truth and reconciliation has to rest on restorative justice, and there has to be an end to impunity for the violence that is used against women. In Rwanda, women have testified against war criminals who still wield power and influence. They have endured the pain of telling, retelling and reliving their stories, often without privacy and security. Women seeking justice need protection and look to the standards set by the ICC. They ask for witness protection, legal support and counselling, as well as separate chambers and female judges to hear cases of women survivors of sexual violence. They ask for sanctions against tribunal staff that do not respect the rights of witnesses. Accountability means being answerable to women for crimes committed against them; it means punishing those responsible and ensuring redress for victims.

But lasting peace requires not only accountability for past actions, but also responsibility for present and future ones. Civilian police and post-conflict judicial institutions, for example, must learn to understand and address the issues such as the trafficking in women and girls, and sexual violence, both of which increase dramatically during conflict and spill over into post-conflict societies. Gender equality and inclusion and freedom from sexual violence are fundamental values on which peacebuilding must be based.

In Rwanda, UNIFEM's support for women leaders has helped to promote women's perspectives in government policies and within parliament, the judiciary and the police. Rwanda today has the world's highest percentage of women judges (50 per cent) and the highest percentage of women in parliament (49 per cent). Our support contributed to the passage of the inheritance bill, which guarantees women and girls the right to inherit property, an important ingredient of peacebuilding. This reform will go a long way in revitalizing the agricultural sector. It will also enable people and communities to invest in economic security as part of human security as rural economies once again are able to produce food and can integrate the internally displaced and the ex-combatants back into the community. More recently in Iraq, support for women's networks helped them secure the reservation in the country's interim law (Transitional Administrative Law) of 25 per cent of National Assembly seats for women. In January this year, women exceeded this, winning 86 of 275 seats or 31 per cent. Similarly, support for women's organizing in Angola, East Timor, and Mozambique has promoted gender-sensitive reviews of legal frameworks and has increased women's participation in the political arena.

Bringing institutional financial institutions on board

Advances in political and legal rights are not matched, however, by significant progress in the achievement of distributive justice. Eight of the 10 countries ranked lowest on the Human Development Index, and half of the countries designated as least developed countries (LDCs), have had major wars in the recent past. Already poor, these countries are further impoverished by violence with the destruction of their infrastructure, livelihoods and productive capacity. The vast majority of countries emerging from conflicts are LDCs and thus deeply dependent on the international financial institutions (IFIs) such as the World Bank and the International Monetary Fund (IMF) for reconstruction. These IFIs have acted as catalysts and guarantees for bilateral donors, and the World Bank in particular has sponsored quick-impact employment schemes and community development. Together with the UN, these multilateral institutions have put in place a results-focused transitional framework (RFTF) for post-conflict countries to be followed by a poverty reduction strategy (PRS).

Despite their considerable efforts to reconstruct war-torn societies and destroyed states, the World Bank and the IMF have tended to underestimate the underlying causes of conflict and the need to give conflict prevention a central place in the PRS and in the country's overall economic strategy. Their approach has been to engage in the costly tasks of reconstructing economies, in order to catch up with years of lost economic growth, and to focus on macro-economic stability. They have treated devastated economies and destroyed states in the same way as peaceful countries in their economic policy prescriptions, regarding armed conflicts as temporary disruptions to an established economic path. The issues of distributive justice among warring parties and along gender lines are not sufficiently addressed, including inequalities in income, assets, employment and access to land. As lead institutions for economic recovery in post-crisis countries, it is essential that they do more to incorporate these issues into their policy frameworks, not only for quick-impact projects or recovery packages but, more importantly, in the development strategies proposed or prescribed to governments.

For women who have long organized for peace on the ground, Security Council Resolution 1325 on women, peace and security represented a long overdue recognition of their accomplishments and challenges. It gave much needed political legitimacy to their struggle. Women were instrumental in the adoption of Resolution 1325 and are breathing life into its implementation. This resolution is not simply a UN document; it is a window to greater protection and promotion of the rights of those who are often the most vulnerable, the most invisible, and who have the greatest stake in peace. It set a new threshold of action by the UN system, and by all member states. However, women's contribution to the peacebuilding and reconstruction process will bear fruit only if conflict prevention and the reduction of political violence become a central part of development strategies to reduce poverty, exclusion and inequalities among groups.

Mobilizing for security and justice: urgent challenges

The UN Charter is a blueprint for conflict prevention. Article 26 of the charter requests the Security Council to formulate a plan for the least diversion towards armaments of the world's human and economic resources. As a conflict prevention measure, there is urgency to complete it in 2005. Member states committed themselves to a core set of norms and values basic to the Millennium Declaration's vision of 'freedom from want and freedom from fear' that underpin their commitment to the Millennium Development Goals (MDGs).

Progress towards the implementation of these goals will be reviewed in 2005, but it is already argued that achieving them would cost too much. This, while military expenditure worldwide is estimated at over US$900 billion, four times what it would cost for all nations to provide decent housing, health care and education to their citizens. The Cold War concept of weapons-based security has often provided the rationale for creating powerful global and national military budgets that emphasize defense over human well-being. We need to shift from looking at global and national security as weapons-based, military security to addressing the roots of conflict and political mobilization, globally and locally. The world can be neither secure nor peaceful until this is taken seriously.

While the human and social cost of conflicts are high for ordinary people, especially women, many individuals, groups and nations, including donor countries, stand to gain from conflicts, through the creation of lucrative war economies, the trade in weapons, employment of armies and peacekeepers, control over oil, diamonds and other resources, and the use of trafficked and forced labour. Any long-term solution for sustainable peace can only be established if there are better economic and political incentives to stop fighting. More important for the development of stable societies is the re-linking of peace to justice, inclusive governance and development with equality along lines of ethnicity, class and gender. Otherwise, a new crop of leaders, with an interest in continuing violence, will begin to mobilize their followers to take advantage of the power vacuum and sow the seeds of hatred and suspicion.

Because the roots of conflict and injustice are multidimensional, involving economic, social, and political forces, conflict and justice must be addressed not just within the agendas of peace and security, and legal reforms, but within a holistic framework that integrates human security, human development, and human rights. So far, however, crisis prevention and conflict resolution agendas have not sufficiently dealt with the conflict-development-rights nexus. The gender discrimination and violence against women that is accepted in times of peace deepens in times of war. At the same time, development strategies and poverty eradication policies have tended to neglect issues related to conflict. Yet, the prevention of conflict is essential for poverty reduction and the prevention of human suffering caused by violent conflict. Conversely, if conflict is to be avoided, the conditions of injustice that fuel political mobilization and social violence must be seriously addressed. In working to implement the MDGs, we must remember that progress towards each and every one of these goals can be destroyed by war and violence.

We now know the factors that can lead to mobilization for violent conflict. We need to create and invest in the necessary conditions that will support a different kind of mobilizing, to bring about human security, justice, and peace. International norms and standards are currently under severe threat, precisely at a time when they are most needed. The world is in need of bold leadership, made strong by vision, sustained by ethics and the moral courage to uphold international principles, based on the rule of law, and the understanding that human development and global security require the commitment of all governments and all people.

One of the best indicators of a country's or community's will to implement their commitments and achieve shared goals is the way in which it treats women and protects and promotes their security and rights. Women's mobilization for the formulation and implementation of Security Council Resolution 1325 clearly shows that change is possible, but a lot more needs to be done in the priority areas identified by women. In the area of protection and assistance, UNIFEM, other UN agencies, national partners, bilaterals and international non-governmental organizations (NGOs), have learned a great deal from pilot efforts to mobilize protection, humanitarian, psychosocial and economic support for women. But lessons learned need to be translated into standard practice. More funds, more expertise, improved monitoring and reporting and stronger accountability mechanisms are necessary to prevent gender-based violence and sexual exploitation.

Immediate and concrete steps

The opportunity now exists to make women and gender perspectives central to peace and reconstruction processes. The UN system as a whole can leverage the political, financial and technical support needed for these efforts to have an impact on peace efforts nationally, regionally and internationally. Ensuring women's representation in peacemaking, peacekeeping and peacebuilding, would be a first step in recognizing the unique and critical contributions that women can make to sustainable peace.

Making Resolution 1325 work means ensuring that the challenges facing women in conflict become a regular item on the political agenda, in thematic debates and every time a country situation is addressed. There must be efforts at every level, from local societies to the international community, to ensure its implementation. There are a number of immediate and concrete steps that can be taken by the Security Council to improve women's protection in conflict and support their role in peacebuilding. These include:

1 Ensuring that human rights verification, observer missions and peacekeeping operations focus on gender-based violations and women's human rights. As the security of women is the best indicator of the security of a nation, any early warning system must take women's voices into account
2 Ensuring that field operations protect and support humanitarian assistance for women and girls, and especially those who are refugees or internally displaced. Special measures to protect women and girls from rape and other forms of sexual violence should be an integral part of humanitarian operations
3 Ensuring that any support offered by the Security Council to a peace process, any investigation of disputes, or any attempts at mediation or settlement, make explicit the need to involve women and address the substantive concerns they bring to the table
4 Restoring the capacity and legitimacy of rule of law institutions as countries emerge from conflict. National judicial, police, and correction systems have often been stripped of their legitimacy for proper function, and have often been transformed by conflict into instruments of repression. Restoring their capacity and legitimacy based on international norms and standards is urgent for the protection of human rights and human security
5 Ensuring that the peacebuilding elements of an operation are gender-sensitive, particularly when designing DDRI programmes, in strengthening governance and public security institutions, in defining the role of civilian police, and in providing electoral assistance. These are the first steps for ensuring that women are central to post-conflict reconstruction

6   Insisting that all peacekeeping personnel be trained to understand their responsibilities to women and children. Mandatory in-service training should be provided as soon as a mission is assembled. This is not meant to be a substitute for what needs to be done at the national level

7   Calling for the establishment of a code of conduct for peacekeeping personnel and of clear reporting on sexual violence in a peacekeeping environment. This should include enforcement and monitoring mechanisms for peacekeeping personnel, through the creation of an Ombudsperson, an Inspector General, or an office created especially for that purpose

8   Promoting timely and effective justice for women by ensuring that all aspects of gender justice are fully integrated in the shaping of new constitutions, laws, and institutions of countries coming out of conflict

9   Reducing institutional and cultural barriers to the implementation of and access to justice for women, to ensure that they do not voluntarily withdraw from engaging with the justice system.

Conclusion

In September 2005, the world's leaders will meet to review progress towards implementing the Millennium Declaration, adopted at the Millennium Summit in 2000. The Declaration outlines a broad vision based on freedom from want and freedom from fear, and recognizes the importance of promoting gender equality as an effective way to combat poverty, hunger and disease and stimulate sustainable development. If we are to find enduring solutions to the challenges identified in the Declaration, the world's women – one half of its population – must be empowered to contribute their knowledge and insights to the process. We must now urgently move forward on implementation, accountability and adequate resources to bring about a world in which all people can live free of want and free of fear.

Security Council Resolution 1325 is a good example of how women, as non-state actors, have been able to bring to the attention of the Security Council situations that have endangered the security of women within particular states. What is needed now is serious and comprehensive implementation, through coordinated partnerships that address current challenges and promote strategies that have worked.

This means having the courage to understand and address the root causes of conflict. It means listening to and supporting people on the ground, being conscious of and responsive to their realities, needs, and aspirations. This must involve not just the UN, but all those who make up part of what we call the international community. In a context where our collective notions of war and peace are shaped powerfully by the media, there is an urgent need to inspire future generations with the remarkable stories of positive initiatives to build peace in the face of war, of ordinary women and men defying all odds to bring justice and hope to their communities. We cannot let our young be inspired by calls to violence.

The alternative to war and terror is an international system based on shared values with effective collective mechanisms for security and justice. As UN Secretary General Kofi Annan said at the opening of the 2004 General Assembly:

> *Today, the rule of law is at risk around the world... too often it is applied selectively and enforced arbitrarily... Throughout the world, the victims of violence and injustice are waiting for us to keep our word.*

Turning words into action is our only hope for a common future.

Notes

1   This text is a shortened version of the 2004 Dag Hammarskjöld Lecture given by Dr Noeleen Heyzer at Uppsala University on 22 September 2004. The lecture is a joint undertaking organized by Uppsala University and the Dag Hammarskjöld Foundation
2   Cited in US Department of State, Trafficking in Human Persons Report, 2004.
3   International Organization on Migration (2001) *Trafficking in Migrants*, Quarterly Bulletin, April.

Part 2
Sustainable Human Development

6

Globalization, Poverty and Security[1]

Jan Pronk

Introduction

I call on the international community at the highest level – the heads of state and government convened at the Millennium Summit – to adopt the target of halving the proportion of people living in extreme poverty, and so lifting more than 1 billion people out of it, by 2015. I further urge that no effort be spared to reach this target by that date in every region and in every country.

United Nations (UN, 2000a, p12)

Kofi Annan made this appeal in his report to the Millennium Assembly, 'We the peoples: the role of the United Nations in the twenty-first century'. These were more than just empty words or a reflection on the state of the world at the turn of the century. The Millennium Assembly of the UN marked the turn not only of the century, but also of the millennium.

In September 2000, the Secretary-General called the heads of state and government to assess the situation in the world at the end of the millennium. In his words:

The arrival of the new millennium is an occasion for celebration and reflection... There is much to be grateful for... There are also many things to deplore, and to correct.

UN (2000a, p3)

In his report, Kofi Annan pointed to economic progress for many as one thing to be grateful for, and ruthless conflict, grinding poverty, striking inequality and a degraded natural environment as the main things to deplore and correct. Poverty figured prominently in the analysis, also because of the relation between poverty and wealth, inequality, conflict and natural resources.

The world leaders gathered at the Millennium Assembly responded by adopting a Millennium Declaration pledging, among other things, to halve world poverty by 2015. They also adopted a number of Millennium Development Goals (MDGs):

- to reduce by half the proportion of people living on less than a dollar a day, suffering from hunger, and without access to safe drinking water;
- to halt the spread of HIV/AIDS, malaria, and other major diseases;
- to ensure primary education for all boys and girls;
- to eliminate gender disparity.

They also adopted a final eighth MDG: to develop a global partnership to achieve the other goals, including specific commitments in the field of trade, finance, aid, debt, technology and essential drugs. The partnership was explicitly meant to imply a commitment to good governance, development and poverty reduction, nationally and internationally (UN, 2000b).

Two years later, at the World Summit for Sustainable Development (WSSD) in Johannesburg, world leaders reconfirmed their pledge by unanimously adopting a Plan of Implementation. In this document, they stressed that 'eradicating poverty is the greatest global challenge facing the world today and an indispensable requirement for sustainable development' (UN, 2002a). They explicitly committed themselves to achieving the goal of halving the proportion of the world's poor and to concerted and concrete measures.

What is all this worth? Does it make sense to set goals and targets at the highest political level, and are the MDGs the rights ones? Do the MDGs help to bridge the gap, in the age of globalization, between the image of progress and the reality of poverty, or will they serve as a diversion in the global battle for riches, leaving the world's poor – to borrow a phrase from Thomas Friedman – as 'road-kill'? (Friedman, 1999).

The Millennium Development Goals

The MDGs are new in many respects. Firstly, together they cover a broad and rather complete terrain of basic human well-being, and represent nearly all the relevant dimensions of poverty; the major element still lacking is poverty resulting from adequate access to energy and natural resources.

Secondly, the MDGs concern the world as a whole, but they are not so global as to become vague or unbalanced. The goal is not to halve the proportion of the world's population that is poor by concentrating only on certain countries: the goal is to reach the target in every region and in every country. They are output targets, concrete and results-orientated, referring to welfare increases and poverty reduction, rather than the means to be used for that purpose.

They are also direct. The MDGs are not growth targets, chosen in the expectation that by meeting them fewer people would stay poor. The aim is

Box 6.1 The Millennium Development Goals

Goal 1
Eradicate extreme poverty and hunger
Target 1
Halve, between 1990 and 2015, the proportion of people whose income is less than one dollar a day
Target 2
Halve, between 1990 and 2015, the proportion of people who suffer from hunger

Goal 2
Achieve universal primary education
Target 3
Ensure that, by 2015, children everywhere, boys and girls alike, will be able to complete a full course of primary schooling

Goal 3
Promote gender equality and empower women
Target 4
Eliminate gender disparity in primary and secondary education, preferably by 2005, and to all levels of education no later than 2015

Goal 4
Reduce child mortality
Target 5
Reduce by two-thirds, between 1990 and 2015, the under-five mortality rate

Goal 5
Improve maternal health
Target 6
Reduce by three-quarters, between 1990 and 2015, the maternal mortality ratio

Goal 6
Combat HIV/AIDS, malaria and other diseases
Target 7
Have halted by 2015 and begun to reverse the spread of HIV/AIDS
Target 8
Have halted by 2015 and begun to reverse the incidence of malaria and other major diseases

Goal 7
Ensure environmental sustainability
Target 9
Integrate the principles of sustainable development into country policies and programmes and reverse the loss of environmental resources
Target 10
Halve, by 2015, the proportion of people without sustainable access to safe drinking water and basic sanitation
Target 11
By 2020, to have achieved a significant improvement in the lives of at least 100 million slum-dwellers

Goal 8
Develop a global partnership for development
Target 12
Develop further an open, rule-based, predictable, non-discriminatory trading and financial system (includes a commitment to good governance, development and poverty reduction – both nationally and internationally)
Target 13
Address the special needs of the least-developed countries (LDCs) (includes tariff- and quota-free access for LDCs' exports; enhanced programme of debt relief for heavily indebted poor countries (HIPC) and cancellation of official bilateral debt; and more generous Overseas Development Assistance (ODA) for countries committed to poverty reduction)
Target 14
Address the special needs of landlocked countries and small island developing states (through the Programme of Action for the Sustainable Development of Small Island Developing States and the outcome of the 22nd special session of the General Assembly)
Target 15
Deal comprehensively with the debt problems of developing countries through national and international measures in order to make debt sustainable in the long term
Target 16
In cooperation with developing countries, develop and implement strategies for decent and productive work for youth
Target 17
In cooperation with pharmaceutical companies, provide access to affordable, essential drugs in developing countries
Target 18
In cooperation with the private sector, make available the benefits of new technologies, especially information and communications

poverty reduction, whatever the level and character of growth. Adopting the MDGs implies that the nature and composition of economic growth should be subordinate to growth itself, rather than the other way round.

Additionally, they are precise and quantified. Not vague, not 'less' poverty. Not qualitative, such as to change and reverse the trend, or to further improve the lot of the poor. The MDGs are very precise: halving percentages in 15 years. Performance against such goals is measurable and accountable.

The MDGs are ambitious. Some might ask: what about the other half, the remaining 50 per cent poor? They might claim that the goals are not ambitious enough. However, the world has never seen poverty halved in the relatively brief period of 15 years. Individual countries may have been rather successful in this respect – China is a case in point – but never the world as a whole.

So it is an ambitious goal, but not over-ambitious. It will require intensive concerted action at all levels, by policy makers and actors. It will require structural change in priorities, investment allocations and resource use patterns. But it is doable. To my knowledge, there are no ecological, physical, technical or other autonomous reasons why it would be inherently impossible to halve poverty rates within a reasonable period. There may be economic or political reasons, but that is always a matter of choice.

Finally, the MDGs represent a Political Target with a capital P and capital T; not just another promise like all those made earlier but easily forgotten. Here we have a set of goals agreed and pledged at the highest possible level. The decision to adopt them was well prepared and well thought through. The goals were chosen consciously, in the awareness of the needs of the poor and of alternative options. All sorts of alternatives had been tried out in the course of the 20th century. But they had not worked well and had not delivered the hoped-for result. That is why, at the turn of the millennium, world leaders chose a radically different approach. They must have felt it: it is now or never.

Is this too rosy an interpretation? Did political leaders really mean all this, and did they realize that they were making a U-turn? Were they aware that expectations would grow as a result? Did they understand that from now on they will be accountable, and that, if expectations – which can be measured in precise terms – are not met, poor people might see this as a betrayal? After all, political leaders had a second chance when they came together at the WSSD in Johannesburg in 2002. But they did not take the opportunity to come back on the promises and commitments made at the Millennium Assembly; they did not dilute the targets or impose conditions on them. They reconfirmed and even expanded them.

Cynical analysts may come to a different conclusion and argue that, in politics, agreed goals and explicit promises have little significance. It is true: politics are a matter of power and interests. But I hope I have made clear that the decision to adopt the MDGs was not made arbitrarily, incidentally or by accident. Those who, as world leaders, had the power to make decisions must have come to the conclusion that it was in their nations' interest to take this course and that the alternative options were inferior. They must also have understood that non-implementation of the goals would have a counter-productive effect. It would resemble the broken promises and unmet targets of the past and lead to even more frustration, resulting in a threat to the stability and well-being of their nations.

So, let us assume that the MDGs represent a serious political commitment. Why then are references to them so often followed by qualifications that they are unlikely to be met or – even more pessimistic – will definitely not be met? Is it a statement of fact, a general disclaimer expressing an attitude of resignation and scepticism, a lack of political will, a prevailing distrust in political leaders or in politics, a lack of insight into changed world conditions or a lack of capacity to translate new insights into a new approach? Or have we become obsessed by the risks of today: security questions and the war against terrorism? Maybe it is all of that. But perhaps the most important reason is that fundamental disagreements exist concerning the very concept of sustainable development, despite a superficial consent reached through talks and negotiations.

A paradigm dispute

Throughout history, dominant paradigms have been contested. The paradigms of those in power are always different from the paradigms of the non-elite. However, genuine paradigm disputes can help in fighting for common ground between interest groups at a higher political level. They can help to disarm powerful elites, and undermine their bias in favour of the status quo, by focusing on the longer-term interests of society. This is true for paradigm disputes both within nations and worldwide. In the field of international development cooperation, a major dispute of this nature took place after decolonization in the 1960s, and after the UN Conference on the Human Environment in Stockholm in 1972. There was a risk that the newly won independence of the young nation states would not be followed by a reasonable degree of political and economic autonomy. The answer was a threefold new paradigm: self-reliance plus the fulfilment of basic human need, plus a new international economic order. None of the three became a reality. Instead, the world experienced a period of neo-colonialism, widening the gaps between rich and poor.

In the 1980s, this led to complete stagnation. Gamani Corea spoke about 'the lost decade of development' (UNCTAD, 1987). The South was told to adjust to new realities set by the North. There was no international cooperation to address world problems such as mounting debt burdens, a deteriorating environment and increasing world poverty. All efforts were paralyzed by the last convulsions of the Cold War between East and West until 1989, when the end of the Cold War created new perspectives for the peoples of all nations. A new paradigm for development cooperation emerged, again defined with the help of three concepts: democracy, eradication of poverty and sustainable development.

When world leaders gathered in Rio de Janeiro for the UN Conference on Environment and Development (UNCED) in 1992, the mood was positive. There was room for change: change for the good – freedom, democracy, human rights, disarmament, peace, development and the protection of the environment. No wonder that the new paradigm of sustainability was widely endorsed: progress for the present generation in all respects and everywhere, without discrimination, but on the understanding that successive generations would be entitled to the same opportunities. We would be obliged to use the resources at our disposal in such a way that they could be fully sustained or renewed for the benefit of our children and grandchildren.

After Rio, we were optimistic, but the optimism did not last long. The world lacked the capacity or the will to translate the new dream into reality. Between the fall of the Berlin wall in 1989 and the summit in Rio in 1992 there was a fair amount of political will. But domestic conflicts in many societies and the erosion of the international public system were weakening the capacity to bring about democracy, poverty eradication and sustainable development. Good governance became the mantra that drowned out the call for sustainable development.

Conflict and globalization

The new conflicts rose mostly within nations, not between them. Some were not new at all, but re-emerged – often after decades of silence. The power struggle between East and West led to a tacitly agreed demarcation of influence, to preserve the status quo, which in turn paralyzed conditions in the South and prevented change. Economic conflicts can be managed within a reasonable period of time, by a good combination of economic growth and (re)distribution of assets and income, creating a perspective of progress for the present generation. However, cultural, social, ethnic, religious or subnational domestic conflicts are rooted deeply in society.

Cultural conflicts, accompanied or sharpened by economic inequalities, outlive generations. They are less manageable than economic conflicts, because there is no way out by means of sharing and redistribution. In an economic conflict there is always a feasible win-win solution: the right path of investment, growth and distribution can make all parties gain. Cultural conflicts are different. Identities are defined in terms of absolute positions, not in terms of shares of total potential welfare. A stronger position of one group in a society – whether a tribe, an ethnic group, a religious denomination, a social class, a sex, a tongue, a colour, a caste, a nationalistic clan, or any group defining its identity in other than purely economic terms – always means that another group will lose. Welfare is a relative concept; it can be increased through intelligent distribution. Power is an absolute concept; total power cannot be increased by means of redistribution. Only when cultural conflicts are not seen as power conflicts but as identity conflicts can a solution be possible, provided that each group considers its identity not threatened but enriched through interaction with the other. Cultural confrontation has to be transformed into a cultural exchange. But as long as this is not the case, such conflicts are longer lasting, less manageable and more violent than either economic conflicts or international disputes.

Over the past decade, violence has not been limited to the original location of the conflict. It has been brought to other countries by the same forces that brought about globalization. That was the second major new phenomenon in the 1990s. Globalization was not discussed at Rio; it had not been discovered. Of course, internationalization was not new: there had been intercontinental transport, foreign investment and trade, international finance, imperialism and colonialism, world wars, efforts to build international alliances, a League of Nations, and the UN itself.

Globalization was not a new process – we had seen it for centuries and had witnessed a stronger pace in the four decades since the World War II. But in the final decade of the last century it assumed a new shape. Internationalization had been an economic and a political process, steered and fostered by means of concrete decisions of policy-makers and entrepreneurs. It was man-made.

But somewhere in the 1990s, internationalization turned into globalization. It achieved a momentum of its own, became less a consequence of demonstrable human decisions, more self-contained and self-supporting. The driving force was twofold. Firstly, there was technological advance, enabling full and fast information and communication everywhere, physically and virtually. Secondly, there were economic global markets linking production, investment, transportation and trade, advertisement and consumption anywhere in the world to any other place. The result was a disregard for national frontiers, a strengthening of global corporations and an erosion of nation states.

Globalization became a cultural affair as well. A reality in the mind of the people: time differences and long distances are no longer barriers for communication. Technology solved this. What used to be far away has come close. Actual distance and time difference are no longer relevant, only the distance between human minds counts. In the WSSD conference centre in Sandton, Johannesburg, most of us felt that our air tickets, cell phones, emails, credit cards and Cable News Network (CNN) connected us with people in comparable conditions in cities abroad, rather than with AIDs victims on the African continent; landless and jobless people in southern Africa.

Global apartheid

Many people are excluded from this global 'community', however. Globalization is neither coherent nor complete. In the 1990s, globalization was boosted by new technologies, rising expectations and a mounting demand from the global market. This unprecedented growth could have helped to enlarge the capacity of the international community to address poverty and sustainability questions. It did not. Instead, globalization led to even more unbalanced development and less sustainable development. Globalization made international cooperation lopsided by directing political attention mainly towards facilitating the workings of the world market and neglecting welfare, social justice and environmental issues.

What has this meant for the poor? During long periods of capitalist expansion, poor people were exploited. But they had an opportunity to fight back, because the system needed them: their labour and their purchasing power, the power to buy goods produced by the system and thereby sustain the very system that exploited them. This common strength of the poor helped to modify exploitation. Development became potentially beneficial to the poor. There was hope in the prospect of incremental improvement. Everybody had the right to hope.

However, these days, we have to conclude that hope is no longer justified. Globalization has changed the nature of capitalism. There are more people excluded from the system than exploited by it. Those who are excluded are seen as dispensable – neither their labour nor their potential buying power is needed. That is the reason why they cannot fight back any more; they have lost perspective. If you believe that your life is worse than your parents' and that there is no hope that your children will do better, then there is no cause for optimism whatsoever.

For many people this is today's reality. They have no land to work on, no job, no credit, no education, no basic services, no security of income, no food security, but ever more squalor, an ever greater chance to be affected by HIV/AIDS, a house without electricity, water and sanitation. Despite unprecedented world economic progress during the last decade, for about 2 billion people there is only the experience of sinking further and further into quicksand. In Johannesburg, President Mbeki called this 'global apartheid' (Mbeki, 2002).

The gap between rich and poor in the world can no longer be explained in terms of a strikingly unequal distribution of income and wealth, which could be modified through world economic growth and a better distribution of the fruits of growth. The gap appears to have become permanent. Rich and poor stand apart, separated from each other.

Under the apartheid regime, people were either white or black: they were part of the system, or they were not. Today, people belong to modernity, or they do not. The world of modernity is western of origin, but stretches towards islands and pockets of modernity in the East and in the South. The worlds of modernity are linked with each other by means of modern communication. Through the culture of modern communication people feel that they belong to modernity, that they are part of it, part of the globalized uniform, western neo-liberal culture of mass-consumption, materialism, images and virtual reality. That modern world is separated from the world next door, physically sometimes just around the corner, but far away in terms of time, mentality, experience and consciousness: poverty, hunger, unemployment, lack of basic amenities in the shanty towns, in the countryside and at the periphery, where pollution is permanent, where the soil is no longer productive, water scarce, life unhealthy.

Winners and losers

Poor people have to live in the worst places of the earth. 'A world society based upon poverty for many and richness for some, characterized by islands of welfare surrounded by a sea of poverty, is not sustainable', President Mbeki has said. Indeed, that is apartheid. On the one side, security and luxury, on the other, deprivation, hardship and suffering. At the beginning of the new millennium, for many people, life has never been so good. At the same time, for many people in our direct global neighbourhood, life is not livable.

Security and luxury on the one side of the fence is being sustained and protected by continuing the squalor, suffering and poverty elsewhere. Not by exploiting the poor (though there still is exploitation – low commodity prices, for instance, and indecent wages for migrant labour), but because the poor are excluded. The western world is afraid that they will cost more than they can contribute. They do not fit into cost-benefit calculations. People living in the slums of Calcutta, Nairobi and Rio de Janeiro, AIDS victims in Africa, landless people in Bangladesh, subsistence farmers in the Sahel, illegal migrants crossing the Mediterranean – all of them lack the capacities needed to contribute to the modern global economy and the buying power for its products. That is why these people are considered dispensable. Well-to-do people are not interested in the ideas of the poor, let alone their fate. The poor are a burden and should not try to come close. They are excluded by the connected from the islands of wealth created by globalization. They are deprived of space and soil, in particular good soil. They are deprived of water, forest, and natural resources. They are burdened by sky-high debts. Their enterprises are denied fair access to global or national markets, which favour foreign companies, providing them with more licenses to operate, higher credits and tax holidays. Globalization takes away living space. The poor are told to stay in, or return to, their homelands, perhaps in occupied territories, separated from each other by arbitrary or economic boundaries drawn by those who do have access to resources, capital and technology.

The pace of globalization has made winners and losers. Real losers and those who see themselves as losers. Globalization is shaking established structures and cultures. Some have the skills to gain access to the modern world market. For others, it is either sink or swim. Many of them, economic asylum seekers for instance, are struggling with the waves of modernity and sink into the undercurrent of the new dynamics. For other people, single females with children in Africa for instance, modernization means uprooting. They are dragged down by the current of globalization.

Resistance

Others resist. Such a resistance can take different forms: protest, economic action, migration, forming alliances or a political counter-offensive at high level. It can also imply the strengthening of a vulnerable culture or an effort to tie religion with politics. It can result in violence, first again those within that culture who choose in favour of modernity and assimilate themselves into the foreign, western culture. Later on, violence may be directed at foreign culture itself. That is the final stage. The more the centre of globalization disregards the periphery, not only the economic and social needs of the periphery, not only the economic and social needs of the periphery, but also its traditions, culture, religion and aspirations, the harsher the resistance. Western promotion of individualism – an attitude of self-sufficiency and self-complacency – is seen by many as arrogant. The excluded feel not only poor and dispossessed, but also defeated, humiliated and resentful.

In the 18th century, such a haughty attitude of the elite brought about a revolution. Today revolt is also in the air. 'If you don't visit your neighbourhood, it will visit you', Thomas Friedman wrote. That visit can take different forms. One is migration to the towns. Another is crime and violence in any metropolis with a dazzling city-centre next to barrios and shanty towns of breathtaking poverty. A third reaction can be terrorism. Migration does not lead to crime, and crime does not result in terrorism, but all three are consequences of uprooting. Even when there is no direct link between poverty and violence, systematic neglect of aspirations and feelings of injustice creates conditions within which violence can flourish. People may acquiesce to violence when they feel humiliated, personally and as a group, once they feel that they are not taken seriously, not respected or recognized as a culture or as a society, once they feel excluded by the new world system. Then they may give a willing ear to calls for violence. Some approve silently, others give support or shelter. Others show themselves receptive to a message of violent action. 'Why not', they may think, 'if the world does not leave us an alternative?'

Those who feel that the system does not care about them may try to seek access to the system, try to clear themselves a way into the system. That has been the aspiration of migrants and of emancipation movements. Often, they were successful. But if your experience is that the system not only ignores you, but brushes you aside, doesn't want you, cuts you off, excludes you, then you may become inclined to consider it your turn: to turn away from the system. 'If the system doesn't want me, then I do not want the system' is a form of logic. People who come as far as this do not even seek access to the system. They turn their back upon the system, denounce it. One step further is to resist and oppose it, to want it undermined: or to attack and undermine it themselves.

Poverty does not necessarily lead to violence. But poverty, exclusion and neglect, the perception of being seen as a lesser people with an inferior culture, being treated as dispensable by those who do have access to the market, to wealth and power, together will lead to aversion, resistance, hate, violence and terrorism; resistance against globalization, which is perceived as perverse, as a curtailment of living space, as occupation; aversion to western dominant values, which steered that process of globalization in the direction of global apartheid; hate against leaders of that process and against those who hold power within the system; violence against its symbols; deadly violence against innocent people within that system; unscrupulous, unsparing violence, fanatically believing: 'this is the only way'.

Is it wholly incomprehensible that people who consider themselves desperate become receptive to the idea that they have been turned into extremists by a system beyond reach? One step further and they become receptive for the arguments of fanatics; they have nothing to lose in a battle against a system that is blocking their future. One more step and they believe that they will gain by sacrificing themselves in that battle. It is hideous, beyond justification, but the notion exists. It should and can be fought, but the most effective way to do so is not by resorting to counter-violence alone, but by taking away the motives and reasons that people may have when surrendering to the temptations of fanatics.

Most people, however poor and desperate, dislike violence. They are disillusioned, but in doubt. Many people in the world have developed a love-hate relationship with the West and its culture. They do not want to make a choice for or against the West unless they are forced to do so – for instance by the West itself. Then resentment overtakes doubt.

After September 11, 2001, the world appeared to reach a crossroads, a choice between two paradigms: security or sustainability. But in reality, sustainability as an inclusive concept implies the mutual trust that justice will be maintained and secured for all people, without discrimination. Sustainable development is the ultimate guarantee of mutual security. This link received explicit articulation in UN Secretary-General Kofi Annan's March 2005 report, 'In Larger Freedom': 'we will not enjoy development without security, we will not enjoy security without development, and we will not enjoy either without respect for human rights' (UN, 2005). The task is to disarm the fanatics without alienating those who doubt. As was pleaded by Kofi Annan when he received the Nobel Peace Prize, that requires building a sustainable, democratic and peaceful world society, within which humanity is seen as indivisible. That concept of sustainability, he added, ought to be based upon the dignity and inviolability of all human life, irrespective of origin, race or creed.

Are we on the right track?

Is there any chance that global poverty will really be halved by 2015? There has been some progress. According to the Human Development Report (HDR) in 2003, 'the past 30 years saw dramatic improvements in the developing world. Life expectancy increased by eight years, illiteracy was cut nearly in half, to 25 per cent, and in East Asia the number of people surviving on less than US$1 a day was almost halved just in the 1990s.' But the report continues: 'Still, human development is proceeding too slowly. For many countries, the 1990s were a decade of despair' (UNDP, 2003, p2). More than 50 countries are poorer now than in 1990. In over 20 countries, a larger proportion of people are going hungry. In quite a few countries, child mortality is increasing, life expectancy is falling, and school enrolments are shrinking. The authors of the report do not hesitate to speak of a 'development crisis' and of 'reversals in survival ... previously rare' (UNDP, 2003, p2). In more than 20 countries, the Human Development Index declined, an alarming phenomenon because, as the authors point out, the capabilities captured by the index are not easily lost.

This means four things:

1   In some places there has been progress. Development has worked
2   In others, there has been regress. In those countries, either development policies have not worked, the countries have not been affected by international economic growth, or they have been affected, but differently: as victims of progress elsewhere, as 'collateral damage'
3   Global inequality has increased
4   In regions experiencing regress this could mean that people fall below any decent level of living, slip through any safety net, lose any capacity to catch up later, lose their dignity as human beings. Indeed, that would be a crisis, a crisis in development, and a crisis in societies. In so far as it would be due to the inherently dualistic character of the global economy, whereby large parts of the world's population are condemned to poverty and despair, it would also be a crisis in world society.

Is this too gloomy an outlook? According to the World Bank, less than 1.2 billion people now live on US$1 or less a day, compared to 1.3 billion a decade ago (World Bank, 2003a). Is that a reason for optimism? Yes and no. Yes, because it shows that high economic growth can lead to less poverty: the fall in the poverty figure was largely due to developments in China, where annual economic growth was 9 per cent in the 1990s, lifting 150 million people out of poverty. No, because excluding China the overall figure increased, from somewhat more than 900 million to about 950 million people. That is a relative decrease, from less than 30 per cent of the population of the developing countries as a whole to less than a quarter.

Is that progress? It depends. In sub-Saharan Africa the poverty figure increased substantially, by 30 per cent in only a decade. In South Asia it is still around half a billion people. That is disappointingly high, four decades after the beginning of coordinated national and international strategies for growth, development and poverty reduction.

In many parts of the world, poverty is high and increasing, despite the fact that the 1990s saw the highest annual world average growth figures since the end of World War II and decolonization. Clearly, the vast accumulations of income and wealth have not been used for sustainable poverty reduction. During the last decade of the previous century, an alarmingly high number of people suffered from worsening living conditions, notwithstanding political promises made at the beginning of that decade.

At the UNCED summit in Rio de Janeiro in 1992, world leaders came together to pledge adherence to the development paradigm of sustainable development. Heads of state and government declared that in the future the world's resources would be utilized in such a way that people would be at the centre and that future generations would not be deprived of the same opportunities as present generations (UN, 1992). We can only conclude that the 'sustainable development decade' of the 1990s – the Fourth Development Decade – was less successful than the First Development Decade of the 1960s.

Still, conventional wisdom is that poverty is on its way out, because the number of people on less than US$1 a day is decreasing. However, what is the significance of the US$1 a day criterion, which has found its way into the MDGs? The authors of the HDR do not take a position on this. They refer to critics who think that this yardstick 'reveals little about income poverty and its trends', but note that others call it 'rough but reasonable'. I belong to the second group in that I believe it is of course necessary to have some global yardstick. But the dollar-a-day yardstick is rough beyond reason. Why not, say, one and a half or two dollars a day? Are people who no longer figure in the poverty statistics, because they now earn one dollar a day, out of poverty for good?

What is the significance of the concept of income poverty anyway? Poverty cannot be captured in terms of money and income alone. If poverty is seen as a lack of opportunity to acquire lasting control of resources in order to strengthen one's capacity to acquire the basic necessities of life – water, energy, food, a safe place to eat, rest, sleep, wash, have sex and go to school, basic health services and medicine in case of illness, a job enabling all this or the income to acquire it by means of exchange, access to economic markets and social networks, knowledge to survive in this world, information and education to acquire more knowledge and to gain the necessary insights to cope with disasters, threats, violence and challenges and, when that is beyond the capacity of the individual, some protection – all that requires more than money, more than an income. It requires assets or entitlements, the value of which cannot be easily estimated in money terms. In other words: rights that ensure access to all these things. These rights certainly cannot be acquired for US$1 a day.

Income poverty is only an indirect indicator of human poverty. Other indicators reveal that there is more stagnation in the battle against poverty than we would expect by looking at the dollar-a-day yardstick only. Some examples: every day 800 million people go hungry. During the last decade, the number of hungry people decreased in China, but increased in 25 other countries (UNDP, 2003, p88). One out of every six children of primary school age in developing countries does not attend school, and only half of those who do start primary school finish it. Close to 900 million adults cannot read or write, one out of four adults in the developing world (UNDP, 2003, p92). In sub-Saharan Africa one in every hundred live births results in the mother's death. In many countries, the already high maternal mortality figures are on the rise. HIV/AIDS, tuberculosis and malaria are killing more people than a decade ago (UNDP, 2003, p97). More than 1.2 billon people do not have access to safe drinking water, while 2.4 billion people do not have adequate sanitation services (UN, 2002b, p7). In the words of one of the participants at the 2003 World Water Forum in Kyoto: more than one-third of the world's population does not have a place to shit. In more formal terminology: they defecate in open areas or use unsanitary bucket latrines. The consequences? Diarrhoea is the world's greatest killer of children and half of the world's hospital beds are occupied by patients suffering from easily preventable waterborne diseases (UN, 2002b, p7).

One of these indicators has been labeled in the HDR a 'shameful failure of development' (UNDP, 2003, p97). In fact, all of them are. The world as a whole has never been as rich as it is today. In the past 15 years, globalization has accelerated without precedent. The opportunities offered by money, capital, technology and communication to enable more and more people to benefit from progress are without precedent. But these opportunities have not been used to correct this shameful failure of the past and bridge the gap between those who benefit from modernity and those without entitlements, thus enabling them to break out of the vicious circle of malnutrition, disease, illiteracy and poverty. On the contrary: if present trends regarding the nature of globalization continue – and there are no indications to the contrary – progress and modernity will not bridge that gap, but widen it further.

I do not criticize the usual poverty yardstick because of measurement difficulties. My criticism of the dollar-a-day yardstick is not so much statistical or conceptual as political. The figures concerned have been published or quoted so often that politicians have been led to believe that the trend was in the right direction. However, there is a large difference between theory and practice, between the statistics showing a decrease in the number of people below the poverty line and the realities of misery. That reality has been put out of sight. During the 1990s, the degree and extent of world poverty were played down and political leaders were lulled to sleep. Were they fooled, or were they fooling themselves by not asking the obvious question: what kind of life can you live on US$1 a day anywhere, in Africa, Asia, in the cities of Latin America, or even in China? Has that question not been raised because of the fear that a more ambitious goal, affecting more poor people, could never be attained without far-reaching changes in the distribution of world income and entitlements, while the US$1 level would only require better governance in the poor countries themselves and a slight increase in development aid? The blame for not meeting a dollar-a-day target level could easily be apportioned to the poor countries themselves, while failing to reach a more civilized goal could be attributable to the richer countries and their reluctance to share with the poor.

Though in terms of macro world statistics – that is, in theory – fewer people now live below a poverty line, which has been selected on political grounds, in practice, poverty has increased in many regions of the world and also in many countries where there has been improvement in macro terms. That can only imply that inequalities have widened. And indeed, that is what has happened: inequality across the world increased during the last part of the previous century, between as well as within nations. The distribution of income among the people of the world, regardless of national borders, has become more unequal. Nowadays, incomes are distributed more unequally among the global population as a whole than in the most unequal countries (UNDP, 2003, p39).

Since the First Development Decade inequality has only increased: while in 1960 the top 20 per cent received 30 times the income of the poorest 20 per cent, at the turn of the millennium this inequality had widened to more than 70 to one. 'Poverty: declining, but still a challenge' – that has been the general message during the last decade, explicitly repeated in the most recent World Development Report from the World Bank (World Bank, 2003b, p2). The political meaning of such a message is: we are moving in the right direction and we should continue to do so, albeit somewhat faster.

However, the direction is wrong. Since 1990, the trend has been negative. The authors of the HDR say this in no uncertain terms: 'What is most striking is the extent of the stagnation and reversals – not seen in previous decades.... (T)he 1990s saw unprecedented stagnation and deterioration. ... Per capita incomes fell in 54 countries... Hunger increased in 21 countries... Child mortality rates increased ... in a way not seen in previous decades...' (UNDP, 2003, pp40–44).

The final step: Meeting the Millennium Development Goals

The MDGs are not just another set of goals. They are different. The MDGs are not the next step, but a final step. At the turn of the millennium, world leaders at the highest political level, looking back on decades full of negotiations, policies and targets at fault, declared that from now on the eradication of poverty shall have first and foremost priority, within all countries and worldwide. Any other interpretation of the Millennium Declaration would be disputable. In the year 2015, no responsible political leader would be entitled to say, once more: 'the goals may not have been reached, but progress has been made and they have helped to keep us alert and the issue alive'.

Heads of state and government have made the MDGs the responsibility of all countries, all national departments and all international agencies, by making them the centrepiece of the Millennium Declaration. There is no higher or broader forum than a summit. The Millennium Declaration is not a legally binding document, but the highest political commitment possible, not made in passing, but with all eyes open.

The MDGs are achievable. It has been said so in many terms, by all political leaders concerned, fully aware of both the challenge and the obstacles. But will they be achieved? The goals were set at a political summit in the year 2000. At the Johannesburg Summit in 2002, where decisions ought to have been made on the implementation machinery, the same political leaders were unable to take any steps further than reconfirming their earlier commitments. No decisions were made concerning the instruments necessary to realize the goals, or on who should do what, or on an effective review and feedback mechanism. Since then, the Millennium Project has presented to Kofi Annan its report outlining what it calls 'a practical plan for the implementation of the MDGs' (Millennium Project, 2005), whose recommendations will be discussed at the Millennium Review Summit in September 2005. Is there any reason to think the outcomes of this summit will be any different?

Let me express some of my concerns.

Firstly, there is no road map. There is much talk of a 'Development Compact', but as yet it does not exist. All references to such a compact in international documents are phrased in terms of 'ought to be' and 'should be'. That is wishful thinking. There is no such thing as a Development Compact, with freshly agreed language on how to focus international trade, finance and technology policy on the implementation of the MDGs, rather than the traditional objectives of the previous decades. The HDR in 2003 devoted to the MDGs is full of questions and recommendations, but has no agreed answers. It is a state of the art document laying out what policies, according to present insights and on the basis of lessons learned, could or should be pursued in trade, debt, industry, science and technology, education, health, water, agriculture, food and nutrition, energy and other resources, the environment and ecosystems, but it cannot point to any new agreement in these fields. It rightly points out that there is a need for country ownership, driven not only by governments but by many actors (local governments, communities, and civil society groups), and a need for a comprehensive approach, bottom up and participatory, worded in 'correct' development language: gender, empowerment, accountability, partnership, social mobilization, a cautious approach towards both privatization and decentralization. But all these references together are not a strategy, only proposals, a Millennium Development Compact 'proposed' (UNDP, 2003, p15).

Secondly, the MDGs are still seen too much as belonging to the traditional field of development policy. It is customary to see development goals as a specific responsibility of developing countries, and the specific governmental departments within these countries, together with the corresponding UN agencies, rather than as a global common responsibility that also includes the northern countries and international institutions like the World Trade Organization (WTO) and International Monetary Fund (IMF). After all, heads of state and government committed themselves to deal with global – that is worldwide – poverty, wherever and with all means, attacking all possible causes, not restricting themselves to foreign aid, but undertaking also to remove national and international constraints: protectionism, monopolistic and discriminatory practices, and other external obstacles preventing developing countries from attacking poverty within their borders. Maintaining such obstacles would make foreign assistance a form of compensation for being kept at a distance, rather than a net investment in poverty reduction. So far, the agenda for the Doha Round on international trade has not been changed in the light of the commitment to meet the MDGs.

Nor are the MDGs a key subject on the agenda of the International Financial Institutions (IFIs). Debt rescheduling should focus on poverty alleviation. However, despite the summit agreements, neither the proceedings of the Paris Club nor the debt-rescheduling programme for the HIPC have been redesigned. There can be no debt sustainability without social sustainability. Debt and poverty are related. Debt reduction and poverty reduction ought to be related as well, by making adequate finance available for both, in an integrated policy. The Poverty Reduction Strategy Papers (PRSPs), introduced by the World Bank and serving as the basis for aid allocations from most donor countries, could be the basis of such an integrated approach. However, the concept and procedures of the PRSPs have not yet been systematically reorganized either. The World Bank assumes current budgetary levels and foreign resource levels as given, rather than making the agreed 50 per cent cut in poverty by 2015 the key objective of its strategy. Instead of one integrated approach to poverty reduction, we now have competing schemes and pathetic efforts to coordinate (UNDP, 2003, pp20–22, 149). All this illustrates that the MDGs are still not the once-and-for-all objectives of the countries and the institutions that have the power to decide.

Thirdly, there is no focus. At the Johannesburg Summit, the UN Secretary-General proposed focusing action on five sectors: water, energy, health, agriculture and biodiversity (WEHAB) and giving priority to policies in these sectors that contribute to poverty reduction. It was an attractive proposal, because sustainable development in these sectors is a precondition for lasting poverty reduction. However, no agreement could be reached on attaching less priority to other sectors. In principle, a comprehensive and simultaneous approach in all sectors would be better than a selective approach. However, if you want to cover everything, you may end up doing nothing. If an overall approach overburdened implementation capacity, it would paralyze action, as now seems to be the case.

Next, there still is a shortage of finance. There is no agreement on the costs of implementation. Estimates have been made for the goals on health and water. A group led by Jeffrey Sachs has calculated that meeting the goals on health would require additional aid of US$30 billion annually (Sachs, 2001). For drinking water a commission chaired by Michel Camdessus calculated that the realization of the target would require US$180 billion annually, but this is considered a gross exaggeration by the Water Supply and Sanitation Collaborative Council (WSSCC), which has presented an annual figure of US$30 billion (United Nations, 2002b, 16) (WSSCC, 2002, p8). It is unclear which parts of these figures would have to be additional to current expenditure. The UN concludes that 'further work is required to have a more accurate and better understanding of the global financial requirements to meet the ... MDGs' (UN, 2002b, p16). That is obvious, but it would have been helpful if that work had been carried out before the goal was set.

Needless to say, none of the MDGs has a financial plan. Nor is there a financial plan to implement the Millennium Strategy as a whole. There are some rough estimates of the additional external assistance required to meet global objectives. They range from US$40 to US$100 billion a year. One of these is the figure of US$50 billion mentioned by a UN commission led by former Mexican President Zedillo (UN, 2001). This latter figure – which was a starting point for the World Summit on Finance and Development in Monterrey, Mexico, in 2002 – is called 'conservative' by the authors of the HDR (UNDP, 2003, p346). That is understandable in the light of the figures for health and water only. However, even this conservative estimate did not persuade the donors and the IFIs to agree on a common finance strategy. The new aid commitments presented in Monterrey by the US and the European Union (EU) were explicitly not intended to help finance a Johannesburg Plan of Action to implement the MDGs.

In addition, foreign aid is missing the mark. Since the Washington consensus became the guideline for aid allocations there is so much emphasis on good governance in developing countries as a precondition for receiving aid, that the assistance itself can no longer help improve the situation within these countries. Rather than aid being used as a catalyst, helping to bring about better policies and better governance, the countries themselves are expected to make such improvements before receiving any aid. Quite a few countries are not in a position to help themselves and they are then deprived of foreign aid. Countries that are able to improve policies and governance to the liking of donors receive aid as a reward. For them this aid is either no longer necessary, because good governance can be rewarded by the market, or it comes too late. In all three situations, as far as poverty reduction is concerned, present-day donor preferences for so-called performance-driven aid allocations are overshooting the mark (Pronk, 2001, 2003).

Poverty reduction will increasingly become more urgent and difficult because of the critical trends in the ecological and physical environment. The loss in global biodiversity, the change in the global climate, and the increasing scarcity of basic resources such as water and energy and distortions of the ecosystems are no new phenomena. However, recent studies seem to indicate that these changes are now moving faster and are having a greater impact than in the past. The poorest people are the first victims: they live in the most vulnerable places, with less productive soils, in arid regions, polluted slums, eroded hill slopes and flood-prone coastal areas and river plains. They are the least protected against environmental crime and the whims of nature. Poverty due to deterioration of the global environment is on the rise. Poverty due to conflicts about increasingly scarce resources will increase, as well. While in international fora, environmental risks seem to have lost the competition for attention against security risks. This imposes a heavy mortgage on the attainment of the poverty goals.

For all these reasons, it is no surprise that we are far behind schedule. As was recently emphasized by Jan Vandemoortele, a UN official working in this field, the MDGs are 'technically feasible and financially affordable. Yet, the world is off-track to meeting them by 2015' (Vandemoortele, 2003, p16). And the authors of the HDR, while stating '(that) all countries can meaningfully achieve the Millennium Development Goals is beyond doubt', present a timeline showing that in most regions most goals will not be achieved if progress does not accelerate (UNDP, 2003, p50 and figure 2.1). That applies not only to Africa, as some might expect, but to Asia, as well (UN, 2003, table 1). And a recent report of internal UN discussions starts with the alarming diagnosis: 'We (the development community) are losing: a dramatic change of direction is needed to reach the MDGs.'

Such a dramatic change of direction requires political leadership. The implementation of the poverty targets should not be left to experts, bureaucrats and diplomats. It should be permanently on the political agenda, within countries and in the international system: the intergovernmental machinery and the relevant global institutions. In these bodies the discussion should not be limited to a review of the state of affairs. All political and institutional power available should be used to apply pressure on authorities and agencies not to shy away from the commitments made by heads of state and government, but to keep their promises. No second thoughts, as is so often the case in international fora, after the political leaders have spoken and left the scene. Where commitments are still political, without yet having been enshrined in legally binding treaties with compliance regimes and sanctions and in institutions with enforcement regimes, there are still political possibilities to ensure implementation. Rather than being confident that the job will be done, the leaders have to stay alert, active, and live up to their commitments.

Notes

1   This chapter has been adapted from the Pastrana Borrero Lecture delivered on the occasion of the UNEP Sasakawa Environment Prize presentation ceremony, New York, 19 November 2002, and 'Collateral Damage or Calculated Default: The Millennium Development Goals and the Politics of Globalization', Inaugural Address, 11 December 2003, ISS, The Hague.

References

Friedman, T. (1999) *The Lexus and the Olive Tree: Understanding Globalization*, Farrar, Strauss and Giroux, New York

Mbeki, President Thabo (2002) Statement at the opening of the World Summit on Sustainable Development, Johannesburg, 26 August 2002

Pronk, J. (2001) 'Aid as a Catalyst', *Development and Change*, 32, vol 4, pp611–629

Pronk, J. (2003) 'Aid as a Catalyst: A Rejoinder', *Development and Change*, 34, vol 3, pp383–400

Sachs, J. (2001) *Macroeconomics and Health: Investing in Health for Economic Development*, Commission on Macroeconomics and Health, World Health Organization, Geneva

UN (1992) *Rio Declaration on Environment and Development: Agenda 21*, June 1992, United Nations, New York

UN (2000a) 'We the peoples: The role of the United Nations in the 21st century', General Assembly, Fifty-fourth session, UN document A/54/2000, 27 March, United Nations, New York

UN (2000b) *Millennium Declaration*, General Assembly, 54th session, UN document A/RES/55/2, 18 September, United Nations, New York

UN (2001) *Report of the High Level Panel on Financing for Development*, General Assembly, 28 June, United Nations, New York

UN (2002a) *World Summit on Sustainable Development: Plan of Implementation*, Johannesburg, 4 September, United Nations, New York

UN (2002b) *A Framework for Action on Water and Sanitation*, WEHAB Working Group, WSSD, August, New York,

UN (2005) *In Larger Freedom: Towards development, security and human rights for all*, Report of the Secretary-General, UN document A/59/2005, 21 March, United Nations, New York

UNCTAD (1987) 'Corea Calls for new development consensus', press release, 17 July, 1987, UNCTAD

UNDP (2003) *Human Development Report 2003*, Oxford University Press, New York

Vandemoortele, J. (2003) 'Are the MDGs Feasible?' *Development Policy Journal*, vol 3, pp1–21

Water Supply and Sanitation Collaborative Council (2002) *Kyoto: The Agenda has Changed*, WSSCC, Geneva

World Bank (2003a) *Global Economic Progress and the Developing Countries 2002*, World Bank, Washington

World Bank (2003b) *Sustainable Development in a Dynamic World*, World Development report 2003, Oxford University Press, Washington, DC

7
Trade and Security in an Interconnected World

Hilary Benn

International trade offers opportunities to reduce poverty

We live in an interconnected world, in which capital, goods, and ideas flow between countries and regions with increasing ease. Greater international openness provides important opportunities for development. These arguments are set out in detail in the two UK government White Papers, *Eliminating World Poverty: Making Globalisation Work for the Poor* (DFID, 2000) and *Making globalisation a force for good* (DTI, 2004). One of the most important of these opportunities is international trade, which, if managed well, has the potential to help lift millions out of poverty. Indeed, openness to trade has been an important factor in the dramatic reduction in poverty that East Asian countries have achieved over the past few decades. In the new global economy, labour is being divided on a global basis and production is becoming ever more specialized and split between different locations. Textiles manufactured in China might be used to make garments in Lesotho, for eventual sale in the US. This increasing globalization of production seems likely to continue.

But this all relies upon a global environment of relative stability and security. A more interconnected world is not necessarily a more stable or secure one. Security and development are intimately linked, as set out in the Department for International Development's (DFID) new security and development strategy, published on 21 March 2005.[1] While globalization provides opportunities for the creation of unprecedented global wealth, it also creates new threats to global and local security. These include the increased likelihood of exposure to economic shocks, such as the South East Asia financial crisis in the late 1990s. As demonstrated by the subsequent financial crisis in Russia,

Box 7.1 Security and trade: An historical perspective

The interdependence of security and trade is not new. There have been periods of increased trade between peoples and regions throughout history – for example, the Roman Empire and the Hanseatic League. Conversely, periods of chaos and disorder, such as the Dark Ages in Europe, saw levels of trade and commerce decline. But what was common to all these periods of increased trade was a system of political and social organization that provided common rules and standards to facilitate trade – underpinned by an environment of relative security. The 19th century saw unprecedented levels of international trade, based around the colonial system, as well as the highest ever levels of migration, although it also saw the pernicious slave trade and the creation of exploitative large-scale extractive economies. Stability at home was an important factor in the UK's economic growth during this period, and together with the role of British sea power in facilitating sea trade routes, led to an enormous expansion of trade between the UK and the rest of the world.

The global trading system broke down at the outbreak of World War I, when major conflict destroyed trading patterns and disrupted shipping lanes. Major global economic depression followed in the 1920s and 1930s, triggering political instability that led directly to further global conflict in World War II – although that war did create a small number of trade winners, such as Argentina and Australia, which benefited from devastated production in Europe. Security concerns, and the desire to avoid further economic instability that could cause future global conflict, were foremost in the minds of the architects of the new global economic order that was established in the 1940s – the Bretton Woods institutions (BWI), including the General Agreement on Trade and Tariffs (GATT).

During the second half of the 20th century, US foreign policy aimed to ensure international economic stability and encourage countries to trade with each other to avoid the prospect of future wars. This policy was especially effective in Europe, ultimately leading to the creation of the European Union (EU). But globalization and economic development, particularly in South East Asia, have brought major changes including the participation of a larger number of developing countries in the global trading system. The rules that govern international trade now have to be worked out multilaterally between a larger number of players. The balance of power in multilateral and regional fora is still held by the major trading powers; and there are still major barriers to developing countries' ability to trade on fairer terms.

crises can spread more quickly from country to country – and, importantly, they impact disproportionately on the poor. The rise of globalization has coincided with the end of the Cold War. This has unleashed demands for greater autonomy in many parts of the world and led to conflicts fuelled by historic, ethnic, religious and economic tensions. There has also been an increase in international terrorism and transnational organized crime. Increased global interconnectedness allows criminal and terrorist networks to operate internationally and transcend national boundaries. Internationalized, organized crime has a growing share of the global economy and increased migration and improved communications facilitate the spread of criminal and terrorist networks. In particular, weak and failing states provide refuges for these networks.

Changes in trading regimes and the knock-on effects of trade adjustment can have social and political implications, as well as significant economic consequences. In a more globalized world, shocks and threats can travel between countries more quickly, through networks that transcend states. Yet national governments are not generally well set up to deal with these shocks, shocks that can have major destabilizing social and economic effects. Globalization has seen a weakening of the relative power of states over events that take place within their borders. And, of course, there are new challenges posed by the emphasis placed on global security since 11 September 2001 that may have significant implications for the free movement of people and goods. We now face the dilemma of how to balance the opportunities of greater openness and interconnectedness with the need for better national and international security.

Insecurity and conflict prevent poor countries from benefiting from trade

Countries that are affected by insecurity and conflict cannot benefit fully from international trade. Unresolved conflict and the legacy of past conflicts marginalize them from global markets. Such countries have only a tiny share of world trade flows, and are unable to integrate themselves meaningfully into the global trading system. Thus, the negative impacts of conflict last long after the end of hostilities. For example, the destruction of transport infrastructure in the Beira corridor during the Mozambique war means that landlocked Malawi is forced to route its exports through South Africa. This results in extremely high transport costs that make Malawian exports even less competitive.

Commodity dependency

Fluctuations in the prices of key commodities can have powerful destabilizing effects on poor countries. Out of 141 developing countries, 95 are more than 50 per cent dependent on commodity exports, including oil, rising to 80 per cent in sub-Saharan Africa. Poor countries are less able to manage commodity price volatility, making them highly vulnerable to commodity price fluctuations. And so far, trade liberalization and economic integration have not enabled most poor countries to break out of their commodity dependency. This vulnerability increases the risks of conflict. It has been argued that primary commodity dependency (measured by primary commodity export earnings as a percentage of gross domestic product (GDP) makes low-income countries particularly susceptible to conflict. Falls in the world prices of tea and coffee are thought to be among the factors that triggered the Rwanda conflict in the early 1990s.

Certain types of commodity are particularly closely linked to the spread of conflict and insecurity. The presence of high value-added tradeable commodities such as oil, rare minerals and precious stones encourages rent-seeking behaviour by predatory politicians and warlords. The capture of assets such as mines, or the exploitation of natural resources such as timber, rare animals and land to grow narcotics, enables militias to pursue their military objectives without having to depend on external sources of funds. The accessibility of basic food supplies, whether through domestic or international markets, is heavily affected by fluctuations in trading patterns – especially for the poor. And unsurprisingly, studies have found that food security is an important determining factor for the onset of civil wars in sub-Saharan Africa.

Conflict trade

Conflict and trade are often intertwined, either through conflict over a particular commodity, or through trade that takes place in the context of conflict. Examples include the illegal diamond trade and illegal logging in countries such as Cambodia and Liberia, where the proceeds of such trade have been used to finance armed conflict. Resource wars have been a major cause of conflict in Africa. Conflicts have been financed by oil and illegally extracted diamonds in Angola, diamonds in Sierra Leone, and high-value minerals in the Democratic Republic of Congo (DRC). The 'curse of oil' has fuelled existing ethnic and regional conflicts in countries as diverse as Sudan, Nigeria, and Iraq. Illegally produced commodities can be traded on legitimate but highly unregulated global markets. Trade in 'conflict diamonds' has been a two-way exchange between illicit arms sales and diamonds, with European brokers involved in transporting the arms in and the diamonds out. Market demand creates a buoyant illicit trade with damaging effects.

The failure of institutions to regulate such trade is an important contributory factor. Poor governance and social exclusion exacerbates these problems in resource-rich countries such as Angola, which still has very high levels of poverty. Shadow war economies spread insecurity and violence along smuggling routes and across borders. Terrorists take advantage not only of weak states, but also of corrupt institutions and criminal networks that exploit the lack of transparency and insularity of conflict trade. The ability to tackle the spread of conflict trade depends not only on measures to sanction rogue companies, control money laundering and improve border controls, but also on the ability of the international community to create development incentives that guarantee economic security and stability in low-income countries.

But progress is possible if the international community focuses its efforts to address these problems. For example, the Extractive Industries Transparency Initiative (EITI), which UK Prime Minister Tony Blair launched in

2002, aims to create partnerships between governments and companies to increase the transparency of payments by companies to governments and the transparency of revenues received by those governments. At the March 2005 EITI Conference, I was encouraged to see that nine countries had started to implement EITI principles, and four more announced their interest or their intention to do so.

Social and ethnic tensions

Changes in trade regimes may have differential impacts on different social or ethnic groups within a given country. For example, the phasing out of the Multi Fibre Arrangement, which gives some countries preferential access to western textiles markets, is likely to have a disproportionate impact on women in countries such as Bangladesh and Sri Lanka. Impacts such as these may exacerbate existing inequalities and lead to heightened tensions, or even violence.

For example, there are concerns that changes to the EU's sugar regime could result in heightened tensions between different social groups in some Caribbean countries, where significant proportions of the population depend upon sugar production for their livelihoods. In Jamaica, where the sugar industry employs 30,000 people directly and 70,000 indirectly, changes in preferences could result in increased unemployment in rural parishes, and removal of public services provided by the industry. This could have a serious impact on already high levels of poverty, and could result in increased migration to cities, pressure on social and security systems and increased social unrest, crime, drugs and violence.

These effects could be more severe in other Caribbean islands, whose economies are even more dependent on sugar. And, in Guyana, such changes could have a disproportionate impact on certain ethnic groups and exacerbate inter-ethnic tensions. This is why effective transitional support from the EU is essential to help Caribbean countries manage the adjustment out of un-competitive sugar production and into other economic activities in which they could enjoy more of a comparative advantage. Failure to do so could risk undermining the stability and security of the region.

Can stronger international trade networks enhance stability and security?

Advocates of free trade have long argued that trade reduces the likelihood of conflict between countries. The French philosopher Montesquieu said as early as 1748 that peace was a 'natural effect of commerce', and the Italian economist Pareto argued in 1889 that customs unions could help to achieve peace between neighbouring countries. After World War II, Monnet, the architect of European Unity, argued compellingly that there would be no peace in Europe unless European countries formed a common economic unit. In Europe at the end of the 1940s, there was an overwhelming desire to prevent the kind of catastrophic destruction seen in World War II from ever happening again. The formation of the European Coal and Steel Community in 1951 was intended to make Franco-German war impossible. Its subsequent expansion into the Common Market and then the European Union helped Europe to achieve an unprecedented period of peace and prosperity. Following the fall of the Iron Curtain, the EU agreed bilateral trade agreements with East European countries that helped stabilize them and prepared them for their eventual inclusion as new member states. The EU has, in this sense, been an enormously successful project, based on an understanding of the links between trade and security. It helped Europe to make a remarkable economic recovery out of the ruins of World War II, and war now seems unthinkable between countries that had been rivals for centuries.

Regional trade agreements (RTAs) have now been established in many different parts of the world. By late 2004, there were about 230 RTAs in existence. These are agreements in which countries agree to reduce barriers to trade on a reciprocal and preferential basis for other member countries. Given the small size of most economies in the African, Caribbean and Pacific regions, and their dependency on a handful of primary commodities, regional integration could in theory offer poorer countries mutual development gains through pooled resources, expanded markets, increased regional trade and investment, greater diversification and greater value added. It could also help to reduce dependency on northern markets and diminish vulnerability to downturns in commodity prices.

But can we expect these other regions to follow the same path as the EU towards economic integration and enhanced regional stability and security? And, critically, has regional integration made these regions any more stable and secure? The answer to the first question is probably no. There is no compelling reason why South-South RTAs should follow the same path towards the same level of economic integration as the EU. They are not starting from the same clean slate as the EU – the near total devastation of European product-ive capacity after World War II. They may not be willing, or able, to pursue certain aspects of integration, such as opening labour markets and allowing the free movement of people across borders, that the EU has. They may also be unwilling or unable to replicate the EU's redistributive regional policies that have helped facilitate economic integration and prevent the marginalization of certain countries or regions. South-South RTAs were created for differing political and economic reasons and their evolution will naturally follow different paths that suit each region's particular political and economic circumstances.

For example, the Association of Southeast Asian Nations (ASEAN) was initially created as a response to the perceived spread of Communism in the region in the 1960s, and although ASEAN has seen a task for itself in main-taining regional peace and stability, it has been careful to pursue a policy of non-interference in domestic conflicts. Conversely, MERCOSUR, made up of Argentina, Brazil, Paraguay and Uruguay, was created with the explicit intention of creating a common market and a common external tariff but also provided a platform for member states to discuss common security policies, such as drug trafficking, nuclear cooperation and military operations. The South Asian Association for Regional Cooperation (SAARC), consisting of India, Pakistan, Sri Lanka, Bangladesh, Bhutan, Nepal and the Maldives has had a more turbulent history, given the large political troubles between and within its member states. However, it has still managed to set up a Poverty Alleviation Fund and facilitate regional cooperation agreements in diverse areas including biotechnology, energy, environment, food security, intellectual property rights, narcotic drugs, suppression of terrorism and preferential trading arrangements. Some less successful RTAs have been signed for purely political reasons but never operationalized, in some cases because of fears that one country within the group will dominate, such as concerns in Uganda and Tanzania that the East African Community could reinforce Kenyan trade dominance in the region.

Box 7.2 International trade and state failure

A major study by the US State Failure Task Force found that the likelihood of state failure is affected by international influences, including openness to trade and membership of international organizations. International isolation and a lack of trade openness significantly increase the chances of state failure. Trade openness and membership of political organizations give an indication of a country's relationship with the international community. Strong ties to the international community minimize the risk that governments will use lethal violence against minorities or political opponents. This helps to explain the link with trade. Countries that have no significant trading relations may escape international scrutiny, while countries that depend on trade must avoid becoming pariahs in the eyes of the international community. Regional groupings such as MERCOSUR and SAARC serve as 'aspirational' clubs and can play a stabilizing role. But countries frozen outside regional integration processes, or with no obvious 'regional club' to join, such as Taliban Afghanistan or Belarus, are much more likely to suffer state failure and isolation.

Although the specific EU model of regional integration may not be applicable to other parts of the world, there is little doubt that national economies are becoming more interconnected and interdependent than ever before. Through interdependence, nations use trade to access one another's resources, instead of using violence to capture them. Economic integration makes conflicts more costly for individual states, as attacking a neighbouring economy becomes just as damaging as attacking one's own. Regional agreements may make military disputes between signatory countries less likely, and there is evidence that the likelihood of hostilities becomes more remote as trade flows rise between signatory countries. For instance, concerns about the threat of the spread of fundamentalism motivated the governments of Egypt, Morocco and Tunisia to negotiate regional agreements with the EU. MERCOSUR, which was originally created to reduce tensions between Argentina and Brazil, also helped lay to rest a possible coup in Paraguay following reaffirmation by the presidents of the MERCOSUR member countries that democracy was a necessary condition for membership in the bloc.

Some economic and trading agreements have been set up with the explicit purpose of preventing further conflict between neighbouring states. The Stability Pact for South-Eastern Europe was created in 2000 after the Balkan wars to create a free trade area to promote economic recovery and integration in a region previously devastated by conflict. And as recently as December 2004, Israel and Egypt agreed a trade deal, with US support, that foresees the creation of five special zones where imports will have free access to US markets, as long as 35 per cent of the goods are the result of cooperation between Israeli and Egyptian firms.

Security after 9/11 presents new challenges to international trade: Especially for poor countries

The world has seen a new emphasis on security since the terrible and tragic events of 11 September 2001. Security is now the overriding foreign policy priority for the US and other countries around the world. But could this shift in emphasis act as a brake on the progressive lowering of barriers that has ushered in a period of unprecedented openness, trade and prosperity? An extreme scenario is one in which new security measures restrict international openness and leave poor countries behind at an even faster pace than the current international trade system.

Exporters and importers have already been confronted with a range of new security measures taken since September 2001. These aim to upgrade port security, enhance airport security systems, and modernize customs authorities. Sea transport is especially vulnerable to security threats. The attack on the VLCC Limburg off the coast of Yemen in 2002 was a grim reminder of the vulnerability of global maritime transport, which handles 95 per cent of world trade.

In 2002, the US introduced the Containerized Security Initiative (CSI) to minimize the risk of a terrorist attack on US ports. Almost 90 per cent of all freight is transported in containers, 244 million of which move annually among the world's seaports. The CSI requires all ports that export to the US to meet stringent security standards. These impose high costs on exporting countries, and, in some cases, could prevent poorer countries from exporting to the US altogether. For example, Durban is the only port in all of Africa that has been accredited by the CSI.

Yet the US is too important a market for many developing countries to lose – for example, 13 per cent of African exports and 20 per cent of Malaysian exports are to the US. The CSI-type approach could spread – both Japan and Canada have already set up reciprocal arrangements. The US is considering imposing further security restrictions on imports, such as the US Customs Service 24-hour rule, which requires all goods to be loaded within a 24-hour period (which many developing country ports will find difficult to meet), and the proposal from the US Food and Drug Administration that an estimated 400,000 foreign food facilities should be registered to prevent a threat to the US food supply.

Box 7.3 Safety on the seas

Moving tradeable goods and services across borders requires smooth and secure modes of transport. These can sometimes be difficult to ensure. For example, the International Maritime Organization (IMO) reports that there were 445 cases of recorded pirate attacks against ships in 2003. The risks and destruction associated with terrorism or war raise the transaction costs of trade. Peace can have a greater beneficial impact on trade than bilateral or multilateral trade agreements. Terrorism, as well as internal and external conflict, can act as the equivalent to as much as a 30 per cent tariff on trade. It has been estimated that a doubling of the number of terrorist incidents in a year is associated with a decrease in bilateral trade by some four percent in the same year. The trade losses incurred by low security can be even higher when legal systems poorly enforce commercial contracts and where economic policy lacks transparency and impartiality.

These security measures could drive up trade costs and shut out exports from developing countries. They must not be allowed to provide an excuse for developed country protectionism, adding to existing non-tariff barriers to trade, such as sanitary and phytosanitary standards. The costs involved are high and disproportionate for small and medium traders in developing countries. The cost of moving goods between destinations and across borders can be as important as formal trade barriers in determining the final cost of goods. Security requirements add to the barriers that developing countries already face, such as high transport costs and poor infrastructure. A study by the World Bank on the impacts of September 11 showed that world welfare declined by US$75 billion per year for each 1 per cent increase in costs to trade from programmes to tighten border security.

Cost sharing and regional partnerships are possible solutions to the new security demands between importers and exporters. The Asia Pacific Economic Cooperation group (APEC) has come up with a regional agreement in the form of the Secure Trade in the APEC Region (STAR). This is a set of standard measures to protect cargo, ships making international voyages, international aviation and people in transit, thereby adopting new technologies to strengthen security without impeding trade. But critically, assistance from the international community is needed to help developing countries meet these demands. A global framework is needed to ensure that the needs of developing countries are addressed as security regimes take shape, and to help facilitate and expand trade, strengthen security and promote national development.

In contrast to freer movement of goods, services and capital, globalization has so far brought down few barriers to the free movement of people around the world. Despite the reduced cost and therefore greater accessibility of international travel, host countries are still unwilling to allow economic migrants access to their labour markets. And yet, greater labour mobility, leading to a greater share of global trade in services, could bring enormous economic benefits to developing countries that are potentially much greater than the potential gains from tariff reductions.

International support is needed to ensure that poor countries benefit from international trade while meeting the demands of the new emphasis on global security

So in an increasingly integrated world, trade between countries and regions seems set to increase – with great potential benefits for poverty reduction. Freer and fairer international trade could bring huge benefits to the world's poor, by encouraging growth, which could provide the resources to fight poverty, and by strengthening international partnerships to provide greater stability and security. But there are also risks that need to be carefully managed.

International trade negotiations need to be sensitive to domestic political concerns, and trade agreements must be built upon political ownership. Trade reforms should reflect national priorities and be sensitive to the political and social realities of individual countries. They must be carefully sequenced and phased to enable poorer countries to adjust their economies and mitigate any negative social impacts. The example of the Caribbean, where trade reforms are likely to have profound social impacts, demonstrates the importance of ensuring that a sound understanding of political and social dynamics is built into national and international trade policies.

Trade reforms must be integrated into national level policies and planning processes, such as Poverty Reduction Strategy (PRS) plans, and not simply imposed by the international community. There needs to be more effective financial and technical assistance for poor countries to help them develop domestic production and trade capacities, and an enabling international trade regime. The Integrated Framework for trade-related capacity building for least developed countries (LDCs) (www.integratedframework.org), supported by a number of multilateral and bilateral donors, is a good example of how donors and governments can work together to help low-income countries integrate trade into their poverty reduction plans.

In recent years, the world has become deeply concerned with security. Secure trade is now as important as free trade. But the one need not preclude the other. If well managed, security concerns could help to improve trade facilitation and investments in infrastructure, provided that there is adequate investment and increased resources for trade adjustment in developing countries. Trade facilitation in particular offers opportunities to increase trade and reduce security risks by making border controls more secure. At the same time, this will make customs clearance faster and more efficient, and increase tariff revenues. For example, in the conflict-affected countries of the Balkans, DFID supported the rapid establishment of effective customs services that helped facilitate trade flows, generated reliable sources of revenues for newly established administrations, and improved security by helping to control the trafficking of arms, people and drugs.

While we must recognize the reality of security concerns, they should not result in unduly onerous conditions on poor countries that make it even more difficult for them to trade fairly. We must ensure that poverty and social impact assessments are factored into trade reforms before poor countries agree to take on new obligations, so that negative impacts such as unemployment, which might otherwise generate tension and possibly fuel conflict, can be managed. It is vital that, in our desire to address immediate security threats, we do not forget the underlying causes of insecurity in an interconnected world – poverty, injustice and inequality – and the urgent need to do something to overcome them.

Notes

1   'Security and development are linked. Insecurity, lawlessness, crime and violent conflict are among the biggest obstacles to achievement of the Millennium Development Goals; they also destroy development. Poverty, underdevelopment and fragile states create fertile conditions for violent conflict and the emergence of new security threats, including international crime and terrorism.' *Fighting Poverty to Build a Safer World: A Strategy for Security and Development* (DFID, 2005).

References

DFID (2000). *Eliminating World Poverty: Making Globalisation Work for the Poor*, DFID, London
DFID (2005). *Security & Development Strategy*, DFID, London
DTI (2004). *Making globalisation a force for good*, DFID, London
Mansfield, E. D. and Pevehouse, J. C. (2000) 'Trade blocs, trade flows, and international conflict', *International Organisation*, vol 54, no 4, pp775–808

Additional reading

Blomberg, S. B. and Hess, G. D. (2004) 'How much does violence tax trade?', May 2004.
Collier P. and Hoeffle A. (2001) 'Greed and grievance in civil war', *World Bank Working Paper No 2355*, World Bank, Washington, DC
Nitsch, V. and Schumacher, D. (2004) 'Terrorism and international trade: An empirical investigation', *European Journal of Political Economy*, vol 20, pp423–433

8

Climate Change: Emerging Insecurities

Melinda Kimble

If we fail to address the challenge of climate change, we cannot achieve sustainable development.

Kofi Annan, February 2005

Introduction

In this chapter, I examine how the challenge of global climate change may reshape security thinking in the next decade. Mitigating the process of climate change demands rethinking how global economies are organized, because the major cause of the accelerating greenhouse effect is carbon dioxide (CO_2) and other greenhouse gas emissions – emissions that result from the burning of fossil fuels, harvesting forests, raising cattle and sheep, or growing rice and other crops. Given the necessity of a technological revolution to change these processes, it is not surprising that no clear consensus has emerged on how to address the problem. While we lack all the tools we need to address it, we are not applying the tools we do have available. Despite the magnitude of the task ahead, global action has been slow.

The existing international framework for addressing the problem, the United Nations Framework Convention on Climate Change (UNFCCC) provides an essential platform for global discussion and consideration of action based on extensive scientific research. At its inception, the UNFCCC envisioned an emissions reduction policy and the major developed countries committed in 1992 to reduce domestic emissions voluntarily to 1990 levels by 2000. In the first meeting of state parties to the UNFCCC in 1995, it was clear the voluntary target could not be met. The parties at that meeting in Berlin agreed to enter a process whereby developed countries would adopt binding targets and the policies to achieve them while developing countries were exempt from targets in the first round of this effort. Although agreement was eventually reached in 1997 in Kyoto, with the adoption of the Kyoto Protocol, the agreement only entered into force in 2005, some seven years after the first step, and with the largest emitter of greenhouse gases – the United States (US) – outside the agreement.

Nonetheless, we are entering a new stage in the global climate debate. The Kyoto Protocol entering into force will establish a market and a price for CO_2 emissions. The largest market will be in Europe as the European Union (EU) trading system begins operation. Voluntary markets are emerging that may be further stimulated by EU regulation. The size of the EU market and its success will certainly shape the future of carbon constraints.

A scientific consensus on the challenge

Between 1993 and 2003, more than 900 peer-reviewed scientific studies have reinforced the consensus of the Intergovernmental Panel on Climate Change (IPCC) that 'anthropogenic activity is contributing to climate change' (Pearce, 2005, p38). In fact, no scientific article has disputed the underlying assumption, the differences focus on the magnitude of the future change and the variations in impact. The clearest fact in these studies is the dramatic change in atmospheric CO_2 since the beginning of the industrial age – roughly 1790. At this point, atmospheric CO_2 was 280 parts per million (ppm). Recent measurements taken at the Mauna Loa Observatory in Hawaii confirm that atmospheric CO_2 has reached 379 ppm (Hanley, 2004) – a significant change in chemical composition of the atmosphere since the start of the Industrial Revolution. This chemical change, or 'carbon loading', of the atmosphere will reinforce the 'greenhouse effect'. This amplification of the phenomenon that creates the essential conditions for life on earth is likely to have the following impacts:

* higher average surface and ocean temperatures;
* more rapid evaporation and then more rainfall (a speeding up of the water cycle);
* more variability and severity in floods and droughts;
* rising sea levels due to water expansion from warming temperatures, and the runoff from continental ice shelves;
* an increased frequency and intensity of extreme weather events (floods and droughts);
* an extended range for tropical diseases, particularly those with insect vectors.

At the end of 2004, the world witnessed a geologic phenomenon – a tsunami unleashed by a high magnitude earthquake in the Indian Ocean – which killed more than 150,000 people and devastated coastal zones from Indonesia to Somalia. In this disaster, 10 of the Maldives' 23 islands were rendered unin-habitable. Similar devastation will almost certainly imperil low-lying coastal zones and island states as sea levels rise and the acceleration of the global water cycle continues to drive extreme weather events. The tsunami also offered dramatic evidence of how natural disasters can eliminate homes and livelihoods, leaving societies with the challenge of not only relief and rehabilitation, but also the need to reconstruct economic and social activity. The costs of this event – already estimated at nearly US$14 billion (*Money Week*, 2005) – could be multiplied many times over with recurrent climate events. In fact, the World Health Organization (WHO) already contends that 150,000 deaths annually are due to extreme weather events brought on by climate change, most of these deaths resulting from water- or vector-borne diseases. If we accept the prediction that more extreme weather events will occur with increasing frequency, then the annual mortality resulting from these factors could rise significantly in the future.

In 2004, the earlier scientific hesitancy to link actual weather events to climate change shifted significantly. New research, applied to specific events, clearly demonstrates a climate change linkage. The most important study in this regard looked at the European heat wave in 2003 – the hottest year on record since 1500 – and demonstrated that the human-induced contribution to the atmosphere has doubled the risk of heat waves of this magnitude (Stott et al, 2004, p610). These findings illustrated that the 2003 July-August temperatures exceeded the level of normal variation to the point that natural drivers could not account for the deviation from the mean. A few weeks earlier, a comprehensive study of Arctic warming (the Arctic Climate Impact Assessment) identified tailpipe and smokestack emissions as the largest contributors to the 'retreats of glaciers and sea ice, thawing of the permafrost and shifts in the weather...' (Revkin, 2004).

More recently, the University of Arizona reported findings that link the extended drought in New Mexico and Arizona to global climate change, and predicted that this would be a long-term trend (Eilperin, 2005, pA3). This analysis confirms an earlier Environmental Protection Agency (EPA) assessment (EPA, 1997) that the southwestern states were among the most vulnerable areas in the US to early climate impacts. The lack of rainfall is directly impacting US farmers and ranchers, but is also taking a toll on the water reservoirs that support the rapidly growing urban populations of Nevada, New Mexico, Arizona, and southern California. The present rapid growth trends in these states cannot continue without an assured water supply.

As scientists establish more complete time series data, we can expect more links to be made, confirming the theoretical assumptions that underlie the complex global warming models that have been predicting these changes for more than two decades. These more explicit connections illustrate that climate change is happening and happening now – and adaptation as well as mitigation will be critical to limit the impact on the planet. More importantly, however, similar climate change events are in progress in developing countries where limited attention is focused on emerging catastrophes. Recurrent drought patterns have been steadily undermining the predictability of annual rainfall, rapidly eroding rain-fed agricultural production and creating famine and hardship in the African Sahel and areas of southern Africa. The pervasive food crises in Ethiopia, Somalia, Eritrea and the ongoing crisis in Sudan have fuelled conflicts and famines since 1979. As rainfall and agricultural productivity have declined, the cooperative state of coexistence among farmers and herdsmen now appears impossible with herdsmen systematically attacking the farmers. The Sudanese conflict among two closely related groups has led to destruction of entire villages and displaced thousands of villagers. Weather phenomenon that compromises expected farm production or reduces forage impacts directly on prospects for survival in these subsistence conditions.

The three centuries of the industrial age have coincided with a period of relatively stable climate – a factor that contributed to the rapid expansion of agricultural production – transforming societies and promoting wealth accumulation, initially in the northern hemisphere, and also within some southern hemisphere regions through colonization. Agriculture, the transformation of agricultural production and the expansion of global trade in food, fibre and natural resources have underpinned the rise of the industrial state, which could not have happened without relatively predictable climate and weather patterns that sustained the expansion of production.

Yet, this essential underpinning of modern agriculture may be the very environmental factor most likely to change in this century, as major productive areas are frequently impacted by less favourable weather conditions. Moreover, the socioeconomic implications for a less productive agricultural system – just as the world's population is projected to grow from six to nine billion by mid-century – could create similar resource conflicts between more powerful states to the political instability we have been witnessing in a number of African states.

The UN Millennium Project – an independent advisory body commissioned by UN Secretary-General Kofi Annan to advise the UN on strategies for achieving the Millennium Development Goals (MDGs), the set of internationally agreed targets for reducing poverty, hunger, disease, illiteracy, environmental degradation and discrimination against women by 2015 – faces its most difficult challenge in Africa. Raising rural incomes and investing in human capacity demands a productive agricultural system. Yet, the African continent last produced as much food as it consumed in 1972; since then, the food balance has continued to worsen with frequent droughts or floods. United Kingdom (UK) researchers have studied a three-year period in Kenya during the 1990s. From 1997–2000, Kenya suffered extensive winter floods and then, a two-year period of drought. These consecutive weather problems cost the Kenyan economy an estimated US$4.8 billion in infrastructure damage, crop and livestock losses, and reduced production. This total represents 22 per cent of annual gross domestic product (GDP) – the cost of climate variability (Jones-Parry, 2005). When this happens in the developed world, crop insurance and government assistance support affected families and communities. For a poor country like Kenya, however, such a safety net is far beyond the government's capacity to respond. Cumulative losses over a decade like this could reverse any development progress rapidly.

A simple prescription for African economic progress focuses on raising African incomes by expanding access to the global market. Although this access is essential, the opportunity guaranteed by a more liberal trade agreement and new trade policies could be lost if Africa's agricultural productivity is further compromised by climate change. While action is essential, much of the solution lies outside Africa's power to respond, and temporary support for the affected communities is difficult to mobilize. The climate cycle is currently driven by the CO_2 emitted two or three decades ago. Even if Africa had the capacity to respond locally, there is no way it could respond to the larger emissions problem given the small contribution Africa has made to the problem. Thus, without a broad global commitment on emissions, the trends already underway cannot be reversed. And to stabilize the climate in a manner that would promote more favorable weather conditions, sustained and collective action is required over decades.

A recent study by Dr Anthony Nyong for the IPCC further confirms the trends highlighted in the panel's 2001 report on Africa, and illustrated by the recent UK studies on Kenya (Nyong, 2005). The continent is continuing to warm with increasing impacts on fragile grassland areas near the Sahara and the Kalahari deserts. Average river flows are declining even as flooding becomes more common in some areas. The visible shrinking of Lake Chad in the Sahel over the last 30 years and the decline of the pelagic fishery in Lake Tanganyika reduced capacity to support the people who depend on these water sources. These situations are further aggravated by rapid demographic growth and the increasing demand for resources. As the trends accelerate, they will only increase the hardship for many Africans and reduce the capacity to adapt to such change. And, as evidenced by the states in East Africa, the combination of climate change, political instability, and resource competition can prove lethal. Moreover, unless more is done to address the underlying environmental problems, there is almost no hope for regaining political and social stability.

Policy divergence

Despite the mounting scientific evidence that climate change is here and could cause major transformations in both developed and developing countries, there is no real consensus on what actions will best address the mitigation and adaptation tasks, nor on what such actions are trying to achieve. Moreover, the current global architecture for environmental cooperation is limited. Although many experts and policy makers recognized as early as 1972 that preserving biodiversity, controlling air and waterborne pollution and limiting environmental degradation would require international cooperation, national environmental rule-making remains in its infancy. The process states settled on for much of the effort was one of 'harmonization' of policy rather than true global enforcement. In fact, the US assumed early in the effort to promote global environmental policy that its own internal policies would become the 'standard' and other countries would follow its lead. This approach meant that international environmental agreements would be easy to ratify domestically, as they would mirror US policy. Early experiences – the Convention on International Trade in Endangered Species and the World Heritage Convention – reinforced these views. Moreover, as environmental regulation invariably imposes costs on business operations, the closer the connection between legislative action, the public and the regulated entity the better.

In 1972, however, few national governments understood the challenge and enormity of environmental protection and the difficulties of reversing business practices through enforcement. The US, in the years since 1969, adopted major pieces of legislation, including the National Environmental Policy Act (NEPA) and later, the Clear Water and Clear Air Acts that are the primary instruments of US environmental regulation. These acts focus on mitigation and operate on a 'polluter pays' principle that is enforced through litigation. The characteristic systemic tensions between government regulation and business operations, however, forced the US over time to explore other methods of regulation as litigation costs rose and public support for such actions waned. The most successful new regime since the beginning of federal environmental policy was the sulfur dioxide regime, aimed at reducing acid rain, which established a 'cap and trade' system for sulfur dioxide emissions from power plants in the US Midwest and Northeast – which has proven highly successful. This experience has critically shaped US thinking on how best to regulate key pollutants and influenced engagement in the global negotiations to regulate climate change, but it was insufficient to keep the US in the international game.

As US regulatory policy was evolving, regulatory regimes elsewhere were diverging from the US model. European states had adopted a variety of environmental policies since World War II, and many states took different approaches. Few European states were structured to use litigation as a basic enforcement tool, and the polluter pays principle was seen as best enforced through taxation or other means of 'internalizing the externality' of pollution. Japan took a similar approach, although it also adopted manufacturing efficiency standards as a tool to induce greater efficiencies in production. European integration complicated the regulatory challenge, but by the late 1980s, most EU countries had agreed on tax and efficiency policies that would support their regulatory regimes.

Developing countries, and the emerging 'economies in transition', faced a more challenging problem. Few had either tax or judicial systems that could effectively enforce environmental regulations. And even though the international system since the 1972 Stockholm Conference had exported model environmental legislation throughout the developing world, there was little capacity to assess environmental problems or regulate them effectively. Thus, as the scientific consensus around the problem of climate change has solidified, at the same time the capacity of states to take concrete action on many environmental problems has eroded.

As an illustration of the difficulty facing global action, the US has only successfully ratified four international environmental treaties since 1992: the

Framework Convention on Climate Change; the International Agreement on Straddling Stocks; the Western Hemisphere Migratory Bird Protection Treaty; and the Convention on Desertification. Major agreements on chemicals, hazardous waste, coastal zone and ocean protection, and, of course, the Kyoto Protocol, remain in limbo. Moreover, given the importance of the US in any regulatory regime, the lack of its participation can only compromise the success of these cooperative efforts. The state of global environmental agreements only reflects the breakdown in domestic consensus in the US around strong environmental action. In fact, recent domestic debates centre on whether or not protections under the Clean Air Act are likely to be reduced. Until this essential political consensus is re-established, the US is unlikely to be able to contribute effectively to multilateral efforts on this agenda. The evolution of the international climate negotiating process underscores the difficulties that faced the US delegation in trying to pursue a constructive negotiating position.

Traditionally, approaches to environmental problems have required a thorough understanding of how and why environmental change is occurring and what its impacts might be. To support the international process, the UK and the US worked with Europe and Japan to establish the IPCC in 1988. This network of scientists and experts was mandated to collect studies and organize an ongoing, systematic review of climate change research, identify gaps in knowledge, and recommend options for addressing the problem. The IPCC's work prompted the creation of an international negotiating process that led to the first international agreement – the UNFCCC, which was signed in Rio at the Earth Summit in 1992.

This instrument organized the international discussion, encouraged countries to contribute studies to the IPCC process, and created the process of national greenhouse gas emission inventories to help identify the sources of atmospheric warming with a view toward eventual limitations through co-ordinated domestic policy actions. The controversy surrounding this issue, however, grew as it became clear that the major factor driving climate change was energy use. Given the vital importance of energy for economic growth, employment and development, regulating energy use in a manner that would impact upon atmospheric chemistry would be a massive undertaking. So massive, in fact, that resistance to such a process was inevitable.

Subsequent negotiations after the UNFCCC entered into force underscored the diverging perceptions of the US and the Europeans on how to address the problem. The EU strongly argued for policies and measures, pressing for a new tax structure that would limit fossil fuel use and called for 'binding targets' on emissions. The US, which had tried to adopt a tax on energy use in the early 1990s and had to settle for a small increase in gasoline taxes that was later rescinded, had no appetite for such an approach. Most problematic, however, was the inability of the US to create a domestic political consensus around the need to regulate CO_2 as an element in addressing climate change.

Key leaders in the Clinton administration strongly supported early action, but divisions existed in the executive branch on how to address the problem. US Congress was resolutely against any environmental agreement that failed to include developing countries such as China, India, Mexico, Brazil and South Korea that were already identified in the treaty as potentially outside an initial regulatory framework. This exception was confirmed early in the process in Berlin, where the parties to the treaty agreed that any limitations on emissions would apply only to the developed countries in the initial phase. As the countries noted above were already major players in climate change due to industrial production or, in the case of Brazil, a major area of global forest cover, this decision further compromised constructive US participation. China was already second in global greenhouse gas emissions, and India sixth. US legislators saw no advantage in supporting a regime that exempted major economic competitors from regulation.

With the election of President George W. Bush, despite earlier campaign promises, it quickly became clear that the White House opposed the Kyoto Protocol. And even though some Congressional leaders were now committed to a US regulatory approach, these leaders could not mobilize majority support. Few observers expect a shift in Congressional attitudes during 2005–2006 that leads to new, tough regulations, but a number of legislative proposals have been introduced for consideration and some of these, especially the recommendations for new incentive programmes and research may become law.

The US rejection of Kyoto threw the international process into a period of disarray as the committed states needed either the US or Russia to ratify the treaty to ensure entry into force. Despite a firm EU commitment, until mid-2004, Russia's position was unclear and the eventual Russian ratification demanded several concessions from the EU, notably an agreement to let Russia continue its internal subsidies on gas. The delay in the process will also make it harder for the EU and Japan to meet the 2012 targets in the first budget period. In fact, the absence of the US and the delay in putting into place needed regulation for control has encouraged more European corporations to criticize the EU decision process. Most significant, however, is whether or not a regulatory regime can be maintained beyond 2012 without the active participation of the US and key developing countries. Despite the controversy over Kyoto, in terms of global emissions, it represents only a small, first step. In fact, it only yields a reduction in emissions growth from the baseline growth forecast in 1997. It was always envisioned by the experts and negotiators that this would set the stage for ever-tighter restrictions on greenhouse gas emissions in the future, reaching a point where global emissions would actually decline. Without the US and major developing country emitters in the process, there is no hope of achieving emission reductions on a scale that can stabilize the climate.

Climate stabilization: A new goal

Given the current constraints on effective international action, it is important that a leading political figure try to recast the debate and clarify the goal of action to prevent climate change. Over the past two years, the opportunity to recast the debate has been seized by the UK Prime Minister Tony Blair.

Significantly, he saw the coincidence of the UK chairing the G8 and the EU in 2005 as a dual platform on which to make the case for immediate action. To set the stage for this effort, he announced early on that his priorities for UK leadership in this period were climate change and Africa. As we can see from the short discussion above, Africa's longer term political stability may be directly linked to the ability of all countries to cooperate actively in limiting the impacts of climate change. Moreover, as this process proceeds, no continent needs more support in the form of assistance for adaptation than Africa. Blair has approached the problem with energy and creativity, but we will limit this discussion to his efforts on climate change.

Building on the work of his own scientific advisory group, Tony Blair has explicitly called for a focus on climate stabilization – an effort that will require that the UK reduce its emissions 60 per cent below 1990 levels by 2050. Similar reductions would be required throughout the developed world. Tony Blair has also challenged the world to limit temperature rise to two degrees Centigrade (2°C), as this would be the maximum level of planetary warming the earth could accommodate. This target equates to a concentration level of 550 PPM of CO_2. To support this conceptual framework, Tony Blair created an International Climate Task Force, chaired by UK Member of Parliament Stephen Byers and US Senator Olympia Snowe. The Task Force's recent report, 'Meeting the Climate Challenge' (Byers and Snowe, 2005), puts these goals in context and reiterates the need for global action.

The UK government is also opening the dialogue on a range of technologies. Blair has been very clear that regulating emissions at the 'pipe end' will be insufficient to attain the needed reductions. All available technologies must be deployed and new technologies developed. UK scientists have even put nuclear power back on the table given its 'no emissions' profile, but there is no guarantee in the UK or the US that public resistance to new nuclear power plants could be overcome without a major effort. The import, however, of Blair's leadership cannot be discounted. He has taken the debate beyond Kyoto, outlined the magnitude of the challenge, and proposed a temperature goal – something other advocates have so far failed to do. The international community must hope that Prime Minister Blair's effort makes progress, especially in re-engaging the US fully in the international effort to address climate change.

Climate security in the US

Despite the history of opposition to action by the US administration, concerns about climate change are growing in the US, and Blair's public efforts can only serve to extend and expand that discussion. In 2000 the National Research Council, and in 2003 researchers at the Pentagon, presented reports that argue there is a growing possibility of more abrupt climate change (Schwartz and Randall, 2003). The most recent report explores the possible impact of an abrupt climate change scenario due to the breakdown of the North Atlantic thermohaline conveyor (more commonly known as the Gulf Stream).

Pentagon researchers have identified eight periods in the past where warming patterns have led to abrupt shifts to cooling in Northern Europe and the Atlantic Ocean, causing glacier advances, more intense cold patterns, and in more recent periods, direct impacts on settled agriculture. The most recent and least severe of these past climatic shifts was the Little Ice Age in the 14th century. The cooling pattern in this period compromised Nordic settlements in Greenland and lowered agricultural production in Europe.

In examining more incremental climate models, the Pentagon researchers cited the need to examine alternative scenarios that would model potential impacts on the largest agricultural production regions in North America and Europe, looking at the political, social and economic consequences of a sharp decline in agricultural production. The Pentagon postulates that such a shift, compromising both supplies of food and fresh water could lead to a breakdown in normal alliances and promote resource-driven conflict. Scenarios that we may well be witnessing include patterns in less technologically advanced African societies that are more vulnerable to weather fluctuations that impact dramatically on subsistence agriculture. The fact that security issues have been added to policy considerations is important, but even these dramatic scenarios have yet to capture the public interest to the point that action on climate change is a topic of public priority in many countries, including the US.

Since 2002, a variety of reports have been issued urging a new energy policy in the US that would address the challenge of energy security, rising energy costs, and climate change through a combination of limitations on greenhouse gases and a variety of new incentives to deploy alternative energy throughout the US. The most recent report, 'Ending the Energy Stalemate' (National Commission on Energy Policy, 2004) is the result of two years of work by the National Commission on Energy Policy. The report recognizes that the US and the world economy must depend on a variety of fossil fuels, primarily natural gas, oil, and coal for much of this century, but if we continue to consume these resources on our current business-as-usual path, we will not only deplete resources more rapidly, but will increase the likelihood of severe climate impacts. And while most studies believe the developed world will adapt at some cost to this warmer future, political insecurity and conflict may be an increasing element of this adaptation. A cleaner, more efficient future could also be a future that constrains global carbon emissions, mitigates many of the incremental climate impacts, and averts the threat of disruptive climate change.

An opponent of the Kyoto Protocol, but an articulate US Senate leader for action on climate change, Chuck Hagel, of Nebraska, has consistently stressed that any global action must realistically accommodate the need for growth and development in developing countries. Given that need, it is vital that developed countries, in Senator Hagel's view, share cleaner technology with developing countries. Like Prime Minister Blair, Hagel has recognized the need for solutions to energy generation, distribution, and transport that reduce carbon intensity, improve efficiency and limit the potential emissions trajectory from the minute a power plant goes online or a car enters the production line. His new legislative proposals address this with tax incentives for American firms to work with developing countries on diffusion and development of these technologies (Hagel, 2005).

The outlook

When we revisit the efforts to mobilize government action on global climate change over the last two decades, one may ask is this method the best way to address a challenge that threatens the foundations of modern economic progress and possibly humanity? In the most classic sense of the 'free rider', a common solution is required, but the magnitude of action is so great and the capacity to mitigate or adapt to the impacts so differentiated that moving collectively is extremely difficult. Even nations that have decided to act – the EU, Japan, Russia, Canada, Norway, Iceland, and New Zealand – will have to mobilize new levels of political will in the next phase unless the US and the major developing country emitters are at the table. While there are some favourable signs that show movement, much effort is required to take the next step. There are opportunities, building especially on the initiatives of UK Prime Minister Blair and US Senator Hagel, among others, that could advance the process more rapidly. To this end, here are some initiatives the international community might take:

1   Establish a Mitigation and Adaptation Fund to supplement the potential resources generated by the Clean Development Mechanism (CDM) that would guarantee loans for developing countries that want to invest in the cleanest technologies for power generation, putting high priority on getting these technologies built-in to new power plants in India and China – as well as other large power users that may be more developed (South Korea, Turkey, Mexico)
2   Work with the EU to leverage its €240 million renewable energy commitment to provide incentives to developing countries that adopt a renewable energy target. Give special preference to the Small Island Developing States for use of these funds in the first five years
3   Use the 14th and 15th sessions of the Commission on Sustainable Development (CSD) to report extensively on energy efficiency and alternative energy use in developing countries to demonstrate the progress in reducing the trend growth in energy and emissions over the last decade
4   Encourage the UN Energy Task Force to develop an analysis of how to maximize clean-energy technology use in development planning and provide pilot initiatives and cost estimates to support countries in diversifying their energy mix to improve efficiency, lower emissions and carbon intensity as a goal of national energy policy
5   Strengthen scientific capacity in developing countries to establish environmental and energy baselines and support the national inventory processes of the UNFCCC to support policy change

6   Support through technical assistance, Overseas Development Assistance (ODA) grants and loans, policy initiatives that promote cleaner fuels and technologies and reduce both explicit and hidden subsidies and fossil fuels

7   Work with the private sector to expand funds available for alternative energy technologies, including exploring the introduction of guarantees, development bonds, and so on.

These activities, if pursued aggressively as part of the UN Millennium Project, hold the potential for building a win–win coalition around technology transfer and development that could lay a foundation for pursuing a new energy paradigm. Given the vulnerability of the global economy – and developing countries – to price and weather variability, this new consensus could set the stage for a major shift in consumption and emission trends making a major contribution to longer term security.

References

Byers, S. and Snowe, O. (2005) 'Meeting the climate challenge', recommendations of the ICCTF, Institute of Public Policy Research, London

'Counting the cost of the tsunami'(2005) *Money Week*, January 7. www.moneyweek.com/article/566/investing/markets/tsunami-reconstruction-cost.html

Eilperin, J. (2005) 'Arid Arizona Points to Global Warming as Culprit', *The Washington Post*, February 6, pA3

Environmental Protection Agency (1997) 'Climate Change: What does it mean for the Central Southwest? A Report on the 30 October 1997 EPA Regional Conference', Government Printing Office, Washington, DC

Hagel, C. (2005) 'Setting A New Course for Climate Change', Speech delivered at Brookings Institution Briefing on Climate Change Policy, 9 February, Washington, DC, http://hagel.senate.gov

Hanley, C. (2004) 'CO_2 Hits Record Levels, Researchers Find', *World News China*, Associated Press, 20 March, www.archive.com/2004/03/21/1400/worldnewschina

Jones-Parry, E. (2005) Statement given at event to mark the entry into force of the Kyoto Protocol, UK Mission to the UN, February 17; www.ukun.org/articles_show.asp?SarticleType=17&Article_ID=866

National Commission on Energy Policy (2004) *Ending the Energy Stalemate*, Government Printing Office, Washington, DC

Nyong, A. (2005) *The Economic, Developmental and Livelihood Implications of Climate Induced Depletion of Ecosystems and Biodiversity in Africa*, Proceedings of the Scientific Symposium on Stabilization of Greenhouse Gases Met Office, Exeter, UK, 1–3 February

Pearce, F. (2005) 'Climate Change: Menace or myth?', *New Scientist*, no 2486, pp38–40

Revkin, A. (2004) 'Warming Trend in Arctic Is Linked to Emissions', *The New York Times Internet Edition*, 29 October, www.nytimes.com

Schwartz, P. and Randall, D. (2003) *An Abrupt Climate Change Scenario and Its Implications for United States National Security*, A report commissioned by the US Department of Defense, October, Washington, DC

Scott, P., Stone, D. and Allen, M. (2004) 'Human contribution to the European heatwave of 2003', *Nature*, vol 432, pp610–614

9

Migration, Development and Security

Devyani Gupta

It is time to take a more comprehensive look at the various dimensions of the migration issue, which involves hundreds of millions of people and affects countries of origin, transit and destination. We need to understand better the causes of international flows of people and their complex inter-relationship with development.

Kofi Annan, 2002

Introduction

With the global movement of people estimated at 175 million (or 2.9 per cent of the world population) at last count (UNFPA, 2002) and the ensuing insecurities this has stirred in many developed countries, we are arguably in the midst of a 'global migration crisis' (Weiner, 1995; Zolberg, 2001). This steadily growing number of people on the move defies our traditional norms of sovereignty and national security, challenging the ability of states to control their borders and suggesting a move to a new more porous global system (Dauvergne, 2003).

But if there is 'chaos' as many suggest, it is not due to or expressed in numbers alone. The problem is a large one partially because it is misrepresented, rendering some of the inadequate measures to address it misguided and failed. The migration 'meltdown' continues to haunt politicians, the media, and the electorate, as it is poorly conceived in both dialogue and practice. Often articulated as an anomaly to the state-centred international system, migration is considered unnatural and as something to be feared. The migrant as an outsider is viewed with considerable suspicion as to his/her intentions that are thought to be dubious at best.

Framed in a manner that breeds cynicism, it is not surprising that migration should hold the negative connotations that it does for many western countries.

Part of the problem is that at present, the immigration debate is a largely one-dimensional affair. Constructed from the perspective of host countries and their voting populations, it pays excessive attention to the *perceived* losses that accompany immigrants and sometimes even criminalizes them. In doing so, it sidelines the *genuine* needs of the host country itself, along with those of the migrants and their countries of origin from the equation.

Governments have been wrestling with immigration for some time now, but as they tackle one aspect of the problem, others surface. For instance, the 'restrictionist' trends in Europe against bogus asylum-seekers and illegal immigrants have had the unforeseen consequence of driving the flow underground, thereby creating a highly lucrative business for human traffickers, which is harder to track and control. In the absence of alternatives, many migrants (whether forced or voluntarily) use clandestine routes to enter states and apply for asylum in the hope of being able to stay – even if they are not bona fide refugees. In an environment that creates incentives for people to lie, the credibility of the applicant and by extension the entire system becomes suspect.

When politicians do attempt to assuage popular concerns over being 'invaded' by outsiders, they are largely met with distrust – after all, these are the same ministers that have on occasion been called into question over their ability to check abuses of our open society. Needless to say, this is an unhelpful starting point for mapping out good governance on migration. Without a reasoned and balanced approach to gaining a better understanding of migration, discussing the dynamics of the migrant's experience and harnessing the positive potential within this powerful force, the presently misguided debate and associated policy responses will continue to be as haphazard as the migrant flows themselves.

The purpose of this chapter is to analyse current limitations in thought and action towards immigration, discuss the migration-development nexus model as a useful construct offering a path away from this 'crisis', and propose measures that may be able to minimize the costs of migration whilst maximizing its benefits.

Migration and development: A force for good?

> *...for those with more, globalisation makes more available, for those with less, there is less. Inequalities are increased, exclusions are underscored.*
>
> Dauvergne, 2003, p10

As a by-product of the noticeably stronger ties that bind the 'global village', migration is an inevitable and (contrary to popular belief) an irreversible certainty. It is both an expression of and facilitated by globalization.[1] This force underscores (and exacerbates) the increasingly visible differences epitomized in the North–South divide[2] and in doing so, tests international geopolitical boundaries.

The so-called 'migration crisis' then is not so much about the abuse of our 'common fund' or evasion of the duties that accompany it, as it is evidence of the gross inequality in our global structures that the migrant attempts to overcome in order to survive. Acute poverty, population growth, high unemployment levels and ongoing conflict situations (to name but a few) provide the *incentives* for people to move, while easier communication and access to transport are the *means* for this human traffic.

That people should move therefore is an irrepressible fact – they have always done so and doubtless shall continue to do so. This is, after all, part of our human instinct, and has long been a strategy to reduce risk by diversifying income sources. It is perhaps fitting that the very process that stimulates the free movement of capital and commodities across international lines (and is thus celebrated amongst developed nations), should also propel labour, and thus people, to migrate. This presents the very problem that stamps a big question mark on the continued absoluteness of state sovereignty.

It is precisely because developed countries are unwilling to address this problem wholeheartedly that the policies designed to curb migration have so far been ineffective. Indeed it has been proposed that the current mismatch between the *aims* of immigration policy and their actual *outcomes* is a by-product of the essentially short-term and tunnel vision approach practiced by government (Cornelius et al, 1994).

By crossing carefully demarcated borders, migrants are thrusting the stark reality of differences between developed and developing nations before us, and in doing so, acting as agents to re-forge the link between the prosperous North and the less fortunate South. Stephen Castles rightly claims that 'migration control is essentially about regulating North–South relationships and maintaining inequality' (Castles, 2004). Until this serious disparity that pervades international society is meaningfully addressed, migration is unlikely to be controlled, or even managed.

As a first step, migration should be accepted as a given and, if possible, even applauded for the opportunities it can offer under the right conditions. To do so, both the prospects and concerns that the fusion of migration and development holds need to be explored as a way of moving forward from this impasse.

Migration and development: Drawing out the linkages

That migration and development are closely linked is undisputed. At a basic level, both terms suggest a change of some form – one based on geographical movement and the other progression to a better society. But aside from semantic similarities, the exact nature and scope of this relationship is as yet unclear and somewhat arbitrary. This is largely because by their very nature, the two processes are constantly changing and moulded by a myriad of unpredictable variables in different settings at any given time. Anticipating the shape they may take and the multiple ways in which they can influence each other is difficult (to say the least). Under such conditions, it is hard to imagine one special 'migration-development' formula that can be successfully applied in all countries for all problems.

Despite its indefinable patterns and resulting difficulties, interest in the realm of possibilities embedded in this union continues to swell. A growing body of empirical evidence demonstrates that migration is both an expression and trigger of development. Some scholars believe that, '...migration is ... a virtuous interaction in which development is enhanced, not only in the destination country, but also in the sending country' (Weinstein, 2001). Often postulated as a good omen, it is thought to *contribute* to development through remittances. These funds sent home by migrants have a strong positive impact on alleviating poverty and driving economic growth.

A study of 74 low and middle-income developing countries, for example, shows that on average, a 10 per cent increase in the share of remittances in a country's gross domestic product (GDP) can lead to a 1.2 per cent decline in poverty (Page and Adams, 2003). Furthermore, the benefits are not restricted to the sending states – host countries also profit from the regular injection of new populations bringing fresh ideas and boosting their economies.

Conversely, in his now famous 'laws of migration', E. G. Ravenstein proposed that migration was in effect *caused by* economic development: 'Migration increases in volume as industries and commerce develop and transport improves' (Ravenstein, 1985). This is often referred to as the *migration hump* – a period when economic and social development improves rapidly causing a significant proportion of the population to migrate (Martin, 1994). As Massey et al (1998) put it:

> ...*international migrants do not come from poor, isolated places that are disconnected from world markets, but from regions and nations that are undergoing rapid change and development as a result of their incorporation into global trade, information, and production networks. In the short run, international migration does not stem from a lack of economic development, but from development itself.*
>
> Massey et al, 1998, p277

Development, then, is accompanied by not only the incentive but also the opportunity and means to emigrate; conversely, migration can boost the financial base of the sending country, thus leading to economic development. The blend of both processes therefore almost appears to be organic.

However, an incomplete conception of *development* is likely to mar the extent to which its fusion with migration can be successful. The present tendency to treat economic growth as synonymous with development fails to appreciate the numerous other socio-political indicators critical to the overall development cycle. This has significant implications for the assessment of any country's position in the development process, the level of emigration that can be expected due to the migration hump, and the actions that should be taken to stimulate rather than hinder further progress.

As the account above demonstrates, our knowledge on the relationship of migration and development is fragmentary at best. Currently riddled with an over-emphasis on fiscal impacts, the orthodox view of development tends to equate it rather simplistically with economic growth. This is both inaccurate and imprudent as such an understanding is in danger of overlooking not only the real catalysts and indicators of development but also the extent to which people are actually enjoying the fruits of economic progress.

For instance, this interpretation does not incorporate the income distribution within a country, which is notoriously difficult to measure both for political and for technical reasons. Where statistics can be found, however, they indicate that many less developed countries (LDCs) have vast income inequalities within their states. A few rich individuals may so distort the picture that the gross national product (GNP) per capita figure corresponds neither to the reality of the low standards of the masses, nor to the wealth of the few.

This can have the unintended consequence of misjudging the socioeconomic conditions in a given country, which in turn can misinform development policies and potentially do more harm than good. That there are often large sections of marginalized and disadvantaged groups in society not sharing in the benefits of economic growth and not being accounted for by this approach underlines its inadequacy in evaluating development. For critics such as Amartya Sen, therefore, economic growth in and of itself is inadequate. It is not the means and end of development – rather, much depends on how this material accumulation is used (Sen, 1999).

Migration: An ideal development tool?

Traditionally, grafting migration and development together in a positive light would have been considered unlikely and even erroneous. Until recently, the mainstream view portrayed migration as the epitome of failed development; the argument being that people generally move in search of opportunities when none are forthcoming in their country of residence. Indeed this perspective holds so much sway amongst some people that they remain firmly attached to its wisdom.

Delving deeper into their argument however, it is not surprising that it continues to be so compelling. A close examination of the linkages between migration and development reveals an ambiguity challenging the heart of the optimists' argument on the positive linkages of migration and development. It suggests that migration is not necessarily the harbinger of development – rather, it can lead to decline. Off-shoots of the migration process such as the much-lamented 'brain drain' cannot be overlooked as a dim likelihood. Issues such as these are a source of great concern and their mitigation must be part of any strategy that seeks development through migration.

Unless such phenomena are reversed, the burden of developing countries is likely to be aggravated rather than alleviated. Referring to a few negative impacts of migration and the seemingly benign policies cultivated by developed countries to address it, this section will unpack some of the ramifications migrants and their countries are likely to bear. The problems elucidated here must feed into, rather than contaminate, policy-making if the future of migration in development policy is to be secured.

At the moment however, developed countries often place migration in direct conflict with development through their pursuit of unequal global structures that in turn attract 'the best and the brightest' to their shores leading to the brain drain phenomenon.[3] This renders the countries (and people) they leave behind even more vulnerable so that 'sending countries ... are pretty much all-round losers: they are deprived of much-needed skills and talent, and forfeit a return in public investment in education' (Boswell and Crisp, 2004, p8). That developed countries, despite being the clear winners in this equation, continue to be anxious about the fact that they must harbour immigrants is an unsurprising yet sorry display of misguided self-interest.

Thus measures to send immigrants back to their countries after a suitable period of time are pushed through quite forcefully especially if, as governments fear, migration leads to permanent settlement. The justification for this position is that if migration is a drain on the financial and human capital of a country, return is the obvious solution that replenishes it. The pretext behind which these governments hide is that development (rather than host country interest) is the motivating factor urging return.

Reports on the subject from influential institutions give credence to this practice by concluding that the long-term costs of the emigration of highly skilled professionals can only be checked with their eventual return (Lowell and Findlay's report, 2001). As a recent paper by the International Labour Organization (ILO) recommends:

> *The work permit scheme should ... operate in such a way as to encourage return migration. Work Permits UK might consider both, making return a condition of issuing visas, and might also discourage employers more strongly from applying for visa extensions.*
>
> *Findlay, 2002*

This advice has been translated into initiatives in many countries such as the 'return of talent' programme that actively encourages the repatriation of highly skilled migrants to their countries as a practical and public display of support for the development of their nations.

It would seem then that the 'free' movement of people should have a time-restriction attached to it. Language and tone on the subject is deliberated in ways that serve to heighten the necessity of return for both the migrants themselves and their country of origin. Indeed Oleson suggests a specific timeline of 10–15 years, at the end of which migrants should return to maximize the benefit to the sending country (Oleson, 2002). That this timeframe mirrors the socio-political interests of the receiving states by ejecting unpopular immigrants after their skills have been fully capitalized upon, is surely more than mere coincidence.

Other commentators, such as Ul-Haque and Ali Khan, even argue for the relative cost-efficiency of 'brain drain repatriation' compared to donor-funded technical assistance (Ul-Haque and Ali Khan, 1997). This is a somewhat worrying signal, as it affords credibility to the idea that migrants can and should shoulder the burden of advancing development in their country without the need for complementary measures such as overseas aid and technology transfers. It heralds a gradual shift from greater donor assistance to one that relies mainly (and then perhaps only) on migrant remittances and skill transfers through their eventual return.

Recommendations such as these, while no doubt well intentioned and carefully reasoned, can clearly prompt unsafe measures that are often less so. Replacing 'brain drain' with 'brain gain' has given temporary immigration ethical as well as commercial sanction. The suggestion that immigrants are sometimes better placed to promote development in their countries through financial and skills transfers allows legitimacy for this position from a humanitarian perspective. Meanwhile, host populations are more likely to be appeased with the assurance that the presence of immigrants here will only be temporary, especially if they yield high economic returns during their short stay. This allows for a more quality controlled sifting process – moral high ground with a distinctly pragmatic twist.

Furthermore, displaying unwavering faith in the ill-advised notion that 'migration can be turned on and off like a tap by appropriate policy settings,' governmental interest in stemming the tide of migration from its very source continues to grow (Castles, 2004). Industrialized states have been vocalizing concern for the root causes of migration, which, if uncovered and eliminated, can prevent the drain on and impediment to the social and economic development of migrants' home countries.

The High Level Working Group on Asylum and Migration (HLWG), for instance, was established in 1998 to address this very issue – a worthy effort, but the intentions behind it were not entirely as noble. Rather than devising viable policy proposals that could have helped to oversee poverty alleviation, conflict resolution, support for human rights and good governance, the HLWG has largely concentrated its efforts on creating and maintaining greater security along the international borders to thwart and reverse immigrant flows.

Along the same lines, there are signs that indicate a willingness to increase development assistance for some states in an effort to combat the 'push factors' for migration thereby helping to reduce the size of immigrant flows. Indeed, a recent inquiry by the International Development Select Committee questioned whether aid can 'prevent migration by promoting local development' (International Development Select Committee, 2003). The six action plans produced by the HLWG at the Tampere summit in 1999 were seen as 'an attempt to pass responsibility for prevention of immigration to the countries of origin of refugees and migrants and the countries through which they pass by tying trade and aid to the prevention and return of 'refugee flows' (Hayes and Bunyan, 2003, p. 72).

Similarly, the European Commission's communication, *Integrating Migration Issues in the European Union's Relations with Third Countries* (COM, 703 Final of 3 December 2002) gives the impression that there is a real risk of making development funding conditional on migration prevention measures. Ultimately, it seems that the aim is to stop future 'unsuitable' migration through 'policies to stimulate economic development [that] may reduce the incentive to emigrate from developing countries' (Coppel et al, 2001).

Finally, even the much-praised remittances are not without their faults. These flows are not an 'external pump that prime every area for an economic take-off' (Widgren and Martin, 2002, p9). Producing what J. K. Galbraith has called 'private affluence and public squalor' or new homes reachable only over dirty roads, these funds can contribute to the growing inequality within developing countries (quoted in Widgren and Martin, 2002, p9). Economic and social divides within a country are likely to be made more visible and reinforced as families of overseas workers significantly increase their incomes, while those without such financial transfers fall further into the poverty trap.

Furthermore, an excessive reliance on remittances can stall the growth of national economies – a flow that, despite its significant size, is still unreliable and dependent on external factors such as the favourability (or lack thereof) of migration policies exercised by the West. Some scholars have also contested the extent to which remittances can be said to contribute to the overall development of a country as they are 'not put to productive use, but mostly spent on unproductive purposes ... or wasted on conspicuous consumption...' (Hermele, 1997). Seen in this light, it becomes important to be cautious in our estimates of the gains that a link between migration and development can offer, especially since this can have considerable repercussions for the future of development aid and practice.

That said, this is but one lens through which to view the migration-development story. This is not to say that the less than hopeful reasoning outlined above is incorrect or dated. Rather, it is simply one truth, however real it may be for those enduring it. While migration can be a harmful force, it can also be a force for good – much depends on how it is perceived, discussed and used. The above-mentioned drains on developing countries should inform immigration policy, rather than hinder it, to provide a more viable and holistic strategy for the future that considers both the opportunities and threats within migration so as to help realize a *sustainable development* goal for all.

Migration for development and security

Acharya and Dewitt offer the *distributive development* model – merging migration and development in a way that is closer to responding to the real sensitivities demanded by migrants, their countries and the receiving states. This approach treats the cause rather than the symptoms of the migration 'crisis' viewing 'the economic problems of developing countries, including conditions that create conflict and lead to refugee exodus, as the function of structural inequality within the international system' (Acharya and Dewitt, 1997).

By injecting a long-term view into immigration policies, this perspective helps to better anticipate future problems, while avoiding the adverse side-effects of some misguided 'quick-fix' arrangements. The recommendations below are neither exhaustive, nor are they without problems, but as a starting point, they are intended to feed into the wider debate that continues on the subject.

Liberalize migration policies

Clearly, any country has at its heart the safety and well-being of its own citizens to consider. While security concerns are understandable, especially in the aftermath of 11 September 2001, nevertheless, allowing such fears to control our mindset and fuel an irrational suspicion of outsiders is unfortunate and unwise.

As a step away from such behaviour, some reformists advocate 'open borders' so as to meaningfully respond to the structural disparities in the international system. As Tarja Halonen recently asserted, it would be self-defeating to ignore the need for greater openness in the movement of labour across international lines (Schifferes, 2004). Authorizing open legal migration channels to meet our labour needs, especially with the growing concerns about our ageing populations, also helps to reduce the possibility of irregular migration.

Liberalize trade policies

Economists tend to be the most vocal supporters of free trade as an efficient means to generate development and reduce unwanted migration. The US Commission for the Study of International Migration and Cooperative Economic Development (1990) concluded that expanding trade between sending and receiving countries is 'the single most important remedy' (quoted in Widgren, 2002). Similarly a joint International Labour Organization (ILO)-United Nations High Commission for Refugees (UNHCR) study found that open markets were the important mechanisms in limiting emigration pressures (Widgren, 2002).

Moreover, a recent Oxfam report convincingly argues that current trade restrictions that only serve to reinforce global inequality and poverty should be removed so as to induce significant benefits for poor countries (Oxfam, 2002). These trade barriers currently cost developing countries the considerable sum of approximately US$100 billion per year – double the amount they receive in aid. Little wonder then that their development is not as swift as it could be.

Address the root causes of migration

As long as immigration policy is based on an inherently state-centred logic that chooses to ignore the role of the fundamentally unequal global structures in fuelling migration pressures, the 'crisis' is only likely to grow. Addressing the root causes of migration should be used to correct the acute poverty and desperate living conditions endured by people in developing countries, so that they are not *compelled* to migrate. This should not be a ploy to contain migration. Rather, the option to move should they choose to do so should always be open to them.

Re-articulating the conception of migration

Migrants are usually vilified and criminalized by the press and public. Recycling inaccurate and highly sensationalized text in their stories, the tabloids seem incapable of exercising restraint and wisdom. That such irresponsible and provocative material is permitted (and even supported by some public figures) is alarming and likely to incite further social tension. Oversight bodies watching over such behaviour and encouraging a more balanced perspective should be set up.

Think-tanks, such as Demos in the UK, also argue for the importance of raising awareness about migration issues and the positive impacts immigrants have on our societies, at educational institutions. This is so that future generations are not raised in the same climate of fear and suspicion as the present one.

Setting up an international regime

There is little in the way of international cooperation on migration at the global level and no international migration regime, partly because the current focus of governments in the post 11 September 2001 world on the real or perceived threat of terrorism places security concerns ahead of development priorities. That said, the very actions of governments in response to the threat of terrorism in fact represent the building-blocks of an international migration regime. As Rey Koslowski recently suggested, part of the reason why the notion of an international regime for orderly migration has gained traction in the post 11 September 2001 world is that it now has a greater security value:

> *Previously, the security threat posed by illegal migration and human smuggling was of the disruptive movements of people. Such movements could provoke immediate border security problems because of their sheer scale or due to the adverse domestic political reactions at the perceived loss of governmental control over borders. Now this threat may come from small groups or even individuals circulating within larger illegal flows. By increasing the share of orderly, properly-documented and pre-screened migration that passes through ports of entry rather than travelling around them, an international migration regime can help border authorities focus their limited resources on travellers and visitors that potentially pose the greatest security risks.*
>
> *Koslowski, 2004*

As a stepping stone to initiating a system much like the refugee regime, the UN Convention on the Rights of Migrants Workers and their Families should be ratified and enforced as a matter of urgency. Bhagwati has also suggested the creation of a World Migration Organization to oversee inter-state and civil society dialogue in producing innovative recommendations, evaluate migration trends and the policy implications therein, analyse emerging issues that impact upon migration, develop and codify standards, and spread best practices (Ratha, 2003).

In the longer term, it is vital to retain the level of international attention currently afforded the migration issue. The release of UN Secretary-General Kofi Annan's March 2005 report, 'In Larger Freedom' has been an important development in this respect, recognizing as it does both the opportunities and challenges presented by migration, as well as the need to understand the impacts of its trends (UN, 2005). Equally important will be the report of the Global Commission on International Migration (GCIM). Launched by the Secretary-General in December 2003, the CGIM has a mandate to place international migration on the international agenda, to analyse the gaps in policy approaches to migration and examine inter-linkages with other issue-areas, and to present recommendations to the UN and other stakeholders (GCIM, 2005). A central aspect of its approach has been a focus on how to strengthen international governance of migration, and the high-level dialogue on the report's recommendations at the 2006 General Assembly will prove a significant forum for action.

Conclusion: A 'win–win–win' situation?

Changes in migration flows will almost always have repercussions (both good and bad) for the development of origin countries. However, in the current climate of profiteering humanitarianism with efforts to curtail the flow of people unless they meet the needs of the receiving state, it is uncertain whether it will do more good than harm. If countries are to be handed the reigns, migration can and will of course be managed, but not necessarily for the benefit of all. As Widgren notes:

> *In thinking about how to manage migration, it is important to remember that most migration is analogous to water dripping, not floods, and durable solutions to 'drip migration' lie in economic growth and peace. Policies that promote trade, investment, aid, as well as respect for human rights, do not eliminate the need for border controls overnight, but they do keep countries on the path toward sustained reductions in migration pressure. Abandoning or neglecting those policies because they work slowly, on the other hand, may invite the very mass and unpredictable migration some industrial countries fear.*

> *Widgren, 2002*

Notes

1   By globalization, I mean the liberalization of international trade, the expansion of foreign direct investment (FDI), and the emergence of massive cross-border financial flows.
2   In using this term I refer to the increasing inequality in economic, social and political security and stability that mars the relationship between developed and developing nations, respectively. Many in the former have grown so accustomed to the privileges that our society affords us that much of the hostility directed towards immigrants can be explained by our unwillingness to share them with the onset of these outsiders.
3   Lowell and Findlay, 2001, p7 suggest that 'brain drain can occur if emigration of tertiary educated persons for permanent or long stays abroad reaches significant levels and is not offset by the feedback effects of remittances, technology transfer, investments, or trade. Brain drain reduces economic growth through loss return on investment in education and depletion of the source country's human capital assets.'

References

Acharya, A. and Dewitt, D. B (1997) 'Fiscal burden sharing' in Hathaway, J. C. (ed), *Reconceiving International Refugee Law*, Martinus Nijhoff Publishers, The Hague, pp111–147

Annan, K. (2002) *Strengthening the United Nations: an agenda for further change*, Report of the Secretary-General, General Assembly, 57th session, document A/57/387, 9 September, United Nations, New York

Boswell, C. and Crisp, J. (2004) *Poverty, International Migration and Asylum*, United Nations University-World Institute for Development Economics Research (UNU-WIDER), Policy Brief No 8, Helsinki

Castles, S. (2004) 'Why migration policies fail', *Ethnic and Racial Studies*, vol 27, no 2, pp205–227

Coppel, J., Dumont, J.-C. and Visco, I. (2001) *Trends in Immigration and Economic Consequences*, OECD Economics Department Working Paper, No. 284, June, OECD, Paris

Cornelius, W., Martin, P. L., and Hollifield, J. F. (1994) 'Introduction: The ambivalent quest for control' in Cornelius, W., Martin, P. L., and Hollifield, J. F. eds) *Controlling Immigration: A Global Perspective*, Stanford University Press, Stanford, CA, pp3–41

Dauvergne, C. (2003) *Challenges to Sovereignty: Migration Laws for the 21st Century*, UNHCR Working Paper No 92, July, UNHCR, Geneva

Findlay, A. (2002) *From Brain Exchange to Brain Gain: Policy Implications for the UK of Recent Trends in Skilled Migration from Developing Countries*, ILO, International Migration Papers no 43, ILO, Geneva

GCIM (2005) Global Commission on International Migration, www.gcim.org/en

Hayes, B. and Bunyan, T. (2003) 'Statewatch: Migration, development and the EU security agenda' in BOND, *Europe in the World: Essays on EU foreign, security and development policies*, May, www.bond.org.uk/eu/euinworld.htm

Hermele, K. (1997) 'The discourse on migration and development' in Hammar, T. Brochmann, G., Tamas, K. and Faist, T. (eds) *International Migration, Immobility and Development*, Berg, Oxford

International Development Select Committee (2003) Inquiry on Migration and Development, November; www.parliament.the-stationery-office.co.uk

Koslowski, R. (2004) 'Possible steps towards an international regime for mobility and security,' *Global Migration Perspectives*, Research Paper Series No 8, October, GCIM, Geneva

Lowell, B. L. and Findlay, A. (2001) *Migration of Highly Skilled Persons from Developing Countries: Impact and Policy Responses*, ILO International Migration Paper No. 44, December, ILO, Geneva

Martin, P. L. (1994) *Migration and Trade: Challenges for the 1990s*, Paper prepared for the World Bank's Development Committee, World Bank, Washington, DC

Massey, D. S., Arango, J., Hugo, G., Kouaovci, A., Pellegrino, A. and Taylor, J. E. (1998) *Worlds in Motion: Understanding International Migration at the End of the Millennium*, Oxford University Press, Oxford

Oleson, H. (2002) 'Migration, return and development: An institutional perspective', *International Migration*, International Organization for Migration, vol 40, no 5, pp125–150

Oxfam (2002) *Rigged Rules and Double Standards: Trade, Globalisation and the Fight Against Poverty*, Oxfam, Oxford

Page, J. and Adams, R. (2003) *The Impact of International Migration and Remittances on Poverty*, Paper presented at the World Bank International Conference on Migrant Remittances, 9–10 October, World Bank, Washington, DC

Ratha, D. (2003) 'Workers' remittances: An important and stable source of external development finance' in *Global Development Finance: Striving for Stability in Development Finance*, the World Bank, Washington, DC

Ravenstein, E. G. (1985) 'The laws of migration,' *Journal of the Statistical Society*, vol 48, no 2, pp167–235

Schifferes, S. (2004) *Can Globalization be Tamed?*, BBC News Online, 24 February, http://news.bbc.co.uk/1/hi/business/3516197.stm

Sen, A. (1999) *Development as Freedom*, Oxford University Press, Oxford

Ul-Haque, N. and Ali Khan, M. A. (1997) *Institutional Development: Skill Transference through a Reversal of 'Human Capital Flight' or Technical Assistance*, IMF Working Paper, WP/97/89, July, International Monetary Fund, Washington DC

UN (2005) *In Larger Freedom: Towards Development, Security and Human Rights for All*, Report of the Secretary-General, document A/59/2005, 21 March, United Nations, New York

UNFPA (2002) *International Migration 2002 – Wallchart*, United Nations, New York

Weiner, M. (1995) *The Global Migration Crisis: Challenges to States and Human Rights*, Harper Collins, New York

Weinstein, E. (2001) 'Migration for the benefit of all: Towards a new paradigm for migrant labor', *International Migration Papers 40*, International Labour Office, Geneva

Widgren, J. and Martin, P. (2002) *Managing Migration: The Role of Economic Instruments*, Centre for Development Research, Expert Working Paper, February, ILO, Geneva

Zolberg, A. R. (2001) 'Introduction: Beyond the crisis' in Zolberg, A. R. and Benda, P. M. (eds) *Global Migrants, Global Refugees: Problems and Solutions*, Berghahn, New York and Oxford, pp1–16

10

Securing a Healthier World

Christine K. Durbak and Claudia M. Strauss

Science knows no country, because knowledge belongs to humanity, and is the torch which illuminates the world. Science is the highest personification of the nation because that nation will remain the first which carries the furthest the works of thought and intelligence.

Louis Pasteur

A ... Government, without popular information, or the means of acquiring it, is but a Prologue to a Farce or a Tragedy; or, perhaps both.

James Madison, 1822

Introduction

Concerns about national security have taken centre stage since 11 September 2001, creating a unique opportunity for governments to evaluate realistically insecurities in global public health. Health is the specific subject of three of the eight Millennium Development Goals (MDGs) (UN, 2000). Priority has to be given to securing a safe environment for all people, particularly those in developing nations and post-Soviet countries in order to reduce the mortality rate among children under five years of age (MDG4); reduction of maternal mortality ratio (MDG5); reverse the spread of HIV/AIDS, malaria and other major diseases (MDG6).

MDG7, on ensuring environmental sustainability, includes reducing by half the number of people without access to safe drinking water. The needs for remediation of HIV/AIDS and malaria are well recognized: however, the need for safe water is one of the cornerstones for securing a healthier world. An estimated 3.4 million people die annually of water-related illnesses; more than 1 billion people lack access to safe water supply; 40 per cent of the world's people lack adequate sanitation, and roughly 40 per cent of the world's nations have unsafe water for fishing, swimming, or supporting aquatic life. In the United States (US), for example, despite 30 years of progress since the passage of the Clean Water Act, 218 million Americans live within 10 miles of polluted water.

According to the World Health Organization (WHO), improving human health 'is at the heart of the matter of development' (WHO, 2003). Reinforcing this, the health-related MDGs are geared toward alleviating the worst conditions of poverty and preventing an increase in the number of people who become severely impoverished. People who suffer from chronic hunger and malnutrition tend to be ill with diseases that can be easily transmitted if not treated. Countries constantly in the state of war and turmoil are in a continual triage situation that prevents alleviation of even the most egregious medical conditions. Communities or nations unable or unwilling to fund medical care and to provide medical assistance, including sterile conditions for medical treatment, create conditions for illnesses to become epidemics. Health security means that governments take responsibility for guaranteeing medical treatment to anyone who needs medical attention. Ignoring or denying treatment to just one highly contagious individual can ultimately cost a government millions to control an epidemic, and industries many valuable workers. The importance of political will for adequate financing in public health cannot be overestimated, and needs to be brought to the attention of political leaders who often misunderstand its necessity.

Throughout the 1990s, the insecure state of global public health became a critical issue although it drew limited governmental attention. The occurrence of unusual outbreaks, such as hantavirus in the American Southwest, or cholera in Peru, pointed to the unexpected rise in infectious disease that had been occurring globally in the latter decades of the 20th century. Vector-borne diseases, such as the West Nile virus, emerged and continue to emerge in new climate zones, such as the temperate mid-Atlantic states of the US. Dengue haemorrhagic fever, which infects almost two million annually, re-emerged in the American region in the 1980s, and by 1997, the *Aedes aegypti* mosquito's geographic distribution was wider than before the eradication programme of the 1950s and 1960s began (Price-Smith, 2001b).

The rise in infectious disease in particular, and health security generally, is increasingly related to a degraded environment (Price-Smith, 2001a). According to the WHO:

> *Poor environmental quality is directly responsible for some 25 per cent of all preventable ill health, with diarrheal diseases and acute respiratory infections heading the list. Two-thirds of all preventable ill health due to environmental conditions occurs among children, particularly the increase in asthma. Air pollution is a major contributor to a number of diseases and to a lowering of the quality of life in general.*
>
> *World Health Report, 2003*

The 2005 Millennium Ecosystem Assessment (MEA) synthesis report warns that the erosion of ecosystems could lead to an increase in existing diseases such as malaria and cholera, as well as a rising risk of new diseases emerging. Worsening ecosystems will also affect the world's ability to meet the UN MDGs.

'Ecosystems are the planet's life-support system. They are fundamental to human health and indispensable to the well-being of all people everywhere in the world,' said Dr Kerstin Leitner, WHO Assistant Director-General for Sustainable Development and Healthy Environments, and member of the MEA Board. 'The work of the Millennium Ecosystem Assessment makes clear how ecosystems and human health are inter-twined – and further highlights how important it is that decisions related to economic development also protect the environment, in order to ultimately safeguard human health' (Millennium Ecosystem Assessment Project, 2005).

The MDGs include a commitment to addressing 'other major diseases', and currently, heart disease ranks at the top of the list. However, if an epidemic on the scale of HIV/AIDS is to be controlled or prevented, then national public health systems in rich and poor countries, in post-Soviet nations and the least-developed countries (LDCs), have to be reinforced with international commitments. A global health surveillance system has to become widespread and reliable, and a robust emergency response network has to be established and utilized.

A realistic assessment of national security needs in this post-11 September 2001 world requires leaders to understand health security, not just in relation to terrorism, but from the perspective of *preventing illness*. Greater communication among ministries of health, environment and finance, as well as increased reliance on medical research and related health and environmental sciences, is needed at this time for realistic public health policies to be created. Expanded transparency within governments and within corporations would facilitate accurate perceptions of real health risks. Together, these measures would go a long way to calm the fears that have been continuously fanned over the past four years. Fear is a useful technique to control a population, but it takes on its own life after a point and turns into paranoia. Paranoia blocks the abilities of leaders and ordinary citizens to differentiate reality from fantasy and to act in a reality spectrum.

Fear reaction and global health security

Since the attacks in the US on 9/11 shocked the country and the world, many Americans lost their sense of security and became frightened in a generalized way. The government's attempts to constantly focus on predicting the possibility of another terrorist attack tend to increase rather than allay fears. Americans generally feel less certain about the future, and this feeling is accompanied by a feeling of loss of control over one's life. Some of these feelings derive from the trauma of 9/11, but a substantial component of current fears also comes from the reality of other domestic issues, including a slow economy in which many people have lost good jobs; a potential upheaval in social safety nets, particularly Social Security; increased costs for higher education at a time when a college degree is a basic requirement for most decent jobs; and growing health care costs, which fewer people can afford.

Fear is not endemic to Americans alone. It is a common human feeling experienced at various points in life, and includes, in particular, the fear of change. If national and international policies are grounded in a perspective of fear, then real danger goes unnoticed or is kept secret for fear of the consequences once the danger is exposed. The Chernobyl nuclear disaster and its ongoing effects on human health exemplify the long-lasting consequences of fear-based decisions, in this case reached by the former leaders of the Soviet Union who knowingly withheld the facts about the explosion and 10-day fire at nuclear power plant No 4 on 26 April, 1986. By hiding information critical to the health not only of the local population of Pripyat, Ukraine, but also to the entire country, as well as to the people of Belarus, Russia, and much of Europe, it is estimated that 4.9 million individuals have been exposed to radiation. That terrible day 19 years ago has had long-term ramifications for human health that will continue to affect future generations.

Unfortunately, there are many examples of governments' intentionally withholding health-related information out of fear of the consequences of exposing themselves to public scrutiny. China's response to the 2003 severe acute respiratory syndrome (SARS) outbreak in Asia is an illlustration of a government's conflict between fear reaction and global health security. The Chinese authorities viewed the release of all negative news as damaging to its international image and a threat to social stability, and as a result, China's position of official secrecy has been blamed for the unnecessary spread of this super-pneumonia around the world (Carrington and Young, 2003). Detecting, treating and containing the severe acute respiratory syndrome (SARS) epidemic put extreme pressure on the Chinese government, as well as the other countries where people developed the disease. The Chinese government finally made an about-face and cooperated with the WHO and other agencies to identify all SARS cases and control this epidemic.

China has been the source of several worldwide flu epidemics over the last century. At the outset of the recent avian flu outbreak, again, the government's initial response was slow, denying the existence of a potentially highly infectious epidemic among fowl that could escalate to human infections. An immediate response would have saved precious time in controlling the disease and saving lives. In mid-March, 2005, officials of the WHO urged governments to prepare for a flu pandemic that could occur as early as 2006. In view of the fact that a strain of avian flu in Asia had killed at least 40 people in the region as of March 2005, the WHO fears that the virus could quickly mutate into a form that spreads easily among humans. Since the WHO warning is based on medical research, including epidemiological studies of the history of flu, the paranoid response of withholding information needs to be controlled.

Paranoia has three main elements: denial, projection and reaction-formation. The official responses to the Chernobyl explosion and to SARS demonstrate denial. Projection, accusing others of one's own actions, continues to characterize the official US reaction against Al-Qaeda. America is doing to perceived terrorists what it thinks will be done to it. Reaction-formation can be seen in the response to a perceived loss of control. Individuals are increasingly creating communities of like-minded people with shared perceptions of reality. The loss of security experienced by US citizens has propelled the nation to create alliances of 'willing' partners who think alike, react together, and ignore existing accords. Extreme fear, or paranoia, also increases suspicion of one's neighbours, for individuals and nations alike. In such a climate, no one can be trusted and the world becomes a dark, dangerous place, a repetition of the Cold War scenario of the last century.

On the other hand, Brazil's response to HIV/AIDS sets a forward-looking path toward achieving health security. Brazil acted early to stem a potential national epidemic with regional implications. In 1996, when the rate of HIV infection was only 1.2 per cent of the country's population, the government offered free retroviral drug therapy to anyone who needed it. Although the cost of this programme was high, the government estimates that it saved an estimated US$2.2 billion in hospitalizations alone. Within five years, the number of HIV/AIDS cases was cut in half. In 1988, the Brazilian government made health as a universal right 'guaranteed by a National Health System based on the principles of comprehensive service, universal access, and social control' (Passarelli and Terto, Jr, 2002). When confronted by an acute public health threat, the government acted quickly to fund its constitutional commitment. Given the extent of the HIV/AIDS pandemic across the globe, in particular in sub-Saharan Africa, Brazil's response is yet more impressive.

Perceiving realistic health threats is the overriding challenge for government and business leaders as well as for all citizens. Taken together, the challenges of making reality-based decisions for the security of global public health are daunting in a climate of fear. Integration of a realistic assessment of a given situation, based on scientific findings and perspective, can balance fear and increase transparency and communication. An additional component for realistically assessing a situation is the reduction of corruption and mendacious behaviour that is fostered in a climate of fear. An important step in this respect is UN Secretary-General Kofi Annan's recent call for 'developing countries to improve their governance, uphold the rule of law, and combat corruption...'. He also called on 'every developed country to support these strategies, by increasing the amount it spends on development and debt relief, and doing whatever it can to level the playing-field for world trade' (UN, 2005a).

Trends for the future

To secure human health, the appropriate model is a public health model, rather a medical model that emphasizes diagnosing and treating diseases. The public health model stresses disease prevention through appropriate measures, including environmental protection. The long-term value of prevention based on validated science, is that it results in the right answers and the best policies to convert what we know into effective action. This alone can save governments billions in health care costs and protect the labour force necessary for

Box 10.1 The tragedy of HIV/AIDS

The HIV/AIDS pandemic now kills more than 3 million people each year and poses an unprecedented threat to human development and security. The disease is wrecking millions of families and leaving tens of millions of orphans. More than just a public health crisis, AIDS undermines economic and social stability, ravaging health, education, agriculture and social welfare systems. While placing an enormous drag on economic growth, it also weakens governance and security structures, posing a further threat.

The epidemic demands an exceptional response. In the absence of a cure, only the mass mobilization of every section of society – unheard of to date in the history of public health – can begin to reverse AIDS. This requires comprehensive prevention, education, treatment and impact mitigation programmes, which, in turn, will not succeed without the personal commitment of heads of state and Government to support and lead genuinely multisectoral AIDS responses.

Since 2000, the world has begun to achieve some successes in the fight against AIDS. More governments have made it a strategic priority and set up integrated administrative structures to lead and coordinate the struggle. The Global Fund to Fight AIDS, Tuberculosis and Malaria now plays a leading role in the global effort, while also focusing attention on and fighting other killer pandemics. Altogether, as of December 2004, 700,000 people in the developing world were receiving antiretroviral treatment – a nearly 60 per cent increase in just five months. This reflects the priority that the international community has now placed on rapidly expanding treatment, and shows that a real difference can be made in a very short time.

However, much remains to be done if we are to have any realistic hope of reducing the incidence of HIV and providing proper antiretroviral treatment to all who need it within the coming decade. Many governments have yet to tackle the disease and its stigma publicly, or are not sufficiently committed to the kind of frank discussion and action on gender equality that is needed. In particular, resources for AIDS remain far short of what is needed to mount a full inclusive response. National governments, as well as multilateral and bilateral donors, must now take steps to meet these costs.

Source: UN, 2005a

development. Central to the field of public health is the focus on anticipating problems.

Global warming

Scientists have long predicted climate change will have its first and most severe impacts in polar regions. The Arctic is more sensitive to climate change than perhaps any other place on Earth. The region warms faster than the global average because dark groundwater, once exposed, traps more heat than reflective snow and ice. Changes in the Arctic provide an early indication of the environmental and societal significance of global warming. It is estimated that the melting of glaciers will raise global sea levels about four inches by the end of the century. Summer heat is melting permafrost, producing major slumping on the coast and along lake shores.

Worldwide implications of sea level rise include severe coastal erosion, higher waves, and storm surges at the shore. In some cases, communities and industrial facilities in coastal zones are already threatened or being forced to relocate, while others face increasing risks or costs. Change in the Arctic climate will also have implications for biodiversity around the world, as migratory species depend on breeding and feeding grounds in the Arctic.

Current scientific research supports the findings of climate change and should not be ignored. National leaders have been slow to accept the urgency of acting on climate change science to prevent or mitigate future disasters, but the general global trend has been to address climate issues. The Kyoto Protocol to control greenhouse gas emissions went into effect in February 2005 (UN, 1997). Global warming is being recognized as a factor in the rise of infectious disease, and growing costs from more frequent and intense weather events are acknowledged by governments and insurers alike. Slowly and reluctantly, governments along with industry are recognizing the inevitably of developing alternative energy sources for the future.

Precautionary Principle

The Precautionary Principle, developed in Germany in the 1980s, can be understood as a 'foresight principle'. The 1992 Rio Declaration encourages political action, 'where there are threats of serious or irreversible damage', and rejects the excuse of 'scientific uncertainty' as a reason 'to postpone cost effective measures to prevent environmental degradation' (UN, 1992). Since 1992, the Precautionary Principle has gained steady ground as a parameter for decisions ranging from food production, to pollution control, to trade regulations. However, with the trend toward broader application, the Precautionary Principle raises complicated issues. The key question is whether it protects public health or is simply an economic argument covered in green.

The global controversy over genetically modified (GM) foods, known colloquially as 'Frankenfoods', illustrates some of the dilemmas that occur when the Precautionary Principle is applied by the developed world toward poorer nations. Grain consumed in North or South America is likely to have been genetically modified. Unlike the Americas, the European Community bans GM foods on the basis of the Precautionary Principle, even though research data demonstrating adverse affects of GM food on human health have not been substantiated. During a drought in Zambia, two-thirds of the corn provided by the UN came from the US and, therefore, included GM corn. The Zambian government decided to leave the corn in warehouses. If the corn was used for seeds, it could lead to the spread of GM corn that would cause Zambia to lose its European market when the drought ended. The potential loss of long-term trade took priority over the potential risks of disease to a chronically malnourished population.

Persistent organic pollutants (POPs)

On May 17, 2004, the legally binding international treaty to control toxic chemicals – the Stockholm Convention on Persistent Organic Pollutants (POPs) – entered into force, providing an unprecedented legal framework to ban or severely restrict the production and use of some of the world's most toxic chemicals (UN, 2001). More than 150 governments have signed the POPs Treaty, which seeks global elimination of the group of POPs known as the 'dirty dozen': polychlorinated biphenyls (PCBs), dichlorodiphenyltrichloroethane (DDT), hexachlorobenzene, dioxin and furans, dieldrin, aldrin, endrin, chlordane, heptachlor, toxaphene, mirex. Because of DDT's controversial use in malaria control, its continued application and production are curtailed but not eliminated. In the countries that have ratified the Stockholm Convention, its provisions have become law.

POPs pose a significant risk to human health and the environment. Poisons without passports, they are particularly hazardous because of their common characteristics. They are toxic to humans and wildlife. They are persistent and remain intact for long periods of time, resisting breakdown. POPs are semivolatile and mobile. They are widely distributed through the environment, travelling great distances on wind and water currents. Through global distillation, they travel from temperate and tropical regions to the colder regions of the poles (IPEN, 2001).

Having a high fat solubility, POPs accumulate in the bodies of humans, marine mammals, and other wildlife. They are found at higher concentrations at the higher levels of the food chain. They are passed from mother to the fetus in the womb and to the child through breast milk. POPs can cause nervous system damage, diseases of the immune system, reproductive and developmental disorders, as well as cancers.

The Stockholm Convention is unique in that it incorporates the Precautionary Principle and requires public participation as key components. It is also a living document in that it establishes a science-based process for identifying and adding chemicals to the initial list of the dirty dozen. Top candidates to be added include lindane (already restricted in the EU) and brominated flame retardants such as polybrominated diphenyl ethers (PBDEs).

Non-governmental organizations

Non-governmental organizations (NGOs) played a key role in the POPs treaty negotiations and are now actively participating in its implementation. The increased number of effective non-governmental, not-for-profit organizations working with governments and other members of civil society assures broader concern for public health safety. This has been one the most important trends since the Rio Summit on Environment and Development in 1992. Working with governments on issues of climate change, environmental degradation, chemical safety, and application of the Precautionary Principle, competent and relevant non-governmental groups can offer their expertise for effective action.

Trends for health security

The outlook for ensuring health security is not grim as long as fear, as the overriding factor in political decision making, is controlled. Positive trends can be reversed within a climate of fear as funds needed for public health are applied elsewhere. Although it takes governments a long time to recognize health problems, even when they are acute, eventually all but the most corrupt do. The expanded involvement of competent and relevant NGOs, along with the profit sectors of civil society, can bring corruption to light, and can also expand communication of sound information to the general public on issues pertaining to public health. Non-governmental actors can play the critical role in curtailing governmental secrecy on matters of health ranging from infectious disease outbreaks to polluted fish hatcheries. As their involvement with governments has grown, non-governmental actors have greater responsibility to insure against corruption and secrecy and foster transparency on every level, including their own ranks.

The news is also an important sector within civil society. It can enhance public knowledge of health issues, including environmental impacts, by featuring many more balanced stories on these topics, or it can collaborate with governments by ignoring critical but controversial health topics. Politicians and media owners influence public perceptions of what is important, and how to understand current issues. Key to changing perceptions about health security is much greater acceptance of scientific data.

The Report of the UN Millennium Project's Task Force on Science, Technology and Innovation, released in January 2005, recommends increasing the capacities of national governments and international organizations to utilize advice from the scientific community (UN, 2005b). Greater reliance on science would assist developing nations to cope in a world increasingly marked by rapid technological change. However, rapid change brought about by new technologies can produce a backlash to those technologies and to change itself. In the current situation, information communication technologies have been both the tool for communicating vital scientific information and part of the reason for an anti-science, anti-intellectual reaction.

Utilizing science more fully in decisions regarding health occurs when leaders are not afraid of the objective findings of the scientists. When leaders fear the consequences of scientific information, they increase the health risks to their population, risks that can almost bankrupt a nation, as the world has witnessed with previous official denial of the HIV/AIDS epidemic. Acting too little and too late imperils the health of everyone.

Conclusion

The greatest impediment to global public health is not recognizing realistic public health threats. The obstacle, as we perceive it, is fear: fear of exposure, fear of consequences, and fear of loss of control. The prevalence of corruption and lack of transparency by governments, companies and some civil society actors, foster this fear and prevent the establishment of a global health security network beneficial to all humanity. We suggest that both government and non-governmental stakeholders in public health conquer their fears and learn to face the facts of reality for a better, secure and healthier future.

References

Carrington, D. and Young, E. (2003) 'Chinese secrecy blamed for super-pneumonia spread', New Scientist, 28 March, www.newscientist.com/article.ns?id+dn3562

IPEN (2001) *POPs Handbook for the Stockholm Convention on Persistent Organic Pollutants, Written and Produced by the Participating Organizations of the International POPS Elimination Network*, Version 4; http://ipen.ecn.cz/handbook/html/index.html

Millennium Ecosystem Assessment Project (2005) *Millennium Ecosystem Assessment*, Island Press, Washington D.C.

Passarelli, C. and Terto, V., Jr (2002) 'Good medicine: Brazil's multifront war on AIDS', *NACLA Report of the Americas*, vol 35, no 3, pp35–42

Price-Smith, A. T. (2001a) *Health of Nations: Infectious Disease, Environmental Change, and Their Effects on National Security and Development*, The MIT Press, Cambridge

Price-Smith, A. T. (2001b) *Plagues and Politics: Infectious Disease and International Policy*, Palgrave Macmillan, New York

UN (1992) *Rio Declaration Principle 15, Precautionary Principle*, UN, New York; www.un.org

UN Framework Convention on Climate Change (1997), *Kyoto Protocol*, UNFCCC, Bonn

UN (2000) *Millennium Declaration*, General Assembly, 55th session, document A/RES/55/2, 18 September, New York; www.un.org/millenniumgoals/

UN (2001), *Stockholm Convention on Persistent Organic Pollutants*, UN, New York

UN (2005a) *In Larger Freedom: Towards development, security and human rights for all*, Report of the Secretary-General, document A/59/2005, 21 March; UN, New York, www.un.org/largerfreedom

UN (2005b) *United Nations Millennium Project's Task Force on Science, Technology and Innovation*, UN, New York

WHO (2003) *World Health Organization Report*, WHO, Geneva

Additional reading

Charles, M. (2004) 'The Power of Acting Early,' *World Ecology Report*, vol XVI, nos. 3 and 4

Garrett, L. (1995) *Coming Plague: The Newly Emerging Diseases in a World Out of Balance*. Penguin, New York

Garrett, L. (2001) *Betrayal of Trust: The Collapse of Global Public Health*, Hyperion, New York

Goldstein, Dr. Bernard D. (2004) 'The Importance of Public Health Principles for Effective Environmental Protection', *World Ecology Report*, vol XVI, nos 3 and 4

Peters, C. J., and Olshaker, M. (1998) *Virus Hunter: Thirty Years of Battling Hot Viruses Around the World*, Anchor, New York

Preston, R. (1995) *The Hot Zone: A Terrifying True Story*, Anchor, New York

UN Commission on Human Security (2003), *Final Report*, 1 May 2003; UN, New York, www.humansecurity-chs.org/finalreport/index.html

11

Biodiversity and Security

Jeffrey A. McNeely

Introduction

In his report, 'In Larger Freedom', UN Secretary-General Kofi Annan observed that:

> *another serious concern is loss of biodiversity, which is occurring at an unprecedented rate within and across countries. Worrying in its own right, this trend also severely undermines health, livelihoods, food production and clean water, and increases the vulnerability of populations to natural disasters and climate change. To reverse these trends, all governments should take steps, individually and collectively, to implement the Convention on Biological Diversity and the Johannesburg commitment to achieve a significant reduction in the loss of biodiversity by 2010.*

> *UN, 2005*

The Millennium Ecosystem Assessment (MEA), launched at the end of March, just after the report of the UN Secretary-General, also highlighted the critical importance of biodiversity in supporting ecosystem services that enable human well-being (MEA, 2005). This chapter examines some of these relationships, demonstrating that biodiversity is relevant to most, if not all, of the other issues being addressed in this book.

The Millennium Project, a report to the UN Secretary-General, has provided a practical plan to achieve the eight Millennium Development Goals (MDGs) (Millennium Project, 2005). One point that is very apparent from this effort is that all the MDGs need to be implemented as an integrated whole if real progress is to be made. This chapter will stress the role of biodiversity in supporting the MDGs, and the costs when biodiversity is ignored.

We also need to consider at the outset that linking environment, health, poverty, migration, hunger and gender issues with security poses at least some risk that these issues will be approached in the traditional way that security institutions approach their problems. But instead of promoting adversarial language and thinking, addressing these problems requires a very different approach, based on cooperative thinking and acting. It is also critically important to recognize the links between these various issues, and one of the important links is through biodiversity and ecosystem services. While the traditional security institutions need to become more aware of broader social issues, the language of sustainable livelihoods, equity, and human rights likewise needs to be brought into the discussion, replacing conventional military language and thinking.

Biodiversity, ecosystem services and human well-being

Simply stated, biodiversity is the measure of the world's variety of genes, species, and ecosystems. 'Biodiversity' only really came into the public vocabulary in the late 1980s. But biodiversity has struck a very responsive chord among scientists, decision-makers, and even the informed public, and the concept has now entered the mainstream. The Convention on Biological Diversity (CBD), signed at the 1992 Rio Earth Summit, now has 188 state parties. The parties have met numerous times and have agreed detailed plans of work for addressing the major biodiversity issues facing our planet (CBD, 2004).

Biodiversity is a comprehensive way of approaching conservation, bringing information, knowledge, awareness, and ethics into a complex mixture of protected areas, agriculture, economics, intellectual property rights, land tenure, trade, forestry, and so forth (WRI et al, 1992). It has enabled us to break away from some of our old approaches, such as excluding people from their traditional lands in the name of 'conservation'. Both academic and civil society have hopped on the biodiversity bandwagon, holding dozens of meetings in all corners of the earth to further develop the concept and build global consensus for the actions required. Hundreds of field projects are now being implemented to address biodiversity problems, involving hundreds of millions of dollars per year from governments, conservation organizations, and the private sector.

Why did we need biodiversity as an approach? What was wrong with the conventional 'species and protected areas' approach? Attempting to conserve nature species-by-species may have begun with Noah and his ark, at least metaphorically. While it may have worked for Noah, however, it was not working very well for us, as indicated by the increasing rate of species loss (for example, Wilson and Peter, 1988; IUCN, 2004). We also now realize the futility of trying to conserve 10 per cent of the planet's land surface as protected areas when the other 90 per cent is being degraded and abused. This is rather like a public health system that stresses the emergency room, with no maternity ward, no out-patient clinic and no preventive public health approach. We certainly need the emergency room, and as the world becomes more like a big city, we will need well-equipped and well-staffed emergency rooms more than ever. But we will also need the rest of the hospital and the public health system if we are going to treat the ills of our sick society. Our emergency rooms – our protected areas and endangered species recovery plans – can provide only part of the answer. For total ecosystem health care, we need the biodiversity approach, leading to wide collaboration among government, biologists, civil society, and the private sector. Most importantly, the new approach also needs to provide real benefits to the people who live with wild biodiversity, and who help create the conditions that provide our planet with its rich biological diversity.

The CBD provides an international framework for cooperation in addressing its three objectives: conserving biological diversity; using biological resources sustainably; and ensuring the equitable distribution of benefits arising. The Convention defines biological diversity as 'the variability among living organisms from all sources including terrestrial, marine and other aquatic ecosystems and the ecological complexes of which they are part; this includes diversity within species, between species, and of ecosystems.' Biodiversity is thus the measure of life itself, and its value is infinite

Biodiversity in situations of insecurity

Many parts of our planet are affected by civil insecurity, often in areas that are of particular interest in terms of rich biodiversity. New Caledonia, Papua New Guinea, Indonesia, Myanmar, Sri Lanka, the Democratic Republic of Congo, and Peru are all recent examples. The implications of civil insecurity on biodiversity are particularly striking in Colombia, which offers both positive and negative elements.

In Colombia, areas of human encroachment and expansion into the biologically important remnant forests are mostly under guerrilla or paramilitary rule, essentially beyond the reach of governmental conservation or development efforts (Davalos, 2001). Explosives detonated along petroleum pipelines cause damage in local watersheds in Colombia, but a more significant problem is the clashes between left-wing guerrillas and right-wing paramilitary groups. Violent conflict can have three types of effects on forests:

- 'gunpoint conservation' includes active exclusion of most productive activities enforced by landmines or civilian curfew;
- the pressure for forest conversion from drug cultivation and cattle ranching in areas beyond the rule of law and/or contested by armed groups;
- the consequences of the collapse of the institutional framework for civilian law.

The National Liberation Army (ELN), a left-wing guerrilla group, enforces forest protection in some parts of the Serrania de San Lucas, purportedly for the role of forests in protecting the local hydrology. The forests also serve to shelter the guerrillas from air surveillance by government forces. They achieve this protection by placing landmines, or at least signs claiming that they have placed these landmines, where they can be seen by villagers. The Revolutionary Armed Forces of Colombia (FARC) exclude almost all agriculture from the southern half of the Macarena range, ostensibly to preserve the wealth and beauty of the forest for future generations, but the forests also house their national headquarters. The protection of such military groups can be very effective. During the 1997 El Niño droughts, farmers seeking to expand their landholdings burned the lowlands of the Munchique National Park, until the FARC threatened to kill the farmers setting fires; the flames quickly died out. Both FARC and ELN tout their environmental interests on their websites, appropriating the discourse of sovereignty over biodiversity on the grounds that their application of these policies also provides shelter from air-raids, protects water supplies, and conserves biodiversity (Davalos, 2001).

The guerrillas appear willing to conserve some of the charismatic wildlife of the region. Far more damaging are the paramilitary groups, essentially mercenaries for cattle ranching and narcotics trafficking interests; once they have cleared a region of guerrillas, they consolidate the landholdings and clear forests for cattle ranching or cocaine cultivation. Violence in the countryside has also reduced population pressure, with rural population increasing just 0.3 per cent per year between 1990 and 1995, despite the countrywide annual population increase of 1.7 per cent. On the other hand, the constant threat of war discourages long-term conservation or management of resources. Areas characterized by conflict have been emptied of villagers, but it also is essentially impossible to practice forest management, restoration, or conservation. Ironically, peace negotiations can lead to full-blown, large-scale unplanned exploitation in areas that are now off-limits because of security considerations.

More generally, environmental stress and competition for resources can be fundamental causes of armed conflict, or at least contribute to it (Klare, 2001; Renner, 2002). Therefore, issues of conserving biodiversity, using biological resources sustainably, and sharing the benefits of such use in a fair and equitable manner – the three objectives of the Convention on Biological Diversity – are critical elements in discussions of national security. Investments in activities such as sustainable forestry, water conservation, land reform, and protected areas management, it can be argued, are vital contributions to peace.

Demilitarized zones, or 'no man's lands' maintained by the military, are often beneficial for biodiversity, at least temporarily. An outstanding example is the demilitarized zone (DMZ) of the Korean Peninsula, a 4km wide forbidden zone stretching 240km across the peninsula; South Korea maintains an additional strip that averages 5.4km in width and totals 1529km^2, to which access is severely restricted. This cross-section of Korean biodiversity provides a sanctuary for a wide diversity of Korea's species, many now rare elsewhere. About 150 Red-Crowned Cranes (*Grus japonensis*) from Manchuria come annually to the DMZ's central basin around Cholwon. Further west, around the truce village of Panmunjom, up to 300 White-Naped Cranes (*Grus vipio*) pass through every winter. It has been found that the Korean demilitarized zone is an essential migratory habitat of these cranes and that they stop at some sites in the DMZ for up to 87 per cent of their total migration time (Higuchi et al, 1996). As Poole (1991) puts it, 'Here the presence of the cranes is especially haunting. These symbols of oriental peace and tranquillity stand sentinel between the gun-toting border guards.'

In the chaotic conditions that often surround violent conflict and its aftermath, conservation is not always given a sufficiently high priority, even though actions taken at this time may be essential to ensuring a productive subsequent environment. This requires appropriate short-term actions that are based on a long-term strategic vision. Methods to reinvigorate the local economy or pay off war debts need to ensure that the environmental costs are minimized; this requires working with all relevant parties, including the military, relief agencies, the private sector, and so forth.

The protected areas and other conservation programmes that have the best relations with local people are the ones that are most likely to be able to adapt to the radical changes that may be imposed in times of violent conflict. But times of violent conflict also mean changes in priorities, and local communities may depend on subsistence activities that would be unacceptable in times of peace. The fact that protected areas are often called 'reserves' is an indication that the resources they are protecting may be considered as a strategic reserve in times of emergency. Conservation staff need to be realistic in such situations, and give higher priority to livelihood security while maintaining a concern about biodiversity conservation. If conservation agencies are able to demonstrate a commitment to the welfare of local communities in times of violent conflict, this may also provide an improved basis for collaboration over the longer term.

It is also important to ensure that other institutions are well aware of how their activities relate to the biodiversity conservation objectives. Relief agencies need to be shown that the environment is also a humanitarian concern, and that problems of refugees can also be problems of an affected protected area.

Finally, a window of opportunity is often open immediately after conflict for updating resource management policies, helping to address problems that may have arisen during the conflict, or even led to it. This often is the moment to improve policy formulation, design new legislation, build capacity among the new staff, ensure that new policies are based on the most relevant information, and design a robust decision-making process (Shambaugh et al, 2001).

Ecosystem services: The benefits people obtain from ecosystems

Like all animals, people are utterly dependent upon ecosystems for their survival. While those living in cities may feel well insulated from nature, the food they eat, the water they drink, and the air they breathe all depend on the services provided by ecosystems. The Millennium Ecosystem Assessment (MEA, 2005) divides these benefits into four general categories of provisioning, regulating, cultural, and supporting (Figure 11.1).

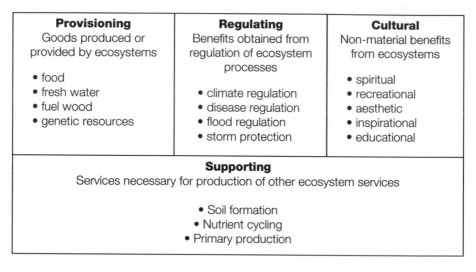

Provisioning	Regulating	Cultural
Goods produced or provided by ecosystems	Benefits obtained from regulation of ecosystem processes	Non-material benefits from ecosystems
• food • fresh water • fuel wood • genetic resources	• climate regulation • disease regulation • flood regulation • storm protection	• spiritual • recreational • aesthetic • inspirational • educational

Supporting
Services necessary for production of other ecosystem services
• Soil formation • Nutrient cycling • Primary production

Figure 11.1 *Ecosystem services: The benefits people obtain from ecosystems*

Ecosystem services have intricate links to human well-being, yet they all derive ultimately from biodiversity (Figure 11.2). Food, for example, depends on nutrient cycling and soil formation, as well as primary production that converts solar energy into plants that are either consumed directly or processed into other forms of food. Adequate food supply in turn leads to health, the basic material requirements for a good life, and ultimately human security. The fact that over 800 million people remain undernourished is a matter of considerable concern, and has led to the MDGs, and a major effort of the UN system to achieve these (Millennium Project, 2005).

As another example, natural ecosystems provide important regulating services such as those that protect coastlines against extreme natural events. It is now beyond dispute in the tragic aftermath of the tsunami that hit the Indian Ocean region on 26 December 2004 that communities that were protected by intact coral reefs, coastal sand dunes and mangrove forests were much less heavily damaged by the tsunami, while those that had lost their ecosystem protection were destroyed.

Biodiversity also helps humans adapt to changing conditions. While the detailed implications of climate change for any particular setting remain generally unpredictable, the reality of climate change is now broadly accepted

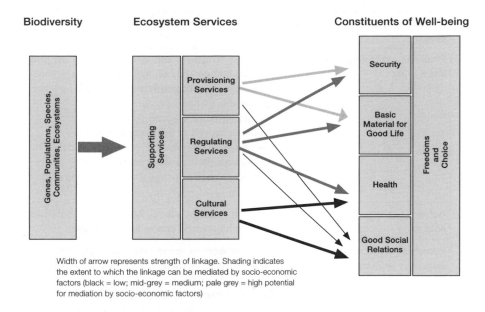

Width of arrow represents strength of linkage. Shading indicates
the extent to which the linkage can be mediated by socio-economic
factors (black = low; mid-grey = medium; pale grey = high potential
for mediation by socio-economic factors)

Figure 11.2 *Linkages among biodiversity, ecosystem services, and human well-being*

(IPCC, 2001), and richer biodiversity means more options for adapting to change.

Climate change will also have significant security implications, as changing temperatures and rainfall regimes affect the productivity of ecosystems, and thereby the carrying capacity of the land for humans. Historically, times of rapid climate change have also been times of insecurity and conflict. While everything possible must be done to reduce the emissions of greenhouse gases that are causing climate change, efforts must also be intensified to maintain productive ecosystems that can enable humans to adapt to the changing ecological conditions and retain or enhance the productivity of the land.

While insecurity can contribute to environmental problems, these same problems can also create incentives for cooperation and collective action. Positive signs of such cooperation include international conventions, such as the Convention on Biological Diversity and the Framework Convention on Climate Change (UNFCCC); environmental reforms, such as improving consumer awareness, the expansion of organic agriculture, and the reduction in the use of hazardous chemicals; and increasing knowledge, as evidenced by the various international assessments, such as the MEA, and the various reports of the Intergovernmental Panel on Climate Change (IPCC).

It is also relevant to recognize that the MDGs are all dependent on environmental sustainability (MDG 7), as indicated in Figure 11.3. Numerous additional examples of links to the environment could also be added.

	Millennium Development Goals	Examples of links to the environment
I	Eradicate extreme poverty and hunger	• Livelihood strategies and food security of the poor often depend directly on functioning ecosystems and the diversity of goods and ecological services they provide • Insecure rights of the poor to environmental resources, as well as inadequate access to environmental information, markets, and decision-making, limit their capacity to protect the environment and improve their livelihoods and well-being
2	Achieve universal primary education	• Time that children, especially girls, spend collecting water and fuelwood can reduce study time
3	Promote gender equality and empower women	• Time that women spend collecting water and fuelwood reduces their opportunity for income-generating activities • Women's often unequal rights and insecure access to land and other natural resources limit opportunities for accessing other productive assets
4	Reduce child mortality	• Water and sanitation-related diseases and acute respiratory infections, primarily caused by indoor air pollution, are leading causes of mortality in children under the age of five
5	Improve maternal health	• Indoor air pollution and carrying heavy loads during late stages of pregnancy put women's health at risk before childbirth
6	Combat major diseases	• Environmental risk factors account for up to one-fifth of the total burden of disease in developing countries • Preventive environmental health measures are as important, and at times more cost-effective, than health treatment
7	Develop a global partnership for development	• Since rich countries consume far more environmental resources and produce more waste than poor countries, many environmental problems (such as climate change, loss of species diversity, and management of global fisheries) must be solved through a global partnership of developed and developing countries

Sources: DFID et al (2002); UNDP (2002).

Figure 11.3 *Key links between environmental sustainability and other goals*

Conserving biodiversity to enhance security

Prevention is generally better than cure, so some countries are recognizing the possibility of using protected areas designed to conserve biodiversity along their borders as ways of promoting peace (for example, Hanks, 1998; Sandwith et al, 2001). In many countries, boundaries are found in mountainous areas that also tend to be biologically rich because of the great variety of habitats and ecosystem types found within relatively small areas, affected by differences in elevation, microclimate, and geological factors. While such ecologically diverse areas are often particularly important for conservation of biodiversity, they also are frequently sanctuaries for combatants in war, especially civil wars and guerrilla wars.

Given that national frontiers are especially sensitive areas where conflict is frequent and biological resources often are especially rich, the idea of establishing protected areas on both sides of the border – as so-called 'peace parks' – has attracted considerable attention, providing a symbol of the desire of the bordering countries to deal with many of their problems in a peaceful way (see, for example, Westing, 1993, 1998; Thorsell, 1990). Zbicz and Greene (1998) have found that transboundary protected areas cover well over 1.1 million km², representing nearly 10 per cent of the total area protected in the world (see Figure 11.4). In addition to indicating the importance of transfrontier protected areas, this also demonstrates how much of the world's land area devoted to biodiversity conservation is in remote frontier areas where risks of conflict historically are highest because of insecure borders.

Many protected areas are located on national borders, and some have adjacent protected areas on the other side of the border, forming complexes that could be the focus of collaboration. IUCN (1997) calls these (perhaps optimistically) 'Parks for Peace'. The following is an indication of how widespread and important such areas are.

Continent Involving 3 countries	Designated PA	Transfrontier PA Complexes	Complexes
North America	48	10	0
Africa	150	36	12
Asia	108	30	5
Latin America	121	29	6
Europe	239	64	8
TOTALS:	**666**	**169**	**31**

Source: Based on Sandwith et al (2001).

Figure 11.4 *Transfrontier protected areas*

Peace parks are far more than a fond hope. Peru and Ecuador fought three territorial wars in the 20th century, but Peru and Ecuador resolved their violent border dispute in 1998 with an innovative plan that included creation of the Cordillera del Condor, including two national peace parks near the most contested stretch of their frontier. Four mediators, the US, Argentina, Brazil, and Chile, helped resolve the hottest regional dispute in South America through binding arbitration. The agreement also granted Ecuador free trade and navigational access to the economically important shipping routes of Peru's Amazon territory. While the agreement fell far short of Ecuador's desire for sovereignty over the disputed territory, leading to demonstrations against the government, many of Ecuador's economic goals were achieved. The area is also the territory of several Jivaro-speaking tribes, who frequently are at war with each other, and against invaders (Descola, 1996; Brown and Fernandez, 1991). The new peace with protected areas will need to involve the indigenous peoples as well (Faiola, 1998), but biodiversity is likely to be a significant beneficiary.

Although peace parks have probably had relatively little independent effect on international relations, transfrontier cooperation on biodiversity issues has the potential to develop into an important factor in at least regional politics by helping to internalize norms, establish regional identities and interests, operationalize routine international communication, and reduce the likelihood of the use of force (Brock, 1991). Peace parks also have significant benefits for biodiversity, through better management of larger protected areas. They seem to be growing in popularity, and a treaty among South Africa, Zimbabwe, and Mozambique was signed in December 2002 to establish the Great Limpopo Transfrontier Park, covering 3.5 million hectares; this was South Africa's fourth transboundary protected area, clearly demonstrating that it considers conservation as an important part of its border defence policy.

Conclusions

National and international security can no longer be conceived in narrow military terms. Ethnic conflict, environmental degradation, and famine leading to civil unrest or massive migrations of refugees, constitute threats to both social stability and the preservation of a productive material base – the planet's biodiversity. Thus governments should assume that reversing deforestation or augmenting food production capabilities in deficit areas can directly and substantially contribute to the security of society. Allocating international resources to environmental monitoring and impact assessment, protection of economically important species, quick response to disasters and accidents, and the minimization and management of waste are all highly appropriate activities that will prevent strife and therefore reduce the likelihood of conflicts leading to war. As Thacher (1984) put it, 'Trees now or tanks later'.

Trying to tease out causality in the relationship between security, conflict, resources, and biodiversity issues is highly complex, because individuals make multiple, mutually constraining decisions that are shaped by interacting environmental and social conditions, all of which themselves have multiple interrelationships. People often learn through conflict, as fundamental interests are challenged. As Lee (1993) points out:

> *Conflict is necessary to detect error and to force corrections. But unbounded conflict destroys the long-term cooperation that is essential to sustainability. Finding a workable degree of bounded conflict is possible only in societies open enough to have political competition.*

In other words, the solution to destructive conflict is constructive conflict that leads to improved conservation of the natural resources upon which people depend.

In seeking to find ways of addressing effectively the relationship between security and biodiversity, it is useful to recall that the list of things that need to be done, projects that need to be undertaken, and people who need to be helped, is virtually endless. A perspective from the environmental side can help to determine priorities by identifying where investments are likely to be most effective. For example, when water is seen as a potential source of conflict, then well-targeted projects aimed at water resources are likely to be a wise investment.

Many biodiversity-related problems are not easily confined within a single country. Large-scale population movements, natural disasters, ecosystem breakdown, climate change, and rising competition over resources are all pervasive issues. Yet many of them can be addressed at least partially through improved management of biological resources.

As contributions of biodiversity to promoting security, the following major actions can be recommended:

- include environmental considerations in security thinking;
- allocate resources to environmental monitoring that will enable more effective identification of environmental problems before they become so serious as to lead to conflict, or at least make solutions extremely expensive;
- protect economically important species of plants and animals, particularly those upon which the rural poor depend;
- respond quickly to disasters and major accidents, mobilizing resources from many sectors to promote such responses;
- conserve energy and seek alternative sources of energy, thereby reducing dependence upon energy sources that cause climate change and may involve or stimulate conflict;
- minimize and manage waste, making societies more sustainable through greater efficiency of consumption
- conserve critical ecosystems, especially those that are irreplaceable or that protect critical infrastructure.

While biodiversity loss, resource scarcity, and environmental damage can all lead to insecurity and conflict, these problems can also mobilize greater

cooperation and actually contribute to improved understanding and cooperation between states. As stated in the preamble to the CBD, 'ultimately the
conservation and sustainable use of biological diversity will strengthen friendly
relations among states and contribute to peace for humankind.'

References

Brock, L. (1991) 'Peace through parks: the environment on the peace research agenda.'
Journal of Peace Research, 28, vol 4, pp407–423.
Brown, M. F. and Fernandez, E. (1991) *War of Shadows: The Struggle for Utopia in the
Peruvian Amazon*, University of California Press, Berkeley
CBD (2004) *Handbook of the Convention on Biological Diversity*, 3rd edition, Secretariat
of the Convention on Biological Diversity, Montreal
Davalos, L. M. (2001) 'The San Lucas Mountain Range in Colombia: How much
conservation is owed to the violence?' *Biodiversity and Conservation*, vol 10, pp69–
78
Descola, P. (1996) *The Spears of Twilight: Life in the Amazon*, The New Press, New
York
Faiola, A. (1998) 'Peru, Ecuador sign pact ending border dispute,' *The Washington Post*,
27 October
Hanks, J. (1998) 'Protected areas during and after conflict: the objectives and activities
of the Peace Parks Foundation,' *PARKS*, 7, vol 3, pp11–24
Higuchi, H., Ozaki, K., Fujita, G., Minton, J., Ueta, M., Soma, M. and Mita, N. (1996)
'Satellite tracking of White-naped Crane migration and the importance of the
Korean demilitarized zone', *Conservation Biology*, vol 10, no 3, pp806–812
IPCC (2001) *Intergovernmental Panel on Climate Change Third Assessment Report: Climate
Change 2001*, Watson, R.T. and the Core Writing Team (eds), IPCC, Geneva,
IUCN (2004) *2004 Red List of Threatened Species*, IUCN, Gland, Switzerland, www.
redlist.org
Klare, M. T. (2001) *Resource Wars: The New Landscape of Global Conflict*, Metropolitan
Books, New York
Lee, Kai N. (1993) *Compass and Gyroscope: Integrating Science and Politics for the
Environment*, Island Press, Washington, DC
Millennium Ecosystem Assessment (2005) *Synthesis Report*, Kuala Lumpur, www.
maweb.org
Millennium Project (2005) *Investing in Development: A Practical Plan to Achieve the
Millennium Development Goals*, United Nations, New York
Poole, C. (1991) 'The gift of no man's land', *BBC Wildlife*, September, pp636–639
Renner, M. (2002) *The Anatomy of Resource Wars*, World Watch Institute, Washington,
DC
Shambaugh, J., Oglethorpe, J., and Ham, R. (2001) *The Trampled Grass: Mitigating
the Impacts of Armed Conflict on the Environment*, Biodiversity Support Programme,
Washington, DC
Sandwith, T., Shine, C., Hamilton, L. and Sheppard, D. (2001) *Transboundary Protected
Areas for Peace and Cooperation*, IUCN, Gland, Switzerland
Thacher, P. (1984) 'Peril and Opportunity: What is takes to make our choice', in
McNeely, J. A. and Miller, K. R. (eds) *National Parks, Conservation, and Development:
The Role of Protected Areas in Sustaining Society*, Smithsonian Institution Press,
Washington, DC, pp12–14

Thorsell, J. (ed) (1990) *Parks on the Borderline: Experience in Transfrontier Conservation*, IUCN, Gland, Switzerland

UN (2005) *In Larger Freedom: Towards development, security and human rights for all*, Report of the Secretary-General, document A/59/2005, 21 March, United Nations, New York

Westing, A. H. (1993) 'Transfrontier reserve for peace and nature on the Korean Peninsula', in IUCN (ed) *Parks for Peace Conference Proceedings*, IUCN, Gland, Switzerland, pp235–242

Westing, A. H. (1998) 'Establishment and management of transfrontier reserves for conflict prevention and confidence building,' *Environmental Conservation*, vol 25, no 2, pp91–94

Wilson, E. O. and Peter, F. M. (eds) (1988) *Biodiversity*, National Academy Press, Washington, DC

WRI, IUCN, and UNEP (1992) *Global Biodiversity Strategy*, World Resources Institute, Washington, DC

Zbicz, D. C. and Greene, M. (1998) 'Status of the world's transfrontier protected areas', *PARKS*, vol 7, no 3, pp5–10

12

Food Security

Henrique B. Cavalcanti

The problem of hunger and poverty remains one of the most pressing and formidable challenges of our time. Apart from causing visible pain and suffering, hunger and poverty also cast a shadow over the future of poor members of society. Extreme hunger is a social shackle which defies every effort of an individual or a society to improve themselves economically and socially.

Jacques Diouf, FAO Director-General (2003)

Introduction

Food security concerns have motivated significant international activity since the early 20th century, and in 1945 inspired the creation of the Food and Agriculture Organization (FAO) of the United Nations (UN). Since its inception, the FAO has spearheaded international efforts to defeat hunger by providing a forum for nations to meet to negotiate agreements and debate policy, by acting as a source of knowledge and information, and by sharing policy expertise with developing countries in order to help them modernize and improve agriculture (FAO, 2005a).

At the time of the FAO's establishment, an estimated 72 per cent of the world population of about 2.5 billion did not have access to a diet of 2700 calories minimum per day, and 83 per cent to a minimum of 30g a day of animal protein. Population at world level subsequently rose to over 6 billion at the start of the new millennium, by which time agricultural production, distribution and trade had improved to the extent that hunger and malnutrition now affect about 1 billion – still a very large figure, representing 20 per cent of the people around the globe.

Acknowledging the enormity of the food security challenge, world leaders have repeatedly committed themselves to the goal of halving the proportion of hungry and undernourished people by 2015. This ambitious proposal first gained traction in the Rome Declaration of the 1996 World Food Summit, reflecting the common outrage that more than 800 million people throughout the world, and particularly in developing countries, do not have enough food to meet their basic nutritional needs:

> *This situation is unacceptable. Food supplies have increased substantially, but constraints on access to food and continuing inadequacy of household and national incomes to purchase food, instability of supply and demand, as well as natural and man-made disasters, prevent basic food needs from being fulfilled. The problems of hunger and food insecurity have global dimensions and are likely to persist, and even increase dramatically in some regions, unless urgent, determined and concerted action is taken, given the anticipated increase in the world's population and the stress on natural resources.*
>
> *FAO (1996)*

This objective later became goal number one, target two, of the Millennium Development Goals (MDGs), launched by the UN at the turn of the century (UN, 2000), and adopted at the 2002 Johannesburg World Summit on Sustainable Development (WSSD) as a relevant item in its Plan of Implementation (UN, 2002).

It is no surprise that eradicating hunger is afforded such importance in the MDGs, since assisting those who suffer from hunger is also an instrument towards the meeting of other MDGs, namely improving maternal health (Goal 5), reducing child mortality (Goal 4) and achieving universal primary education (Goal 2). Indeed, conditions of hunger and malnutrition run counter to the concept of sustainable development with regard to the rights of both the present and future generations. In that respect, special priority must be given to vulnerable individuals and groups like mothers and children, who are subject to negative effects that are often cumulative and irreversible in terms of equity, health and well-being, life expectancy, physical and intellectual development, competitiveness and productivity.

Despite determined efforts to solidify the achievement of the MDGs as *the* overriding international priority – most recently with the release of the UN Millennium Project Report, which outlines what it describes as a practical plan for their achievement – results for the hunger goal have been unevenly obtained by countries in most continents. Indeed, over 70 per cent of the 122 developing and in-transition countries where data are available are either lagging, far behind or not on track to meet the goal. According to the Plan of Action adopted at the 1996 World Food Summit sponsored by FAO in Rome, food security only exists 'when all people, at all times, have physical and economic access to sufficient, safe and nutritious food to meet their dietary needs and food preferences for an active and healthy life' (FAO, 1996). To achieve these requirements, it is imperative we understand the complex and multi-disciplinary nature of food (in)security.

Availability, access and stability: together these three pillars cover all aspects of food security, from production, transport, storage and distribution, to final consumption. Food security involves practices and measures related to the assurance of a regular supply and adequate stocks of foodstuffs of guaranteed quality and nutritional value. This requires effective national and international trade and credit policies, and necessitates monitoring, risk assessment, rehabilitation from natural disasters, protection from the effects of human conflicts, and reform of structural or institutional deficiencies.

Food insecurity, by contrast, is a component of the general state of human insecurity, fuelled by inequality and poverty, often expressed in terms of income levels. It denies minimal conditions for the exercise of citizenship and is detrimental to the concept of human dignity. Providing food security thus demands preventive planning and action on the part of government at all levels – with the direct participation of society and the support of international partners and the private sector – aiming at those who are under conditions of temporary or permanent risk. Broadly defined, food security can only be achieved if every person, family, community and nation is considered in the process and at the same time play a responsible role, as sustainable consumers, in ensuring its efficiency and effectiveness.

Shocks in food security

In addition to the dimensions of food security outlined above, the Committee on Food Security's (CFS) CFS's 2005 assessment of the world food security situation states that, 'while chronic hunger is a consequence of structural deficiencies, transitory hunger is a result mainly of shocks to food security' (FAO, 2005b). Any viable strategy to eradicate hunger and ensure food security must take account of and find solutions to a range of shocks:

- *Natural disasters*: The escalation of natural disasters such as droughts, floods and earthquakes can destroy assets and jobs, undermine investments in agriculture and push otherwise food-secure families into acute hunger (FAO, 2004a)
- *HIV/AIDS*: As made clear by the UN's Hunger Task Force, there are important two-way interactions between malnutrition and HIV/AIDS: 'Undernourished people infected with HIV/AIDS develop the full symptoms of the disease more quickly than people who are fed well. People suffering from the disease need good nutrition to fight it off. Yet one of the earliest effects of AIDS is reduced consumption of food in affected households.' The spread of HIV/AIDS limits the capacity of people to work, erodes the capital base, undermines the productive capacity of a country, and has a devastating impact upon smallholder agriculture (UN Millennium Project, 2005, and FAO, 2004a)
- *Conflict*: Violent conflict poses particular challenges for long-term food security. According to the FAO, 'conflict is one of the most common causes of food insecurity. The number and scale of conflict-related, food security emergencies is increasing, and the role of human-induced conflict

in escalating a natural hazard, such as a drought, to a food security emergency has grown in importance over the last decade' (FAO, 2005b). Over the past two decades, civil conflict has created food emergencies in Angola, Burundi, Republic of Congo, the Democratic Republic of Congo, Côte d'Ivoire, Guinea Bissau, Liberia, Sierra Leone, Sudan and Uganda (UN Millennium Project, 2005). The civil war in Sierra Leone, in particular, demonstrates how conflict can impact upon access to food, as food distribution was used either as a means of encouraging people to remain in or return to their towns (by the revolutionary forces) or as a political tool to demonstrate control (by the government) (UN Millennium project, 2005b).

Monitoring the dimensions of food security

Cereal production, including that of wheat, coarse grains and rice, is a reliable indicator of dietary energy for most developing countries. The 2004 CFS assessment report indicates a substantial increase in global cereal production from the preceding year and would thus attenuate the impact of the continuous reduction in global cereal stocks observed in the past five years (FAO, 2004a). However, it is important to stress that no one indicator is sufficient to describe all aspects of hunger and food security. Rather, taken together, various indicators can help provide a picture of the different dimensions of food security, both at the global level and within countries.

For instance, taking a different, albeit complementary, approach is the Oxford Commission on Sustainable Consumption. Its 2004 report recognizes changes in food consumption patterns – being distorted by farm subsidies – as one of the growing pressures upon the sustainability of the planet in view of the ever increasing human demand. Even so, changing the way we consume, according to the commission chairman, the Rt Hon John Gummer MP, is easier said than done because the way we consume goes to the heart of our lives and our enjoyment of them:

> *As a result, efforts to change the ways we consume may simply fail or have very painful political consequences, if they are not shaped and managed carefully. For this reason, policies on sustainable consumption have been a neglected subject since the Rio Summit a dozen years ago. The Commission's report grapples with the issues and sets out a basis on which governments and other institutions can deal with them, looking particularly at the transport, housing and food sectors to identify ways in which consumption can be made more sustainable.*

> *Oxford Commission on Sustainable Consumption, 2004*

Another example is measurement of food deprivation, for which the FAO has established three key parameters for each country: the average amount of food available per person, the level of inequality in access to that food and the minimum number of calories required for an average person. Data are compiled from 'food balance sheets', taking into account a mix of age, gender and body sizes. People whose daily food consumption falls below minimum daily requirement are considered undernourished. Evaluation is presently being complemented by information on income, food consumption and anthropometrics (FAO, 2004b).

Overview of current food security situation

Food security assessments are based on a combination of information acquired from such indicators. The UN Secretary-General's 2004 Report to the General Assembly indicates that the food security situation has improved or stabilized in Northern Africa, Latin America and the Caribbean, in Eastern, Western and South-East Asia, in Commonwealth of Independent States (CIS) countries in Asia and in Europe, and in other transition European countries, where malnutrition affects 15 per cent or less of total population. However, certain countries in some of those regions were not able to meet the required individual performance in the period 1990–2001. On the other hand, in sub-Saharan Africa, in Southern Asia, in Oceania and in CIS countries in Asia, where the undernourished represent 20 per cent or more of total population, progress has been either minimal or negative for the same timeframe (UN, 2004a).

Recent estimates indicate that about 1 billion people worldwide are undernourished, with over 800 million in developing countries, the figure having fallen by 19 million in the 1990s. Regionally, however, only Latin America and the Caribbean regions have seen a decline in the number of hungry people since the mid-1990s.

The 2005 assessment report of the world food security situation, published by the CFS of the FAO, states that the number of countries facing serious food shortages throughout the world – so-called 'hunger hotspots' – stood at 36 as of March 2005, with 23 in Africa, seven in Asia/Near East, five in Latin America, and one in Europe. Particular concern is reserved for Eritrea, Sudan, Kenya, Côte d'Ivoire, Guyana, Haiti, Afghanistan, Iraq and Palestine (FAO, 2005b).

Challenges and opportunities in 2005 and beyond

Perhaps the main food security challenge for 2005 and beyond is the implementation of a strategic plan such as the UN Millennium Project, directed by Prof. Jeffrey Sachs, with the setting up of an appropriate institutional arrangement capable of mobilizing ongoing initiatives, instruments and executing bodies, and motivating all actors on the national and international scene to collaborate effectively towards the common goal of hunger reduction (UN Millennium Project, 2005). The Project Task Force on Hunger, coordinated by Dr Pedro Sanchez and Professor M. S. Swaminathan, describes five principles and consequently makes seven recommendations 'determined partly by past successes and failures and partly by recent international agreements and initiatives to reduce hunger', that should guide the formulation and implementation of national poverty reduction strategies, to be drafted with a critical focus on policy and investment needs (UN Millennium Project, 2005b).

The five principles include forging a global partnership, promoting good governance, mainstreaming gender equality, adopting a people-centred approach, and investing in science and technology. By contrast, the resulting recommendations aim at measures to be taken at the global, national and local levels that relate to moving on from commitments to political action, reforming policies and enabling environments, increasing agricultural productivity, improving nutrition for the hungry, reducing the vulnerability of those subject to shocks, raising incomes and ensuring market access to the poor, and restoring and conserving natural resources.

Building on the recommendations of the Millennium Project report, the UN Secretary-General's report, 'In Larger Freedom', goes some way in setting the agenda for ensuring food security by calling for National Strategies that target 'Smallholder farmers and others living in impoverished rural areas'. Specifically, Kofi Annan recognizes that such people 'require soil nutrients, better plant varieties, improved water management and training in modern and environmentally sustainable farming practices, along with access to transport, water, sanitation and modern energy services' and recommends that 'in sub-Saharan Africa, these elements must be brought together to launch a twenty-first century African green revolution commencing in 2005' (UN, 2005a)

Smallholders farmers are an important aspect of Brazil's 'Fome Zero' (Zero Hunger) Program, launched in 2002. This plan integrates federal, state and municipal levels of government, the private sector and social organizations in developing and implementing 'structural, specific and local' actions to assist an estimated 30 per cent of the population that require nutritional support in about 1200 out of a total of almost 6000 municipalities, especially in the northeastern region. Structural measures include agrarian reform, family allowances for food and schooling, all-inclusive social security, and expanded water supply services.

More recently, in 2004, the programme and its many policies and projects were formally integrated into the Ministry of Social Development structure, with the purpose of improving coordination of all measures at the federal level on poverty eradication, social inclusion and inequalities, and hunger reduction. A National Council on Food and Nutritional Security – and its companion Councils in all the federative states, where two-thirds of its members are non-governmental representatives – advise the president of Brazil or state governors, respectively, on food security policies, while the Zero Hunger Committees, organized in similar fashion, are responsible for overseeing the programme's implementation.

At the local level, municipalities are urged to create their own councils, or alternatively to establish inter-municipal associations to develop projects on smallholder farming, small loan cooperatives and digital inclusion. Over 500 such initiatives are in place since 2003, attending to about 10 million people, also involving setting up food banks, low-price restaurants, producer markets, and the so-called urban agriculture. Local progress is monitored by volunteer Operational Councils and supported by volunteer action groups that collect and distribute donations and food supplies (Rocha, 1996, and FAO, 2002).

The international scene and its many fora provide a variety of possible courses of action, sufficient both in number and focus, and adaptable to specific cases and circumstances that in all cases require careful planning, coordination and regular appraisal. Each of the following events and their conclusions and initiatives will contribute in some way to relevant discussions and decisions in 2005.

Within the UN system, the issue of hunger is approached from different perspectives, all of them pertinent to the subject. Two major collective bodies – reporting to the Economic and Social Council (ECOSOC) – have the task of following up on the international commitments discussed in this chapter. These are the Commission for Social Development (CSD), which will review progress on the 1995 Copenhagen Declaration and Plan of Action adopted at World Summit on Social Development (WSSD) and prepare for the Decade on Poverty in 2006, and the Commission on Sustainable Development (CSD), which keeps track of the advances on Agenda 21 and engages in a two-year cycle of thematic appraisal of the 2002 Johannesburg Plan of Implementation, taking on poverty and hunger as a cross-sectoral issue on all other topics (UN, 2005b).

As executing agencies, there are several UN and Bretton Woods institutions (BWI) and mechanisms that deal directly or indirectly with hunger, its causes and effects, such as food and agriculture, health, labour, children, education, science and culture, regional development, environment, and other issues, through their governing bodies, specialized committees and units, and country representatives. In a recent decision by the UN Secretary-General, the United Nations Development Programme (UNDP), which regularly publishes the Human Development Report (HDR), was designated to coordinate and monitor the various efforts to implement the Millennium Development Goals.

Other relevant international commitments on the agenda to be discussed in 2005 are finance, trade, the role of women, and the question of collective security, all of which bear strong links with the poverty and hunger targets:

- *Finance*: An International Conference on Finance for Development held in Monterrey, Mexico, in 2002 developed the so-called Monterrey Consensus. The consensus aims at promoting growth and sustainable development by mobilizing domestic and international financial resources, as well as utilizing the instruments of foreign trade, technical and financial cooperation, foreign debt management, coherent and consistent financial, trade and monetary systems in support of development, and the eradication of poverty and hunger. Specific reference is made to the need for developed countries to provide annually the equivalent of 0.7 per cent of their gross national product (GNP) to overseas development cooperation and to assist Heavily Indebted Poor Countries (HIPC) (Monterey Consensus,

2002). This is part of Key Recommendation no. 7 of the UN Millennium Development Project

- *Trade*: The negative impact of the present global trading system on the efforts to alleviate poverty in developing countries, through the imposition of trade barriers, was recognized in the international conferences held in Monterrey and Johannesburg. To that effect, the 2001 World Trade Organization (WTO) Doha Declaration recommended that signatories place needs and interests of developing countries at the core of negotiations over a new trade round. A meeting to review Doha is scheduled for December 2005, having in mind the possibility of concluding the Doha development round by 2006 and of discussing those negative impacts (WTO, 2004)
- *Role of women*: The significant role of women in the process of combating poverty and hunger was recognized, among many other topics, at the Fourth World Conference on Women, held in Beijing in 1995 (UN, 1995). In 2005 there was a 10-year review of Beijing which enabled effective input to the UN Secretary-General's deliberations in producing his report, 'In Larger Freedom'. Noteworthy are the references to women's contribution to family welfare, and the social recognition of maternity in the context of society; the Secretary-General recognizes that 'empowered women can be some of the most effective drivers of development' (UN, 2005a)
- *Collective security*: The quest for peace and world security was the object of a report prepared by the High-Level Panel on Threats, Challenges and Change, submitted to the UN Secretary-General in December 2004. The task set the panel by Kofi Annan was to consider the security threats facing the world in the 21st century and make recommendations on collective responses to them. It addresses directly the so-called 'soft' threats of poverty, infectious disease and environmental degradation, and makes specific reference to food security:

> Current trends indicate persistent and possibly worsening food insecurity in many countries, especially sub-Saharan Africa. Population growth in the developing world and increased per capita consumption in the industrialized world have led to greater demand for scarce resources… Feeding such a rapidly growing population will only be possible if agricultural yields can be increased significantly and sustainibly.
>
> UN, 2004b

These themes and others drawn out in the panel's report will play a significant role in the Millennium Review Summit in September 2005, and will no doubt provide guidance on how the international community should work together in the roadmap expected to come out of that summit.

Trends in food security

There are advantages in setting global targets such as the MDGs, not least because they demonstrate in a simple manner how overall access to food has advanced in terms of individuals, even though unequal results have been obtained at the regional and national levels in accordance to specific difficulties encountered. Moreover, a global perspective helps to retain a sense of purpose for the world community and the responsibility of the rich and the not so rich in providing for the less privileged.

At the same time, a global appraisal of the worldwide hunger situation, as referred to an objective set for 2015, would permit an overall evaluation of the capacity to prevent and face food emergencies, and to overcome structural obstacles, through institutional strengthening and capacity building at the national level, and also of international technical and financial cooperation where needed. A detailed complement to the global approach exercise would be provided by the analysis of specific regional and national scenarios. In that respect, three main trends could be examined, as follows.

Food supply, trade and the environment

Continuous improvement in agricultural practices and a potential to increase food production through scientific advances and the expansion of land use for cultivation in certain continents are positive prospects for the world as a whole. Trade restrictions would be gradually lifted as result of the Doha process, and they would particularly favour developing countries that rely on food commodities for export. Compliance with national regulations and international commitments regarding the environment tends to be further enhanced and encouraged, as a requirement for financial assistance and a fundamental tool for sustainable development. A movement to more regional food security would also reduce ecological footprints caused by long-distance transport of goods, and in that sense, developed countries should look at their consumption patterns, not only in general, but particularly with regard to food imports from developing countries that may have a direct impact on the availability of water for local use and local agriculture.

Structural features: Economic, social and political

Not all sovereign countries are able to solve the problem of hunger on their own. That would partly depend, in physical terms, on their capacity to produce and achieve a favorable trade balance in foodstuffs. Most developing countries have not reached that stage of relative autonomy, and some do not have the means to pursue MDG 2. These are the least developed among the low-income countries, and will require a special approach that encompasses measures on tariff-free trade, debt relief, and official development assistance, as proposed in MDG 8.

Other vulnerable nations have not shown the capacity to maintain a reasonable rate of growth, and will rely on specific economic and social development assistance programmes to face their internal hunger situation. Favoured trade conditions as contemplated in the Doha process may be a good starting point in helping activate the economy in those countries.

Large territorial developing countries with a sizeable population may also require specific strategies adaptable to their circumstances. Five of those, namely China, India, Brazil, Indonesia and Nigeria, totaling about 40 per cent of the world population and a reasonable share of the world poor in absolute numbers, may comply with the proportional goal of MDG 2 and yet require a longer time schedule to resolve questions of domestic regional imbalances and to curb the tendency for rising inequality.

Conservative monetary policies currently adopted to control inflationary pressures have been opposed by public opinion especially in slow-growth indebted nations, both at home and abroad. This may eventually become instrumental in the introduction of more flexible practices that would favour faster growth and increase employment opportunities

The frequent participation of non-governmental organizations (NGOs) in the decision-making process, and the upsurge of partnerships between government and the private sector on matters related to poverty and hunger, is likely to increase in many countries, as good governance practices settle in.

Finally, resolution or mediation on cases of civil strife and other conflicts, whether internal or among nations, will remain a major challenge due to matters of national sovereignty, non-interference policies and the permanence of spheres of influence.

Coordinated action at all levels

There are several constraints to be managed in order to meet the target, such as the limited 10-year timespan, relatively scarce human and financial resources, protracted medium-term progress anticipated for some of the key initiatives, inherent complexity of case-by-case strategies, and so on. Coordinated and decentralized action would inevitably be exercised, both horizontally and vertically within the national framework, among providers of international bilateral and multilateral assistance, and between both groups. This is especially important with respect to early warning and rapid response to natural disasters and in dealing with serious health issues, such as HIV/ AIDS, both relevant causes of emergency situations. UNAIDS has shown how stakeholders can react well to coordination when included in the decision-making process.

Efficient coordination will also enhance project performance on matters of budgeting and disbursement of financial resources. In order to start the process of assessing the needs of low-income countries, the UN Millennium Project has proposed a list of fast-track candidates, 82 per cent of them in Africa and Asia-Pacific, based on several criteria that include governance qualities, economic policies, productive use of aid, and willingness to submit their policies and institutions to regular peer reviews in accordance to agreed values, standards and codes.

Implications of these trends

The trends described above, taken simultaneously at the global scale, are generally favourable to the implementation of the hunger target. Nonetheless, should it not be met as foreseen, there will be a negative reflection on the welfare of a significant number of people in many parts of the world, both in medium- and low-income countries.

Moreover, regardless of the considerable indirect gains obtained by reducing the number of hungry people, the benefit:cost ratio of stepping up the present rate in order to meet the challenge would be clearly positive, according to a macro-economic study conducted by FAO. A faster pace in the effort to combat hunger would mean adding 200 million people to the hunger-free population by 2015.

Taking into account only the extended life expectancy resulting from the availability of higher quantities of food, the total discounted value of food production would reach an estimated US$120 billion per annum, compared with US$24 billion per year in public investment toward that goal.

Food supply and the environment

Trade negotiations on agricultural products between developed and developing nations and their respective blocks may continue to be difficult for political, economic and even for cultural reasons, since rural areas are often the repository of national traditions and way of life. More flexibility on both sides will probably be required in order to have the Doha process come through and benefit those developing countries that rely on food commodities for exports.

A significant increase in food production is quite compatible with the inclusion of hunger-free human contingents. However, care must be taken in certain cases not to aggravate a condition of growing scarcity of water supply for basic needs in several countries (especially since irrigation for agriculture already represents over 60 per cent of demand in many parts of the world), and not to add further threats to the environment caused not only by the improper use of fertilizers and pesticides in agricultural activities, but also by damages to ecosystems, such as deforestation, soil exhaustion and danger to individual species in expanded production areas.

Compliance with national regulations and international commitments regarding the environment, which are highly desirable, may be overlooked on the premise that they would be an impediment to economic growth, in many cases considered as a fundamental requirement for a stable condition of food security. In view of the apparent increase in the incidence of natural disasters, as population continues to grow and becomes more exposed to risk situations, further effort should be made to implement preventive measures and modern early warning systems.

Structural features: Social, political and economic

Sorting out the most extreme cases and directing aid to more vulnerable countries seems a logical move in setting priorities. Acknowledging the positive impact of including a small number of significantly large countries, and creating a parallel strategy to meet those more complex challenges, would be helpful in meeting the target. More could also be expected from the involvement and strengthening of regional organizations to act as honest brokers in conflict prevention internally and across borders. The move towards more food security in regions can have a positive impact on building peace and reducing the possibility of war. The European Union (EU) is a good example of this.

The participatory decision-making process is still at an experimental stage in many developing countries for political and administrative reasons, especially at the central level. Organized society and private sector participants must be legitimate and representative and their contribution, and equally that of governments, must aim at the common good. Participation, by its very essence, is more time-consuming, and that should be taken into account in devising timeframes and in harmonizing products with disbursements in business contracts.

Coordinated action at all levels

A concerted effort between developing countries at the national level and developed partners through international cooperation provides a valuable opportunity for the UN to play a leading role in advancing a most important target with profound human repercussion. A promising experiment with Africa, the most critical region, in establishing specific criteria for the selection of priorities and stimulating cooperation within the region, should be closely examined to be followed and fully supported by other regions.

The outlook: Suggestions for the future

It is not by chance that hunger and poverty are associated in MDG 1. They are closely inter-related, more so in less developed countries, in rural areas, and increasingly in large urban centers. Food supply figures seem to indicate that it would be possible, quantivately, to eliminate hunger in the world. There is also enough money worldwide to eradicate poverty and consequently hunger. In a certain middle-income country, where about 30 per cent of the population lives below the poverty line, an average monthly contribution of US$5 per capita from the other 70 per cent would presumably allow the poor to rise above that level. On the other hand, the estimated amount in international cooperation required annually to meet the target represents a fraction of the US$900 billion a year spent on military budgets.

At this time, world performance to meet the hunger target has not shown to be sufficient, although concrete proposals to accelerate and attribute the necessary credibility and continuity to the process are under way and shall be examined at different meetings in 2005. Having in mind, for instance, the scope and depth of analysis of the main issues and the selection of instruments provided by the UN Millennium Project, it would be logical to take this document as a necessary reference for the drafting of the overall strategy and the guidance for preparing national plans designed to meet the 2015 target.

There are perhaps three relevant aspects in the Millennium Project that should be underlined and warrant final remarks: fast-track priorities; funding from domestic and external sources; and involvement of local participants in the process.

Selecting fast-track countries for a quick startup is a positive idea, although the criteria initially adopted for their identification, with the best of intentions and with sound reasoning, would inevitably contain temporary features that might change as time progresses and should thus be constantly revised. There is a wide range of indicators that can be assembled and compounded, and given different weights that could also vary throughout project implementation as a pre-condition for scheduled disbursements. Unless the chosen sample of fast-track countries provides a representative picture of the various models, and a diversified pattern of project management and donor-recipient relationship, the first round may hide some of the more difficult aspects of the work and lessons learned may not be sufficiently informative for tackling what may be the tougher way ahead. Maybe adding a few not-so-reliable, but significant countries at first would require more courage but yield a worthwhile contribution to the cause.

The decision to launch a programme of this magnitude and critical importance should be followed by the initiative to create an organizational structure of considerable managerial, financial and political competence, and high-level technical support. One of the main challenges for this setup would be to run a well-coordinated multilateral and bilateral funding, project-based, and fully transparent compact, where each contributor would have a certain degree of freedom of choice but also a firm commitment to the general rules and procedures so that time schedules and amounts would be consistently delivered. Counterpart obligations would also be closely monitored. A number of sectoral executing agencies, either national or international, would respond to a central coordinating organization responsible for overall performance.

Finally, it would be fair to say that social inclusion for all, in the strictest sense, depends on our ability to eradicate hunger and poverty. That can only take place at the community level, and preferably in the community where one belongs, or is invited to belong. Transparency in this case becomes a much simpler and almost visual matter, because the most efficient assistance and proper evaluation of results is rendered by direct contact between donor and beneficiary, as some of the most successful programmes have shown.

References

Diouf, J. (2003) Statement of the FAO Director-General to the Committee on World Food Security, 16 May, FAO, www.fao.org

FAO (1996) Rome Declaration of the World Food Summit and the Plan of Action; www.fao.org/docrep/003/w3613e/w3613e00.htm

FAO (2002) Joint FAO/IDB/WB Transition Team Working Group, Report on Brazil's Fome Zero Program; www.fomezero.gov.br/download/FinalReport.doc

FAO (2004a) Committee on World Food Security, Assessment of the World Food Situation, September, CFS:2004/2, FAO, www.fao.org

FAO (2004b) State of Food Insecurity (SOFI), Undernourishment around the world; www.fao.org/docrep/006/j0083a/j0083200.htm

FAO (2005a) FAO, www.fao.org

FAO (2005b) Committee on World Food Security, Assessment of the World Food Situation, March, CFS:2005/2; www.fao.org/docrep/meeting/009/J4968e/j4968e00. htm

Monterey Consensus (2002) International Conference on Financing for Development, 5th Plenary Meeting on 22 March 2002, UN document A/CONF.198/11, United Nations, New York

Oxford Commission on Sustainable Consumption (2004) Report, 3 November; www. mansfield.ox.ac.uk/report.pdf

Rocha, S. (1996) 'Poverty studies in Brazil – A review', Texto para Discussão no. 398, January, IPEA, Rio de Janeiro

UN (1995) Beijing Declaration and Plan of Action, 4th World Conference on Women, Special Session of the UN General Assembly; www.un.org/women.watch/daw/ Beijing/official.htm

UN (2000) *Millennium Declaration*, General Assembly, 54th session, UN document A/RES/55/2, 18 September, United Nations, New York

UN (2002) World Summit on Sustainable Development, *Plan of Implementation*, Johannesburg, 4 September, United Nations, New York

UN (2004a) Report of the Secretary-General to the Commission on Sustainable Development/ECOSOC, Overview of Progress, document E/CN.17/2004/2, United Nations, New York

UN (2004b) *A more secure world: Our shared responsibility*, Report of the High Level Panel on Threats, Challenges and Change, UN document A/59/565, 2 December, United Nations, New York

UN (2005a) *In Larger Freedom: Towards development, security and human rights for all*, Report of the Secretary-General, United Nations, New York

UN (2005b) 'Commission on Sustainable Development', 43rd session, document E/ CN.5/2005/L.5, United Nations, New York

UNDP (2003) *Human Development Report 2003*, Oxford University Press, New York

UN Millennium Project (2005) 'Investing in development: A practical plan for the achievement of the Millennium Development Goals', www.unmillenniumproject. org/reports/fullreport.htm

WTO (2004) Doha Work Programme, WT/L/579, 2 August, WTO, www.wto.org/ English/tratop_e/dda_e/ddadraft_31jul04_e.pdf

13

Water Security: What Role for International Water Law?

Patricia Wouters

Water is essential for life. Yet many millions of people around the world face water shortages. Many millions of children die every year from waterborne diseases. And drought regularly afflicts some of the world's poorest countries. The world needs to respond much better.

UN Secretary-General Kofi Annan, 2005c

Introduction

The international community recognizes the need to improve the management of its global water resources, and the UN 'Water for Life Decade', announced by UN Secretary-General Kofi Annan in March 2005, demonstrates, in many ways, the increased focus on issues related to water security and resources.

The notion of 'water security' is not a new one, but is being reconsidered in current global discourse – a reinvigorated concept inviting closer study. In the United Nations Environment Programme's (UNEP) report on Environment and Security, 'Understanding Environment, Conflict and Cooperation', UNEP executive director Klaus Toepfer states that:

maintaining environmental quality and improving degraded environments are preconditions for achieving sustainable development and meeting the Millennium Development Goals. They are also crucially important for enhancing human well-being, including security. The United Nations Environment Programme has therefore been interested in promoting understanding of the relationship between environment and peace.

UNEP, 2004[1]

But what is water security in this context, and how does this concept contribute to the world 'responding much better' to the problems it faces over water?

What is water security?

...emphasizing that water is critical for sustainable development, including environmental integrity and the eradication of poverty and hunger, and is indispensable for human health and well-being.

UN General Assembly, 2005

The term water security has never been defined precisely, although it has been used in many contexts. For instance, Eric Gutierrez argues that the concept of water security is not simply about dwindling supplies:

A comprehensive definition goes beyond availability to issues of access. Access involves issues that range from a discussion of fundamental individual rights to national sovereignty rights over water. It also involves equity and affordability, and the role of states and markets in water's allocation, pricing, distribution and regulation. Water security also implies social and political decision-making on use – the priority to be accorded to competing household, agricultural or industrial demands on the resource.

Gutierrez, 1999

Another more recent example: this year's World Bank Water Week Conference was convened under the title, 'Water Security: Policies and Investments'. The bank's website introduced the topic as follows:

The preconception that all water problems can be solved with infrastructure is as questionable as the assumption that, in the right institutional environments, problems can be solved with minimal infrastructure. Rather, countries need to develop their institutional environment and invest in infrastructure in parallel. The balance between the two interventions is different in different settings. In all of the countries and many dimensions of water it works in (water supply and sanitation, irrigation, water environment, water resources management, hydropower), the World Bank helps countries to balance infrastructure and institutions.

World Bank, 2005

At the bilateral donor level, the UK Department for International Development (DFID) has produced a Strategy for Development (March 2005), which recognizes that 'security and development are linked' and that 'insecurity is a barrier to achieving the Millennium Development Goals'. 'DFID's role is to promote the security of the poor locally, nationally and internationally, as part of our work in reducing poverty' – and asserts that more can be done: 'reducing conflict and promoting poor people's security is not yet a regular feature of our programmes or partnerships' (DFID, 2005). Thus, the notion of water security is strongly embraced by multilateral and bilateral donors and also appears at the forefront of the NGO agenda – but what does it mean, and how shall we address the attendant challenges?

For the purposes of this chapter, security is defined as 'the state of being secure, assured freedom from poverty or want' (Sinclair, 2000). This can also be understood from the term *secure*, defined to mean: 'free from danger, damage; free from fear' (Sinclair, 2000). In this light, the notion of water security can be understood as 'the state of having secure access to water; the assured freedom from poverty of, or want for, water for life'. This definition introduces a number of issues, including notions of the right of all people to enjoy secure access to adequate supplies of drinking water and sanitation, within the context of water-related environmental requirements.

Water as a right

> *Water is vital for the life and health of people and ecosystems, and a basic requirement for the development of countries, but around the world women, men and children lack access to adequate and safe water to meet their most basic needs. Water resources and the related ecosystems that provide and sustain them are under threat from pollution, unsustainable use, land-use changes, climate change and many other forces. The link between these threats and poverty is clear, for it is the poor who are hit first and hardest. This leads to one simple conclusion: business as usual is not an option. There is, of course, a huge diversity of needs and situations around the globe, but together we have one common goal: to provide water security in the 21st century. This means ensuring that freshwater, coastal and related ecosystems are protected and improved; that sustainable development and political stability are promoted, that every person has access to enough safe water at an affordable cost to lead a healthy and productive life and that the vulnerable are protected from the risks of water-related hazards.*
>
> *World Water Forum, 2000*

The global aspiration that people should have basic water rights is captured both in the UN Millennium Development Goals (MDGs)[2] – agreed to by 191 states at the Millennium Summit in 2000, which included their commitment to reduce by half the proportion of people without access to safe drinking water by 2015 (UN, 2000) – and in a complementary target, to halve by 2015 the proportion of people lacking improved sanitation, agreed in 2002 at the World Summit on Sustainable Development (WSSD, 2002).

This goal is discussed more comprehensively in a declaration issued by the UN Committee on Economic, Social and Cultural Rights in 2002, described by former World Health Organization (WHO) Director-General Gro Harlem Brundtland in one interview as 'a major boost in efforts to achieve the Millennium Development Goals (Capdevila, 2002). The declaration provides that access to water is a 'human right' and that water is a public commodity fundamental to life and health. Adopted by the UN Committee as a 'General Comment', it further stipulates that water, like health, is an essential element for achieving other human rights, especially the rights to adequate food and nutrition, housing and education:

> *The human right to water entitles everyone to sufficient, affordable, physically accessible, safe and acceptable water for personal and domestic uses. While uses vary between cultures, an adequate amount of safe water is necessary to prevent death from dehydration, to reduce the risk of water-related disease and to provide for consumption, cooking, personal and domestic hygienic requirements.*

> *UN, 2003a*

Building on the General Comment, the UN World Water Development Report, 'Water for People, Water for Life', adopts as the principal challenge that of 'ensuring basic needs and the right to health' (UN, 2003b). The report was produced by a joint project of 23 specialized agencies and other UN entities, and other water-related collaborative mechanisms and initiatives.

Given this background, it may appear surprising that the 2005 UN Commission on Sustainable Development (CSD) – in its discussions on water and sanitation in preparation for the September 2005 Millennium Review Summit – did not agree to reaffirm that right. What seems clear is that the identification of the normative content of the 'right to water', coupled with real issues tied to the ability of some states to implement this right, may have undermined a global consensus to agree that this is a universal duty that is opposable on states – that is, in international legal terms, considered to be a rule of *jus cogens* or as an obligation *erga omnes* (Woodhouse, 2004).

Nevertheless, the now readily identifiable and globally endorsed water agenda – both top-down and bottom-up in its genesis – appears embedded in the world's development initiatives and aspirations. Access to water is directly linked to the health and wealth of populations, demonstrated from the beginning of time by the location next to water of emerging new communities (Caponera, 2003). This link between access to water (broadly construed) and economic development is clearly outlined in a 'Make Poverty History' campaign report:

> *An immediate annual injection of at least US$50 billion is needed per year to allow countries to make progress towards the MDGs. As much as US$94 billion extra may be required if countries are to meet the targets in full. Without proper funding, 30,000 children will continue to die needlessly every day from causes associated with extreme poverty: A child dies every 15 seconds from water-related diseases.*

> *Make Poverty History, 2005*[3]

At the heart of this discourse on water security are three important elements:

1 Water security is based on three core freedoms: freedom from want, freedom from fear and freedom to live in human dignity[4]

2   Ensuring water security may lead to a conflict of interests, which must be capable of being identified and effectively dealt with at the international, national and local levels
3   Water security, like water, is a dynamic concept, and one that needs clear local champions and sustained stewardship.

These key points can be discussed from a number of perspectives. I propose to look at these from a water law angle, and to demonstrate the importance of this discipline in the effective achievement of water security. It must be acknowledged from the outset that water law is not a panacea for the world's water problems – clearly it is not; there exist a number of world-views through which we can understand these challenges. However, existing practice – both internationally and nationally, and, at the operational and theoretical levels – is marked by an absence of the effective integration of cross-disciplinary expertise, including, water law as an integral component of solution-oriented actions. Although things are changing,[5] there remains much scope for improvement. While this chapter will focus on the water law aspects of water security, it is critical that this must be seen to be nested within that broader interdisciplinary context.

What is water law?

Considering the international agenda for the issues related to the more effective management of the world's water resources, we are faced at once by the sometimes conflicting aspirations of an interdependent international community and the individual needs of sovereign states. In such a context, water law must be construed in the broadest possible sense, to include all areas of law, at the national and international level, that might impact upon the legal regulation of water resources (supply and sanitation). At the international level, this would include not only water treaties[6] but also those agreements that governed the use of international waters, directly or indirectly – such as environmental, trade and commerce, and boundary treaties. At the national level, the law that governs water use (supply and demand) covers a broad spectrum – from constitutional law (e.g. the South African Constitution), to administrative, planning, environmental, health and so forth. In the UK, for example, identifying the sum total of all of the rules and regulations that cover water supply and services is an enormous task – an exercise that should be made much easier!

From a legal perspective, the complementary but distinct systems of international and national law are at the forefront of any discussion involving international relations, with sovereign state actors. In the area of water law, this requires study under three broad headings: international water law (involving state-state relations), national water law (domestic legal system for regulating water within state borders), and transnational water law (a newly emerging area of water law concerned with the rules that apply to third party involvement with the national state's regulation of its water resources, including such actors as multinationals, donors and non-governmental organizations (NGOs)) (Wouters et al, 2003).

For governments to best meet their obligations related to water under the MDGs, it is essential that each of these areas of water law is understood and applied effectively.[7] The following discussion examines why this is necessary and how it is linked to water security.

What role for water law in the water security discourse?

...the goals of the Decade should be a greater focus on water-related issues at all levels and on the implementation of water-related programmes and projects, while striving to ensure the participation and involvement of women in water-related development efforts, and the furtherance of cooperation at all levels, in order to help to achieve internationally agreed water-related goals contained in Agenda 21, the Programme for the Further Implementation of Agenda 21, the United Nations Millennium Declaration and the Johannesburg Plan of Implementation, and, as appropriate, those identified during the twelfth and thirteenth sessions of the Commission on Sustainable Development.

UN General Assembly, 2004

The current global discourse on water is very much tied to action plans and focuses on seeking operational mechanisms to implement, inter alia, the MDGs. As attractive as this appears, a rigorous examination of the listed objectives of the MDGs and emerging global water initiatives reveals conflicting demands and approaches. This is especially true at the local level. For example, where there is inadequate water to meet agricultural demands and other uses – say for grazing livestock, or sustaining a fishery or maintaining in stream flow requirements – which use is to prevail? The potential conflict-of-use scenario becomes even more complicated when occurring across state boundaries. What water security can the government of Uganda or Zambia provide at the national level for its citizens, where most of their national waters are shared transboundary resources? What position on water security for Mozambique, which, downstream on 11 international watercourses, relies on upstream state activities – most recently with catastrophic consequences for its people during the raging floods of 2002? The situation becomes even more complex when shared transboundary groundwater is involved (Daibes-Murad, 2005). What water security for upstream and downstream states at the sub-national level, for example, in China, on the Tarim Basin, where the downstream now runs dry?[8] Or, given the current terrorist-related threats in the USA, how do sub-national entities deal with water security issues?[9]

Questions related to humanitarian law connected to water also arise at the international level – what protection for water during times of international conflict? The International Committee of the Red Cross (ICRC) has found that 'armed conflict deprives millions of people of drinking water. When water reserves are contaminated, damaged or destroyed, the results can be disastrous as thirst and disease add to the misery of war' (ICRC, 2004a). This view is supported by Théo Boutruche in 'The Status Of Water In The Law Of Armed Conflict'. He concludes that:

> *...the lack of a proper and autonomous legal framework for protecting water would appear to be explained, on the one hand, by the many roles that water can play – for example, as a weapon, target or victim – and, on the other, by the very manner in which it is treated in international humanitarian law. Water is taken into account only in connection with that body of law's basic objectives of protecting victims of war and regulating the conduct of hostilities – and even then only in its capacity as one of man's basic needs, or as a danger, or as part of the natural environment. Water as such is not given legal protection. This arrangement may be inadequate, but it is enough to serve as a firm basis for improvement. In view of research carried out recently on international rules on the use of water in peacetime, a fresh look should be taken at the status of water in the law of armed conflict.*
>
> *Boutruche, 2000*

In the area of transitional water law, the global debate challenges world trade law and scrutinizes the roles of the public and private sector in their obligations to meet water security objectives around the world. Often, the poorest pay the highest price for water, placing them in a cycle of water insecurity.

Thus, many issues arise when a state seeks to ensure that the three core freedoms fundamental to ensure water security – freedom from want, freedom from fear and freedom to live with human dignity – are met in a sustainable manner. Conflicts arise on many levels, which require, in an international transboundary watercourse situation, expertise in the three distinct, but complementary, areas of water law – international, national and transnational. In keeping with the central theme of this book, this chapter will now focus on water security at the international level, and thus concentrate on the area of international water law.

Water security and international water law

International rivers cover the world, with more than 250 major watercourses shared by two or more states. Given the world's growing population and the increasing demands on the quality and quantity of fresh water, the likelihood of conflicts is very high. According to some forecasts, the future withdrawal of the world's water supply for domestic, industrial and other uses will increase by at least 50 per cent by 2025, leading to a global water crisis caused by the severe water shortage, especially in developing countries (UNWire, 2002). How can water security be achieved in this context?

International water law, as noted above, is concerned with sovereign state relations over water. Connected to this are national government concerns over

---

Box 13.1 Maura's story

Maura Hassan lives in Tabata, a poor area of Dar es Salaam in Tanzania. Although she has water pipes connected to her home, she is unable to get any water through them. Since the water supply to the area has been privatized, she has been receiving bills for water she hasn't used. Her last bill was for US$400.

Maura is forced to buy water from a well dug by a private individual. Although this is much more expensive than piped water and she has no guarantee that it is safe to drink, she has no choice, since the water connection to her house doesn't work. Other local families can't afford to buy any kind of water, and are forced to use the local shallow wells. People who bathe in them start to itch, and those who drink from them need expensive medicines to treat their subsequent illnesses.

How does aid fit in? Aid flows to Tanzania were made conditional on the government privatizing the water system in Dar es Salaam. The move has increased water prices and made poor populations more vulnerable to waterborne diseases such as cholera.

The British government is heavily implicated in the deal. The water supply has been handed over to Biwater, the UK water multinational. The British taxpayer, through the Department for International Development, funded the pro-privatization advertising campaign. A hostile Tanzanian public was subjected to a media campaign promoting the sell-off, at a cost of £430,000.

Source: Make Poverty History, 2005

issues of respective legal entitlement and obligations, or, in short – *who* is entitled to use *what* water?[10] The analytical framework for examining how international water law works has been developed and discussed in detail elsewhere, and provides the template to evaluate the potential for achieving water security (UNESCO, 2005). In essence, when a transboundary watercourse state seeks to develop its national water policy, including its position on shared freshwater, the following list of issues needs to be addressed:

1 *Scope:* Which waters are included? Which other state parties are involved?
2 *Substantive Rules:* Which rules govern the use of shared waters?
3 *Procedural Rules:* Which rules of procedure govern the use of shared waters?
4 *Institutional Mechanisms:* Which body (with which mandate) is charged with managing the shared regime?
5 *Dispute Avoidance/Dispute Settlement and Compliance:* What mechanisms are available to ensure the parties are able to comply with the rules that apply?

The successful response to these matters – ideally by agreement among watercourse states – is one solid step towards ensuring water security at the international, national and, thus, local levels. There is a direct connection between a transboundary watercourse state's ability to provide its population with adequate drinking water and sanitation and the existence of an operational (legal) framework guiding the use of its shared waters.

Rules of international law governing transboundary waters and the 1997 UN watercourses convention

Agreement by transboundary watercourse states on matters related to scope, substantive rules, procedural rules, institutional mechanisms and dispute avoidance/settlement will provide a solid foundation upon which to ensure water security at the local level. In many ways, the 1997 UN Watercourses Convention provides a credible framework agreement for addressing the five fundamental issues outlined above, and states should move forward with its ratification. Article 5 of the convention requires states to participate in the use, development, and adequate protection of international watercourses in an equitable and reasonable manner.[11] In addition to the provisions to prevent and mitigate harmful conditions (Article 27) and emergency situations (Article 28), the convention also deals with international watercourses and installations in times of armed conflict:

> *International watercourses and related installations, facilities and other works shall enjoy the protection accorded by the principles and rules of international law applicable in international and non-international conflict and shall not be used in violation of those principles and rules (Article 29).*

The convention also requires states to fulfil their international obligations through indirect means if there are 'serious obstacles', such as military hostilities or no diplomatic contact (Article 30). The convention further contemplates the necessity to limit exchange of information on the watercourses when it is vital to national defense or security (Article 31).

Given the scope of these provisions, calls for a 'new' global watercourses convention are not entirely justified and could result in an unnecessary distraction for states. This is especially true for developing nations, who have limited resources in their departments of affairs and face difficult challenges in dealing with the existing 'treaty congestion' on environmental matters – a situation that hinders, rather than enables, states to get on with effective implementation of water security at the domestic level. With 109 states supporting the UN resolution that adopted the UN Watercourses Convention, and the nearly 30 years of study undertaken on the topic by the International Law Commission (ILC) – which represents legal systems from around the world – surely states should be called upon to ratify this existing instrument before they pursue a similar (and arguably unnecessary) exercise?

The challenge for a transboundary watercourse state to ensure water security at the national level is linked directly to issues of *international* water security

– the extent to which it can rely on secure access to its shared water resources. Again, the 1997 UN Watercourses Convention – and the many international treaties concluded on the basis of this framework agreement – provides the foundation for such international water security. This is especially true where conflicts of use arise, and also in situations where watercourse states do not enjoy friendly relations, or, where there exists an inequality of power. The existing governing rules of international water law (best understood through the analytical framework identified above) provide a level playing field and platform for cooperation over shared waters, and this message needs to be embedded in the water security discourse.

The core rule: 'Equitable and reasonable use'

At the heart of this legal framework, and instrumental for achieving water security, is the governing rule of international water law – that each watercourse state is entitled to an 'equitable and reasonable use' of its shared freshwater resources (Wouters, 1999). The rule, necessarily flexible to meet the needs of the resource, finds precise definition through application on a case-by-case basis. It requires the consideration of all uses and all needs across the basin, with a decision on what qualifies as 'equitable and reasonable' determined in each particular situation. This methodology is set forth in the ILA Helsinki Rules, which were adopted in Article 6 (3) of the 1997 UN Watercourses Convention. (See also Articles 5, 6, and 7, UN Watercourses Convention.) All factors are considered to be equal in weight, although there may be a priority of use accorded to 'vital human' needs, and, possibly also, to vital environmental needs. Article 10 of the UN Watercourses Convention – 'Relationship between different kinds of uses' – provides direction in this regard: '1. In the absence of agreement or custom to the contrary, no use of an international watercourse enjoys inherent priority over other uses. 2. In the event of a conflict between uses of an international watercourse, it shall be resolved with reference to articles 5 to 7, with special regard being given to the requirements of vital human needs.' In the statement of understanding attached to the convention, this is taken to mean 'in determining vital human needs, special attention is to be paid to providing sufficient water to sustain human life, including both drinking water and water required for production of food in order to prevent starvation'. Such an approach, endorsed broadly by the international community – including a significant number of watercourse states – offers important insights on how issues of individual water security are dealt with within the framework of international water law (UNESCO, 2005).

Box 13.2 What is a lawful use?

Article 6 (3) 'In determining what is a reasonable and equitable use, all relevant factors are to be considered together and a conclusion reached on the basis of the whole'

Source: 1997 UN Watercourses Convention

Supporting the primary rule of equity and reason are procedural rules (requiring prior notification of proposed uses and exchange of information) (Jones, 2005), institutional mechanisms (to be established by states to ensure joint cooperation in development activities) and dispute avoidance/settlement/compliance mechanisms (fundamental for ensuring the peaceful implementation of the agreed legal regime) – which together provide a transparent, enforceable and responsive framework that provides the operational side of water security, at the international level (Peace Palace Papers, 2003). The UK government, under its DFID Knowledge and Research Programme, has funded the development of an operational tool that facilitates a transboundary watercourse state to develop its national water policy in line with its international legal entitlements and obligations. The Legal Assessment Model (LAM) provides transboundary watercourse states with a pragmatic methodology – interdisciplinary in nature – to determine its national legal entitlements and obligations related to the use of its shared transboundary water resources (UNESCO, 2005).

Using international water law in support of water security

The core freedoms of water security are best secured in states with sound governments and governance. Where these elements are not solidly in place, enforceable legal regimes can provide transparent entry points to ensure the enjoyment of such fundamental freedoms. For example, in times of armed conflict, rules of international humanitarian law provide for the securing of water for the human population. Humanitarian organizations such at the International Red Cross have provided water for millions around the world – in 2003, the ICRC met the water needs of some 19 million people. Its water and sanitation activities aim to ensure that victims of armed conflict have access to safe water and proper sanitation' (ICRC, 2004b). Ensuring basic human dignity during conflict is the mandate of ICRC, and the provision of water is one of its core activities in this task.

Many developed countries have stable governments in place and work towards sound governance, and yet face ongoing challenges in meeting their water security imperatives. In this context, the rules of international water law provide a solid foundation upon which to develop cooperative arrangements that enable meeting their goals of water security. The 1997 UN Watercourses Convention, coupled with the applicable rules of customary international law – and in particular, the primary rule of 'equitable and reasonable use' – offers states concrete building blocks in their quest to ensure *international* water security (Wouters, 1999; Peace Palace Papers, 2003). This approach is strengthened through the rules of international law linked to the peaceful settlement of disputes, and watercourse states are recommended strongly to study the compulsory conciliation ('fact-finding') provisions of the UN Watercourses Convention in this regard (Wouters, 1999; Peace Palace Papers, 2003; and see Article 33, UN Watercourses Convention).

The way forward: A new generation of water leaders

In his March 2005 report, 'In Larger Freedom: towards development, security and human rights for all' (UN, 2005a), UN Secretary-General Kofi Annan calls upon governments to:

> *recognize the need for significantly increased international support for scientific research and development to address the special needs of the poor in the areas of health, agriculture, natural resource and environmental management, energy and climate*

UN, 2005b

With respect, this request to governments fails to go far enough. There is a significant and damaging divergence between developed and developing country approaches to resolving water resource issues. As has been discussed in detail elsewhere and demonstrated in many cases, simply *increasing* development aid is not the answer. Tearfund asserts that most international aid money for tackling the global water crisis is going to wealthier countries rather than the billions of people in the poorest countries who lack access to safe water and sanitation: 'Our research clearly shows that aid is not being delivered to the poorest people most in need of safe water and sanitation,' says Joanne Green, Tearfund's water policy adviser. 'Africa will currently miss by 35 years and 95 years, respectively, the Millennium Development Goal of halving the number of people without access to water and sanitation by 2015. Aid needs to be re-doubled, but also re-focused on the poorest countries to get us back on track' (Tearfund, 2005).

The real problem lies more with *how* support is provided, not *how much more is provided*. Successful implementation of a sustainable level of water security is linked directly to local capacity to identify and to respond to ongoing local issues and needs. In the context of water law, experience in the field reveals a profound lack of understanding of the fundamental principles of international, national and transnational law in most developing countries. This means that expertise in these areas often comes from foreign consultants, brought in on short-term contracts, who, despite their best intentions, cannot provide long-term support and sustainable solutions. There is a clear need, consequently, to develop innovative strategies and systems that work with local expertise to provide more effective mechanisms for long-term capacity development. The rules of the game must be identified and established from within the country, in line with its security and development needs, and, not imposed from 'the commercial and financial interests and mindsets [that] have prevailed within the international economic institutions' (Stiglitz, 2002).

The development, implementation, modification and ongoing nurturing of states' national water policy must come from within. Ensuring long-term stewardship of this regime requires national, in-county expertise. There is a real need to facilitate the development and support of a new generation of water leaders *in-country* – educated within an interdisciplinary curriculum, mentored by leaders in the field around the world, but supported as leaders within their home state.

Several initiatives seek to meet this challenge, but the international community, generally, and donors, in particular, have yet to embrace fully this idea.[12,13] Discussion during the closing plenary session of the Stockholm World Water Week 2002 yielded broad base support for this approach,[14] but funding for 'training the trainers' programmes, including developing regional centres of excellence in water law, has not been forthcoming.

Water security must be evaluated at the user level, at the local level. Water law is a necessary element to ensure the fundamental freedoms at the heart of water security. We need a new generation of in-country water leaders capable of understanding and articulating local issues, and who are able to draft and implement relevant and responsive rules of water law at the international, national and transnational levels. This is one pragmatic proposal for ensuring the effective achievement of water security worldwide. Let us together find the way forward for this activity.

Notes

1   See also Postel, S. (2002) 'Waters 1: Farms versus cities and nature', and Gleick, P. H. (2002) 'Water and conflict: Fresh water resources and international security', both in Wolf, A. T. (2002) *Conflict Prevention and Resolution in Water Systems*, Edward Elgar Publishing Limited Collection, Northampton, MA.

2   For the UN Millennium Development Goals, see www.un.org/ millenniumgoals/.

3   See also OXFAM, www.oxfam.org.uk/what_you_can_do/campaign/mdg/ mph.htm; Tearfund www.tearfund.org/Campaigning/Make+poverty+ history/; and also the G8 Evian Report, where G8 member states agreed to 'address core issues of human dignity and development'; see /www. g8.fr/evian/english/navigation/2003_g8_summit/summit_documents/ implementation_report_by_africa_personal_representatives_to_leaders_ on_the_g8_african_action_plan.html.

4   This approach is based upon *In Larger Freedom: Towards development, security and human rights for all*, Report of the UN Secretary-General (2005), document A/59/2005, 21 March; available at www.un.org/largerfreedom/ report-largerfreedom.pdf

5   See the innovative HELP (Hydrology for the Environment, Life and Policy) programme, introduced under the UNESCO IHP programme, which is founded upon the principles of inter-disciplinary approaches to water resources management, including water law; see www.unesco.org.

6   Such treaties include those international agreements dealing with allocation, use and development of shared water resources, such as the 1997 United Nations Convention on the Non-Navigational Uses of International

Watercourses (UN Watercourses Convention), the UN Watercourses Convention 36 ILM 700 (1997) and the 1995 Mekong Agreement, Agreement on the Cooperation for the Sustainable Development of the Mekong Basin, 34 ILM 864 (Mekong Agreement, 1995).

7 On the broader point of state responsibility for development, the UN Secretary-General is unequivocal in his March 2005 report: 'Each developing country has primary responsibility for its own development – strengthening governance, combating corruption and putting in place the policies and investments to drive private-sector-led growth and maximize domestic resources available to fund national development strategies. Developed countries, on their side, undertake that developing countries which adopt transparent, credible and properly costed development strategies will receive the full support they need, in the form of increased development assistance, a more development-oriented trade system and wider and deeper debt relief. All of this has been promised but not delivered. That failure is measured in the rolls of the dead – and on it are written millions of new names each year.'

8 See Wouters, P. et al (2004) 'The new development of water law in China', *University of Denver Water Law Review*, vol 7, pp243–308.

9 See US Newline, Medialink Worldwide (2005) 'Water Security Officials Explore Monitoring Technologies at Congress': 'Officials charged with protecting North American water supplies examined the latest contamination warning technologies today during the third annual Water Security Congress, hosted by the American Water Works Association (AWWA). AWWA estimates that US water utilities have spent more than US$2 billion since 9/11 to upgrade the physical security of treatment plants and infrastructure. Utilities are also upgrading defences against cyber-attacks on water systems and revisiting emergency response plans... Utilities are taking many proactive steps to safeguard our water supplies and infrastructure, but we also need to be ready to respond. The Water Security Congress is an ideal forum to address all these issues.'

10 This must be considered in the broader context of virtual water, meaning that the focus is not on sharing water per se, but instead with how a transboundary watercourse state's national policy related to water use is best identified and applied. This introduces also the notion of 'sharing benefits', a concept that is part of the governing rule of 'equitable and reasonable utilization'.

11 'Adequate protection is meant to cover not only measures such as those relating to conservation, security and water-related disease, but also measures of control in a technical, hydrological sense of the term, such as those taken to regulate flow, to control floods, pollution and erosion, to mitigate drought and control saline intrusion'. See Report of the International Law Commission on the work of its 46 Session (1994) UN document A/49/10, United Nations, New York.

12 The Universities Partnership for Transboundary Waters, in connection with UNESCO, seeks to develop an international curriculum in the area

of transboundary waters that will assist in meeting this objective; see Universities Partnership for Transboundary Waters, a consortium of universities from 10 countries specializing in transboundary waters research and work; see http://waterpartners.goe.orst.edu/

13   The University of Dundee, under its 'Water Law, Water Leaders' executive-style postgraduate degree programme, seeks to support the development of regional water leaders, through delivery of taught courses in regional basins. See www.dundee.ac.uk/water

14   The Universities Partnership will support this approach during its sessions at the Stockholm World Water Week, scheduled for 27 August 2005.

References

Boutruche, T. (2000) 'The status of water law in the law of armed conflict', *International Review of the Red Cross*, no 340, pp887–916

Capdevila, G. (2002) *UN Consecrates Water as Public Good, Human Right*, Global Policy Forum, www.globalpolicy.org/soceon/ffd/gpg/2002/1127water.htm

Caponera, D. (2003) 'National and international water law and administration', *Kluwer Law International*, The Hague

Daibes-Murad, F. (2005) *A New Legal Framework for Managing the World's Shared Groundwaters: A Case-Study from the Middle East*, International Water Publishing, London

DFID (2005), *Fighting Poverty to Build a Safer World: A Strategy for Security and Development*, DFID, London

Gutierrez, E. (1999) *Boiling Point: Issues and Problems in Water Security and Sanitation*, Water Aid Briefing Paper, Global Water Partnership, London

ICRC (2004a) 'World water day: 20 years of commitment', ICRC news, 04/37, 19 March, www.icrc.org

ICRC (2004b) *Six of the ICRC's top water and habitat operations in 2004*, Report on the work of the ICRC in Liberia, Ivory Coast, Russian Federation, Georgia, Iraq and Afghanistan, www.icrc.org

Jones, P. (2005) *Allocating Transboundary Water Resources: Procedural Problems and Solutions* [Working Title], IWLRI, Dundee

Make Poverty History (2005), www.makepovertyhistory.org

Peace Palace Papers (2003) 'Universal and Regional Approaches to resolving International Disputes: What Lessons learned from State Practice?', in *Resolution of International Water Disputes*, International Court of Arbitration, *Kluwer Law International*, pp111–154

Sinclair, J. M. (2000) *The Times English Dictionary*, First Edition, Harper Collins, London

Stiglitz, J. (2002), *Globalization and its discontents*, Penguin, London

Tearfund (2005) 'World Water Day: Aid is not reaching the poorest says new report', press release on the launch of *Making every drop count*, www.tearfund.org

UN (2000) *Millennium Declaration*, General Assembly, 55th session, UN document A/RES/55/2, 18 September, United Nations, New York

UN World Summit on Sustainable Development (2002) *Plan of Implementation*, 4 September, Johannesburg, United Nations, New York

UN (2003a), 'General comment', E/C.12/2002/11, 20 January; www.unhchr.ch

UN (2003b) *Water for People, Water for Life*, World Water Development Report, UN sales number E.03.II.A.2, United Nations, New York

UN (2005a) *In Larger Freedom: Towards development, security and human rights for all*, United Nations General Assembly document A/59/2005, 21 March, www.un.org/largerfreedom/report-largerfreedom.pdf

UN (2005b) *Annex – Decision for Governments*, Report of the Secretary-General, document A/59/2005, 21 March; www.un.org/largerfreedom/report-largerfreedom.pdf

UN (2005c) 'Water for life decade', Message of the Secretary-General for World Water Day, 22 March; available at www.un.org/waterforlifedecade/worldwaterday.html

UN General Assembly (2004) *International Decade for Action, Water for Life, 2005–2015*, Resolution A/RES/58/217, 9 August, United Nations, New York

UN General Assembly (2005) *Resolution on Water for Life Decade*, document A/RES/59/228, 16 February, United Nations, New York

UNEP (2004) *Understanding Environment, Conflict and Cooperation*, 6 October; available at www.unep.org

UNESCO (2005) *Sharing Transboundary Waters, An Integrated Assessment of Equitable Entitlement – The Legal Assessment Model*, UNESCO Technical paper, UNESCO, New York

UNWire (2002) *Water: Good Policies Can Avert World Crisis*, Global Water Outlook to 2025, www.unfoundation.org

World Bank (2005) *Water Security: Policies and Investments*, Water Week 2005, 1–3 March, Washington DC, www.worldbank.org/watsan/waterweek/

World Water Forum (2000) 'Ministerial Declaration of The Hague on Water Security in the 21st Century', March 2000, www.waternunc.com/gb/secWWF.htm

Woodhouse, M. (2004), 'Threshold, Reporting and Accountability for a Right to Water under International Law' *University of Denver Water Law Review*, pp171–199.

Wouters, P. (1999) 'The legal response to water scarcity: The UN watercourses convention and beyond', *German Yearbook of International Law*, vol 42, p293

Wouters, P., Vinogradov, S. and Jones, P. (2003) *Transforming Potential Conflict into Cooperation Potential: The Role of International Water Law*, UNESCO publication presented at the Kyoto World Water Forum, March 2005, UNESCO-HLP

14

Urban Safety: A Collective Challenge for Sustainable Human Settlements Development

Anna Tibaijuka

Crime, violence and insecurity: A daily concern for urban dwellers

Crime and victimization occur in all countries of the world, and the probability of being a victim of crime is substantially higher in urban areas. Approximately 60 per cent of city dwellers in Europe and North America, and 70 per cent in Latin America and Africa, have been victimized by crime over the past five years. Globally, one in five people is likely to be a victim of a serious contact crime such as robbery, sexual crime or assault.

Overall, recorded crime rates are stabilizing or even decreasing in the countries of the North, but not all types of crime have decreased. Property crime has decreased or stabilized, but the risk of being a victim of a violent crime such as homicide, assault, rape, sexual abuse and domestic violence has continued to rise worldwide. Although there are large variations between countries and cities, on average, urban violence makes up at least 25 to 30 per cent of urban crime in many countries. Women in developing countries are twice as likely to be victims of violent aggression as men, while in other regions the risk is a little lower.

Crime and insecurity are serious threats in developing countries, where they further compound other factors such as poverty and social exclusion that already limit quality of life. Corruption in the public sector is higher in Latin America (21.3 per cent) and Africa (18.8 per cent) than in other regions threatening economic and social well-being.[1] A victimization survey conducted in Nairobi revealed that close to 30 per cent of business people admit to having bribed an official in 2002 (UN Habitat, 2002). Corruption facilitates the growth of organized crime, particularly where public administration has inadequate political, legal, and ethical frameworks to ensure accountability and transparency in decision making.

Corruption is significant because it erodes the trust that a society needs to function effectively, excluding the poor and accelerating their disengagement from wider society. Corruption is a central reason why societies grow more insecure deepening social cleavages, increasing social exclusion and societal fragmentation (World Bank, 2000).

Box 14.1 Corruption in Nairobi's informal settlements

Corruption rules in Nairobi's informal settlements. The majority of slum dwellers are forced to pay (often too high) rent rates to local chiefs and rich property and land owners. These chiefs and landowners have created a Mafia-style system through which the residents are forced to abide by the rent rates and conditions they dictate (and enforce through the use of youth gangs). Landowners often refuse their tenants to hold meetings to prevent them from organizing resistance to their power base, which forces the residents to live in houses of poor quality, under unhealthy and low-standard living conditions. This system of extortion exacerbates levels of insecurity and violence, which subsequently diminishes social and community structures.

Jane Weru, Nairobi

Delinquency most commonly involves young offenders, and the majority of offences are committed by youths between the ages of 12 and 25. Over the past decade, youth delinquency has become increasingly violent. Youths are faced with increasing peer pressure that is breaking traditional societal values. They are recruited by organized crime, and the numbers of youth gangs are growing substantially. However, it is important to distinguish between youth gangs and groups of street children, whose delinquent behaviour is sporadic and driven by the need to survive.

The increased availability and use of firearms lends heavily to the increase in urban violence. Violent crime and murder rates are generally much higher in cities where weapons are widely and easily available. Post-conflict countries often become the source of large numbers of illegal weapons and hubs for weapons smuggling to neighbouring countries. The presence and proliferation of illicit weapons not only increases the likelihood of continuing violence and more violent crime, but also has a serious impact on the recruitment of child soldiers.

Human security: An urban development perspective

Globally, more than 1.6 million people die from violence every year (WHO, 2004) and about 2.8 billion people suffer from poverty, ill health, illiteracy and other maladies. Urban security challenges are becoming more complex, and a plethora of actors are attempting to play a role in addressing such insecurities.

There is need to broaden the focus to include human security, which means protecting vital freedoms. Protecting people from threatening situations, building on their strengths, demands an integrated approach. Human security connects freedom from want, freedom from fear and freedom to take action. There are two general strategies: protection and empowerment. Protection requires developing norms, processes and institutions that systematically address insecurities, while empowerment enables people to become full participants in decision making. Protection and empowerment are mutually reinforcing, giving people the building blocks of survival, dignity and livelihood, enabling them to participate in governance and make their voices heard. In an urban development perspective, this requires building strong institutions, establishing the rule of law and empowering people.

Human security in the city: Exclusion, social fragmentation, anxiety and fear

Crime, violence and insecurity present major challenges for the social and economic development of cities. Delinquency and violence in urban areas is no longer viewed exclusively as a criminal problem, but also as a developmental problem.

Insecurity contributes to the isolation of groups and to the stigmatization of neighbourhoods, particularly those containing the poor and more vulnerable. It creates conditions of fear, hinders mobility and may be a major stumbling block for participation, social cohesion, and full citizenship. Furthermore, insecurity erodes the social capital of the poor and the social fragmentation results in a decline in social cohesion and an increase in social exclusion. Social exclusion prevents certain groups from equal and effective participation in the social, economic, cultural, and political life. There is a close connection between social exclusion and poverty. Most of the excluded groups – women, children, the elderly, widows, and AIDS sufferers – are cut off from networks that provide access to power and resources, making them vulnerable and increasing their risk of being poor. The vicious cycle of poverty encourages social stigmatization and marginalization from institutions, leading to greater poverty, having a profound negative impact on quality of life (World Bank, 2000).

Poor people in urban areas often report weakened bonds of kinship and community, as well as increased corruption, crime, and lawlessness. The poor also speak about decreasing trust and the inability of families to cooperate with one another. When state institutions cannot provide a secure and predictable environment, groups may rally to provide security for their members in response.

A lack of trust in society's institutions tends to reinforce people's desire to seek security within groups, rather than within society, which in turn exacerbates a cycle of insecurity, social exclusion, and increased levels of conflict and violence. Social fragmentation permeates society, evidenced in domestic violence at the household level, crime and violence in the community, and corruption and civil conflict at the state level.

At the community level, social cohesion is an asset that provides security, regulates behavior, and improves the standard of living of the community as a whole. Social cohesion and civic engagement are preconditions for better schools, safer streets, faster economic growth, more effective government, and healthier lives.

The decline in social cohesion is linked to lack of economic opportunities. Poor people frequently report a general feeling that lawlessness has increased, accompanied by significant upheavals in norms of acceptable behaviour. At the extreme, general lawlessness escalates to crime and violence, which become a vicious cycle, fed by the absence of police and a functioning judicial system. In an environment of declining trust, people note the weakening of community groups.

Box 14.2 Crime and Violence in Jamaica

A group of youths in Jamaica argued that everyone in their community was branded either a criminal, or an accomplice to one, so that they are disrespected by outsiders and the police alike, and cannot secure a job. They perceived this leading to hunger, frustration, and idleness, which encourages gang war and gun violence, with death or imprisonment as the ultimate price. When contract work was available to the local male work force, crime and violence declined, increasing again once the contract ended.

Jamaica, 1997; World Bank, 2000).

Social exclusion and poverty are deeply connected. Poor people remain poor because they are excluded from access to the resources, opportunities, information, and connections the less poor have. In addition, poverty makes it harder for poor people to gain access to the networks and resources they need for survival.

Exclusion perpetuates stress factors such as domestic violence, family violence, violence against women, and child abuse, which maintain the cycle of violence. The large number of street children is also a result of family crisis. These children have ruptured their social and emotional ties with the family. A moral frame of reference that is no longer provided within the family context also accounts for the increase of teenage gangs, delinquents or criminals in neighbourhoods. This behaviour instils anxiety and fear in the population.

Where an absence of cohesion within neighbourhoods has allowed deviant behaviour to take root, inhabitants adopt defence mechanisms such as lynching (mob justice) and the growth of vigilante groups. Furthermore, there exists in numerous neighbourhoods, behaviour that legitimizes anti-social acts such as possession or drug trafficking.

Slum life and human security: The struggle for livelihoods

Rapid urbanization, globalization and population expansions, in combination with the lack of capacity, resources and good governance in many developing countries, have resulted in largely unplanned cities and growing levels of poverty and disparity between rich and poor. Consequently, many cities are faced with growing disadvantaged neighbourhoods characterized by severe social and economic exclusion. In deprived areas, poor health, crime, vandalism, drugs, unsupervised youths, litter, pollution, and lack of services add to the lack of safety and security. There is growing evidence that these problems reinforce one another to create a spiral of decline. In communities where an increasing portion of the population is excluded from society, individuals, especially youths, see themselves condemned to alternative models of success and peer recognition, which sometimes imply illicit and criminal activities, but may also lead to violent behaviour (Vanderschueren and Vezina, 2003).

Living conditions in disadvantaged neighbourhoods make a life free of violence practically impossible, and the inhabitants' lives become a daily struggle. When a neighbourhood is facing a surge in crime, a sufficient level of social cohesion can enable the implementation of very positive local prevention initiatives. Conversely, where social cohesion is absent, crime can lead to the formation of a statute-free zone and neighbourhood protection groups are rapidly transformed into dangerous vigilantes.

Economic hardship and deprivation are often correlated with crime. In particular, both property and violent crimes are related to problems of economic hardship among the young. Unemployment and under-employment are important issues. Employment in the informal sector therefore becomes the solution for many, which translates into lower salaries, dangerous work, and low employment security. In this context, the boundary between what is legal or lawful and what is illegal and illicit becomes unclear.

Evidence also suggests that violence against women increases if the economic situation of households deteriorates as a result of macro-economic changes. For example, in a district in Uzbekistan, over 50 per cent of family conflicts arise due to unemployment. It is not so much poverty and unemployment that cause violence, but rather the costs of poverty and unemployment in the form of stress, loss of self-esteem and frustration that can cause crime, violence and abuse. In many cases, violence is caused by changes in livelihood patterns that put households under pressure to develop new survival strategies that can strain intra-household solidarity and lead to crime and violence.

Poor people suffer more from violence and petty theft than the wealthy. In these circumstances, violence and insecurity issues can be regarded by poor people as more important than housing or income issues. There is no direct correlation between poverty and crime, but it is important to acknowledge that on the one hand, poor people experience a number of risk factors that are closely inter-linked with the causes of crime. On the other hand, victimization levels of the poor are often higher than those of the population in general. In addition, the impact of crime on the poor is far more devastating and dramatic because it often threatens their livelihoods and maintains their cycle of poverty.

Crime and the fear of crime are the major causes of lack of urban investment. Both the individual improvement of standard of living (such as the acquisition of a radio) and the economic investment of entrepreneurs (such as in buildings, or infrastructure/equipment) are hindered by the likelihood of theft and violence. This is compounded by the inability of the poor to protect themselves, and repeat victimization, and heightens the sense of helplessness against crime. The lack of fallback systems (such as insurance, counselling or savings) make the impact of crime, be it emotional or material, much more severe and difficult to overcome than for wealthier residents. Therefore, economic development and investment is a key to crime reduction.

The impact of insecurity on cities and threats to urban dwellers

The feelings of insecurity common in many urban populations (insecurity with respect to employment, health, the future of children, domestic violence, and the risk of impoverishment, and so forth) derive from an impression of abandonment, powerlessness and disbelief in the face of crime and the multiplication of minor acts of delinquency or vandalism. Because of its emotional character, the perception of insecurity blows facts out of proportion, encourages rumour, and can even cause social conflicts. The feeling of generalized fear can create a climate that may threaten the democratic foundation of a community or society.

At the city level, insecurity has resulted in the abandonment of certain neighbourhoods, the development of an *architecture of fear*, the stigmatization of neighbourhoods and defence mechanisms – for example, lynching. More positively, insecurity has also led to the development of self-defence and new social practices.

While all social classes are affected by insecurity, research shows that insecurity affects the poor more intensely because they do not have the means to defend themselves. Urban violence erodes the social capital of the poor and dismantles their organizations, thus preventing social mobility. The increase in the overall costs of insecurity accounts for approximately 6 per cent of gross national product (GNP) in the North and 10 per cent in the South.

A call for action: Towards new and sustainable responses from local authorities

Two general approaches to advance the security of people can be observed. Firstly, by reinforcing security through repression – by increasing police manpower, increasing prison sentences and zero tolerance measures, which include curfews for minors or the lowering of the age of legal responsibility. Secondly, by acting preventively – involving the decentralization of the fight against insecurity through the delegation of police responsibility, either to local authorities or civil associations, or both.

The repressive approach has the advantage of having immediate effects, which can satisfy the short-term demands of public opinion. People are increasingly demanding more police manpower and more repression, thinking that the increase in prison populations constitutes an effective neutralization of serious offenders. It is evident that the cost of repression is much higher than that of prevention, however, and that repression only has a short-term, limited effect.

Addressing safety concerns improves city development

Addressing safety concerns through prevention practices improves city development, bringing together a wide range of community members – residents, businesses, and government agencies – to define problems, identify solutions, carry out plans, and evaluate results.

Programmes aimed at building community responsibility and including communities in crime prevention strategies are critical in improving the city and welfare in the built environment, protecting the public's life and health. There is a general consensus that if the urban environment is planned, designed and managed appropriately, certain types of crime can be reduced.

Crime prevention and tackling the causes of crime are usually more cost-effective than traditional crime control measures, such as incarceration. Economic evaluations of crime prevention programmes show that:

*   Actions encouraging the social development of children, youths and families reduce delinquent behaviour with returns ranging from US$1.06 to US$7.16 for every US$1 spent
*   Actions aimed to reducing opportunities for victimization have produced returns ranging from US$1.83 to US$7.14 for every US$1 spent (US Department of Justice, 2000).

As well as decreasing delinquency, reducing the number of offences, and increasing social integration, prevention generates economic benefits such as: more people employed, economic investment in the community, less social and health care assistance required. In The Netherlands, a simulation model comparing four scenarios to reduce crime by 10 per cent showed that investing in prevention through social development was more effective than the addition of 1000 police officers (US Department of Justice, 2000).

The need for a more comprehensive and holistic approach

The responsibility of crime prevention and control was entrusted for a long time only to the criminal justice system. Several developed countries devoted significant resources to increasing police manpower and the capacity of the prison system and using new technologies. In spite of these major investments, delinquency and violence kept growing in the 1960s and 1970s.

In developing and transition countries, the growing urban crime trend went hand in hand with strong urban growth and the proliferation of unplanned areas. These countries have limited resources to invest in the modernization of their criminal justice system. Underpaid police officers, lack of equipment, overcrowding of courts and prisons and corruption are some of the problems requiring urgent solutions.

One response has been the rapid development of the private security industry. However, this response has often resulted in a climate of fear and social isolation and fragmentation.

Confronted with the increase in crime, it became clear that this traditional approach was not sufficient and sustainable. Local authorities were called upon to develop a more comprehensive solution, and were under pressure to respond to the request of the population to ensure a safer environment and better quality of life in cities. Urban safety has become a key challenge for the sustainable development of local communities.

Over the years, cities have moved towards establishing local safety coalitions/partnerships, bringing together key parties to respond to the increasing crime and violence. Safety is seen as a common good, and everybody's responsibility to promote and develop it.

Taking action on the causes of urban violence and insecurity requires an integrated, comprehensive and coordinated approach. The model relies on the key role of the local authorities to mobilize partners (such as municipal services, police services and the justice system, schools, social and health services, housing agencies, the private sector, non-governmental organizations (NGOs) including women and youth organizations, basic community service organizations, traditional leaders and religious groups) and to develop a local strategy and action plan adapted to the needs of the community. The focus is on local solutions to problems, the joint development of a prevention plan, and the involvement of all stakeholders. Local government should support the action of local communities, developing their capacities and promoting integrated and coordinated partnerships and actions.

Safety: An integral part of city planning

It is crucial that the municipality fully integrates and mainstreams safety in its strategic urban planning processes and delivery of services. An increasing

number of cities are organizing planning exercises with communities to prepare inclusive urban development plans. Safety has been identified as a priority
issue in many city/community consultations, and municipal/city planning is
refocusing on the quality and management of public urban space – for example, street trading and markets, parking and public transport, street lights,
and recreational areas and parks can be reorganized to contribute positively
to urban safety.

It is essential for local authorities to consult community members, develop
a culture of partnership among the various institutional and community actors,
as well as contribute to the social inclusion of at-risk or marginalized groups.

Safety and good urban governance

Good urban governance is a tool to enhance citizenship and give it full meaning. Tackling crime and insecurity are issues of good urban governance and at
the same time benefit greatly from the interaction among urban development
actors. Good governance needs safe cities: where inhabitants are free from
fear. In safe cities interaction between people and the public institutions becomes possible, and creates an enabling environment for better inclusion of
the inhabitants.

Tackling crime and insecurity effectively requires actions that involve
civil society and mobilize institutional partners to share responsibilities and
to encourage new modes of integration and regulation. Addressing urban
crime and violence requires good governance – for example, the development
of solidarity practices, city consultation processes and institutional reform,
which enhance citizenship and inclusion.

The challenge of change: Safety and security furthers human development

Community safety is:

- a consistent priority for citizens;
- usually among the top three priority issues identified in local consultations;
- the general responsibility of all agencies but the specific responsibility of
  none;
- cutting across prevailing structures;
- dependent on joint action.

The preventive approach faces many challenges. First and foremost is the
reluctance of governments to invest in it. Another major obstacle is the absence
of a legal framework to facilitate preventive actions. Cities wishing to use a
preventive approach often do not have the legal or financial capacity to do
so. These challenges can be overcome by mainstreaming community safety
and crime prevention at the local level. Mainstreaming community safety is
recognized as the key to achieving sustainable community safety.

International consensus exists regarding the central role local authorities should play in providing security for its inhabitants. Local government can play an instrumental role in the design and implementation of local crime prevention initiatives and in mobilizing and managing broad-based crime prevention partnerships. Although local governments should ideally take the lead in local crime prevention, they are often not in a position to fully take up this role due to governance, management and capacity problems. Among the most common constraints faced by local governments are:

1   a lack of decentralization (the issue of subsidiarity);
2   limited financial resources;
3   limited human resources;
4   weak management;
5   weak governance;
6   corruption, fraud, bribery and abuse of office;
7   a lack of public confidence and trust in local government;
8   limited delivery of basic, municipal and social services.

Mobilizing the financial resources necessary for the implementation of safety initiatives is a great challenge. There are three important goals on which to focus:

1   provide the basic support required for the development of a safety initiative;
2   provide financial support for implementation;
3   ensure sustainability by linking the safety initiative to programmes addressing poverty and exclusion, good governance development, women, youth, child and family support programmes.

Any advance in urban safety and security and crime prevention initiatives requires coordination, and the commitment of all involved partners is essential for the success of the initiatives. It is important, therefore, to set up the necessary conditions for proper management. Urban safety covers a vast area requiring various competences in the fields of law enforcement, urban planning and management, social development and community action. This can be achieved in a number of ways.

Understanding crime and insecurity

A diagnosis of the local crime situation and safety needs is required to understand crime and insecurity in an area. The local safety diagnosis identifies the main forms of insecurity and their causes as perceived by the inhabitants, allows priorities to be set and a shared approach agreed upon.

The diagnosis identifies the causes related to urban planning and those of a social nature (behaviours, attitudes, living conditions, gender) by analysing the differences in the perception of safety based on gender and age. Problems and their causes must be placed in their social and economic context in order to gain a better understanding of the specific characteristics of each neighbourhood and identify the challenges.

Understanding institutions – state and civil society

A specific institutional diagnosis analyzes the main responses to insecurity problems from government and local institutions, as well as from civil society organizations, and identifies partners implementing various safety initiatives.

Governments at all levels should nurture community-based anti-crime efforts. We must go beyond a response by our criminal justice system to prevent crime in cities, by bringing together those responsible for housing, social services, recreation, schools, policing and justice to tackle the situations that cause crime (European Forum for Urban Safety, Federation of Canadian Municipalities, the United States Conference of Mayors, 1989). The central role played by local authorities is pivotal because:

- Local authorities are the level of government closest to the people and should ensure that their citizens have a say in the day-to-day running of their affairs
- They have a mandate in areas that are considered potential causes of crime and insecurity such as city/town planning, environmental design, housing, and provision of basic services, health and education
- Crime and violence develop at the local level
- Local government can facilitate grass-roots action and community participation.

Creating a local coalition and sustaining and supporting the local partnership

Local authorities have a key role to play in creating local coalitions responsible for implementing joint actions for the reduction and prevention of violence and urban insecurity. The local authority is the public institution that is closest to the people. It is the place of civic participation and commitment, and should ensure a high quality of living for its inhabitants as well as foster development and community participation.

Key partners to join the safety coalition include: the police and justice system, education, health, housing and transport; civil society institutions, NGOs, religious institutions and churches that heavily influence morals and values; business leaders, chambers of commerce and trade associations should also be approached. This partnership requires the sharing of experiences and expertise as well as building an alliance between government institutions, civil society and the private sector.

It is important to involve all members of a community and sometimes it may also be important to reform the institutions and attitudes that may be at the root of delinquency. For example, an inefficient police force fosters delinquency, domestic violence offenders contribute to the continuation of violence against women and children, unsafe schools encourage crime and an inadequate justice system leads to impunity, indirectly encouraging deviant behaviours.

Municipalities engaging in urban safety initiatives have two specific challenges: (1) to coordinate the process and implementation; (2) to ensure the sustainability and institutionalize the cooperation.

Safety should be a municipal interdepartmental priority. All the programmes and services offered by the municipality should be considered from their impact on safety at the local level. For example, urban renewal projects are opportunities to apply the concepts of safety planning, social development targeting groups at risk, community empowerment and good governance.

Institutions such as the police and justice system may support the action of cities in the field of safety and prevention by decentralizing and encouraging local and community policing, the establishment of local district courts, alternative sentencing to incarceration and measures for the reintegration of young offenders.

Civil society may contribute to the sustainability by developing a culture of partnership and participating in the joint efforts on the local level.

Developing a strategy for action and coordinating initiatives

The local crime prevention strategy is the product of the safety diagnosis. The strategy deals with the various causes and manifestations of violence and insecurity in an integrated and coordinated manner. Short- and long-term actions should be identified. The priority concerns in the community should be taken into account, promoting partnership and coordination of implementation. Urban safety and crime prevention strategies have mainly been built along four components:

1 *More efficient enforcement of the law and municipal regulations* – police establishing a closer relationship with the population and decentralizing police operations, promoting alternative sentencing and local justice mechanisms and conflict resolution by traditional leaders

2 *Urban planning and municipal management* – integrating and mainstreaming safety planning principles into the development of the city

3 *Social development* – targeting groups at risk, contributing to the reintegration of young delinquents, preventing violence against women and children and promoting the social and economic integration of youth as a non-violent solution to conflicts. This includes victim assistance, initiatives focusing on street children and youths confronted with drug and alcohol problems, providing support to single-parent families and young mothers, as well as support for continuing school, promoting employment training and integration initiatives in cooperation with relevant economic organizations

4 *Promoting good governance, citizenship development, citizen participation and renewal of values* – these actions promote community empowerment and specifically the involvement of women and youths.

Protecting and empowering groups at risk – addressing the security concerns of disadvantaged communities

Crime affects different groups in different ways, both as potential victims and potential offenders. Urban insecurity and crime affect youth and women in particular. The crucial role for local authorities in preventing violence against women should involve:

1 Integrating a gender-based approach in policies and programmes (sensitization campaigns, services and shelters and improving the city's physical environment in order to make it safer)
2 Contributing to a better understanding of gender-based violence (GBV) and the development of adequate tools: collection of disaggregated data, qualitative surveys on violence against women to fill the information gaps, women's safety audits and exploratory walks
3 Promoting partnerships between all stakeholders and promoting consultation and participation of women in project activities
4 Promoting the documentation and exchange of practices and lessons learned.

There is now sufficient evidence that the conditions under which children and young people grow up are crucial for their mental and physical health, and emotional, social and intellectual development (Shaw, 2001). The quality of early childhood care and conditions, and parental and family relationships, are especially important in shaping their lives. In adolescence, access to schools, to good role models, leisure and recreational facilities, the availability of employment opportunities, and health care, are all important.

There are common factors that place children and young people *at risk* of becoming involved in crime and of being victimized. These risk factors vary with gender. The common *protective* factors that strengthen children and young people's resilience in the face of difficult living conditions include good parenting, a stable and supportive home, a healthy and supportive environment, and good schooling (Hawkins et al, 2000; Shaw and Tschiwula, 2002).

Severe urban overcrowding and decay, increasing poverty and unemployment, family and community breakdown, ongoing wars, disease, child and youth exploitation, and transnational trafficking and crime are multiplying the severity and range of risks to which children and young people in cities are exposed.

The cumulative impact of these cross-cutting problems in cities, and on the growing numbers of youth affected by them, is enormous. The breakdown of social controls in the family, school, and neighbourhood has contributed to increased crime and insecurity in urban areas. The development of ghettos and areas of lawlessness controlled by local gangs, and increasing numbers of street children, have resulted in an increasing resort to deterrent and tough criminal justice responses, as well as private security and vigilantism.

Each government needs to develop a *policy in relation to all youth* that addresses:

- social inclusion and participation that empowers youth;
- the re-insertion of groups of youth at risk;
- the development and implementation of a comprehensive national youth policy;
- full and representative youth participation, including youth at risk;
- the creation of family support mechanisms for the reintegration of youth at risk;
- the education and training of youth at risk;
- the development of comprehensive job-training and job-creation programmes for youth;
- specialized police officers to work with at-risk youth in partnership with local services;
- youth courts;
- diversion programmes, such as mentoring, education and job training, as alternatives to custodial sentences.

Conclusion: Institutionalization and sustainability

Institutionalization is a long-term process that requires influential supporters; the success and sustainability of local crime prevention initiatives is very much determined by the quality of governance and service delivery by local government. Institutionalization means a *mainstreaming* of structures and attitudes so that safety and crime prevention are integrated into municipal (and public) policy making, planning, design, and working and implementation modalities as inter-sectoral priority concerns that require coordinated efforts. It means *reform*, so that policies, laws, regulations supporting community safety and crime prevention, inter-agency collaboration and participatory action for local crime prevention are developed, formally adopted and implemented.

People only become supporters of the cause once they grasp the issue. Sustainability implies an *attitudinal shift*, in order that safety and crime prevention are understood and adapted to maximize a positive impact on community safety. It requires a *strengthening of local* governance, through the adoption of policies, laws, regulations in support of local government empowerment, improvement of local governance, municipal service delivery. And it demands *public and political support*, an expansion in awareness, knowledge and capacity for crime prevention and the improvement and maintenance of community safety so as to effectively address the issues, identify lessons learned, replicate successes and sustain efforts and investments in the long run. The media and civil society are instrumental in this sense.

Finally, urban safety is a central quality-of-life issue and an integral component of good governance. Safety is a daily need (UN Habitat, 2003). Whatever the reality, the fear of crime has changed the nature of cities, transforming an urban community into one characterized by enforced segregation through gated communities and walled enclaves, stigmatization and exclusion.

Notes

1   Measured by the International Crime Victim Survey (ICVS) of the United Nations (1997).

References

European Forum for Urban Safety, Federation of Canadian Municipalities, the United States Conference of Mayors (1989) 'Agenda for Safer Cities', Final Declaration of the European and North American Conference on Urban Safety and Crime Prevention, October, Montreal

Hawkins, J. D., Herrenhohl, T. I., Farrington, D. P., Brewer, D., Catalano, R. F., Harachi, T., and Cothera, L. (2000) 'Predictors of youth violence', *Juvenile Justice Bulletin*, Office of Juvenile Justice and Delinquency Prevention, Washington DC, pp1–11

Shaw, M. (2001) *Investing in Youth: International Approaches to Preventing Crime and Victimization*, International Centre for the Prevention of Crime, Montreal

Shaw, M. and Tschiwula, L. (2002) 'Developing citizenship among urban youth in conflict with the law', *Environment and Urbanization*, issue 14, vol 2, October, pp59–70

UN Habitat (2002) 'Crime in Nairobi, results of a city-wide victim survey', *Safer Cities series* no 2, p23, www.unhabitat.org

UN Habitat (2003) *Safer Cities: A Collective Challenge for Sustainable Human Settlement*, Background Paper prepared for the International Conference on Sustainable Safety, Durban, South Africa, November, www.unhabitat.org

US Department of Justice (2000), *Investing Wisely in Crime Prevention – International Experiences*, International Centre for the Prevention of Crime, Montreal

Vandershueren, F. and Vezina, C. (2003) 'Reviewing safer cities: Safer cities concept, approach and achievements to date', Background Paper presented at the Durban International Conference, 'Sustainable Safety: Municipalities at the Crossroads', www.unhabitat.org/programmes/saftercities/plenary.asp

WHO (2004) *Global Campaign for Violence Prevention*, World Health Organization, Geneva

World Bank (2000) *Voices of the Poor – Can Anyone Hear Us?*, World Bank, Deepa Narayan, March

Part 3
Global Governance

15

America as Empire: Global Leader or Rogue Power?[1]

Jim Garrison

Introduction

People used to think of the United States (US) as a global leader. Now a majority of the world thinks of it as a rogue power. Why? The answer to this question has, to a large degree, to do with what the US has become. The re-election of George W. Bush in November 2004 made it indelibly clear to the international community that the US is no longer what it was. Indeed, under Bush, the US has become what it was founded not to be: established as a haven for those fleeing the abuse of power, it has attained and now wields nearly absolute power. It has become an empire. This is meant as a statement of fact, not a judgment of national character. It is a way of understanding America, not an indictment against the American people. Indeed, by opening up the possibility of viewing the US as an empire, one opens up a far larger frame of reference to understand America's history, its role in the world, and its future responsibilities. It certainly helps in understanding what is going on in Iraq.

What is an empire?

Historian Michael Doyle provides a succinct, behaviouristic definition of empire: 'effective control, whether formal or informal, of a subordinated society by an imperial society' (Doyle, 1986). Empires are thus relationships of influence and control by one state over a group of lesser states. This can take a variety of forms, ranging from territorial annexation and direct political rule, to economic domination and diplomatic oversight. Empires are as old as history itself and characterize the earliest stages of human development. For reasons deeply buried in the human psyche and soul, human beings have always competed against one another, and the victors have established dominion over the vanquished and exploited that relationship to their own benefit. Almost every people on earth has at some point expanded and conquered, or contracted and been conquered, often many times over and in a variety of combinations.

Of all governing institutions, empire is the most complex and extensive in scope. Empire stands at the apex of the social, economic and political pyramid, integrating all the people, nations and institutions within it into a unified order. An empire well run is the greatest accolade a nation can receive. An empire squandered is the most damning legacy it can leave behind.

From the fall of the Berlin Wall to the fall of the Twin Towers

Policy analyst Michael Ignatieff states in his article 'American Empire' in the *New York Times Sunday Magazine* that the US 'is the only nation that polices the world through five global military commands: maintains more than a million men and women at arms on four continents; deploys carrier battle groups on watch in every ocean; guarantees the survival of countries from Israel to South Korea; drives the wheels of global trade and commerce; and fills the hearts and minds of an entire planet with its dreams and desires' (Ignatieff, 2003).

Surprisingly, the inordinate and unique power of the US was not immediately recognized when the Berlin Wall came down in 1989 and the Soviet Union disintegrated. While a few observers recognized that America had entered what columnist Charles Krauthammer called a 'unipolar moment', most commentators predicted that the demise of the Soviet Union and the end of the Cold War would lead to a return to the age-old balance of power.

Such a view was completely understandable. The last 1,500 years of European history have been essentially multipolar, with the major European powers incessantly competing with one another but without any single power ever gaining undue advantage, whether during the medieval era of city states or the modern era of nation states. Even Britain at its prime during the 19th century was constrained by France, Russia, Spain and Germany. During the reign of Queen Victoria from 1837 to 1901, which marked the apex of British imperial power, Britain had to fight 72 separate military campaigns to keep its rivals at bay and its colonial holdings intact. The very notion of *realpolitik* is predicated upon the assumption of a balance of power between major states.

That the US has broken out of this multipolar framework to attain unipolar global dominance is an extraordinary achievement in the annals of history, not attained by any power since the time of Rome, 2000 years ago. Because the world had become so used to thinking in multilateral and multipolar terms, it took some time for the novelty of the historical situation to sink in.

Talk of American weakness dominated the 1992 US presidential elections, with the ultimate victor, Bill Clinton, focusing on fixing the ailing American economy, while his rival for the Democratic nomination, Paul Tsongas, repeatedly declared, 'The Cold War is over and Japan won'. Margaret Thatcher expressed the commonly held view that the world would evolve into three regional groups: one based on the dollar, one on the mark, one on the yen. Henry Kissinger solemnly predicted the emergence of a multipolar world. Asians, along with some American Asian enthusiasts such as James Fallows, spoke exuberantly of the rise of the 'Pacific century'.

The Clinton administration (1993–2001) was essentially a transitional period when the US was emerging as what French Foreign Minister Hubert Vedrine called a 'hyperpower', but was still essentially multilateralist and collaborative in its mentality and behaviour. Clinton's main focus was the integration of the global economy under American hegemony, but he seldom used the power the US had at its disposal, seeking rather to work collegially with American allies on issues of common concern. While believing that the US was the 'indispensable power', as then-Secretary of State Madeleine Albright was fond of putting it, Clinton exercised this indispensability with discretion. He initiated limited military actions against Iraq and the Sudan and led the European coalition in Kosovo, but by and large he remained committed to multilateralism and to upholding the international treaties negotiated by his predecessors. These included the Comprehensive Test Ban Treaty and the Antiballistic Missile Treaty, signed by Presidents Kennedy and Nixon, to limit America's nuclear capabilities. Clinton also negotiated and signed the Kyoto Protocol on Global Warming that would constrain the emission of hydroflurocarbons into the atmosphere. All these framed US strategic interests in the context of collective security considerations.

In general, the 1990s were marked by a strong commitment to international law, working within the context of the UN system, and upholding pre-existing treaty obligations. The US was certainly the senior partner in all deliberations, but the emphasis by Americans and the larger world community was on the importance of partnership, as much as on American seniority.

Then came the events of 11 September 2001. The response by the new Bush administration dramatically altered this equilibrium by heightening asymmetries already there but unobserved because unexercised. Right at the point that it was emerging as the undisputed superpower, the US was attacked unexpectedly and with devastating impact by non-state actors virtually invisible to the American intelligence apparatus. In one of the strangest syn-chronicities of modern history, a nation that thought itself invulnerable was made, without warning, completely vulnerable. Its response was to strike out with an overwhelming application of military power in Afghanistan and Iraq, and make it clear to friend and foe alike that there is one undisputed military power in the world: the United States of America.

Since 9/11, the US has emphasized national security concerns and pre-emptive military responses in a war on terrorism that President Bush has declared as the highest priority of American domestic and foreign policy. Multilateralism, in which the coalition defines the mission, has been replaced by unilateralism, in which the mission defines the coalition. Deterrence, where there is an assumed balance of power, has been superseded by preemptive strikes, whereby the US hits first against potential adversaries.

The invasion of Iraq

The events of 9/11 reframed global affairs within the context of national security and the war on terrorism. The invasion of Iraq reframed global affairs yet again within the reality of overwhelming American military might. What is extraordinary is that the US exercised its strength and global reach by seizing the most strategic area in the Middle East.

US military forces now occupy the area along the Tigris-Euphrates river basin and are building four 'enduring' bases to consolidate their power. This is where the Neolithic revolution and the domestication of plants and animals began 10,000 years ago. This is where the first human civilization at Sumer, in the environs of present-day Baghdad, developed 6000 years ago, and where the first empire under Sargon the Great, also around Baghdad, held sway 5000 years ago. This is where Abraham was born. It is where, closely to the west, Judaism and Christianity had their origins, with Islam originating just to the south. Zoroastrianism and Baha'i arose to the east. The Tigris-Euphrates river basin is the cradle of Arab civilization, and the site of the early Muslim Abbassid dynasty. The armies of Alexander the Great marched here, as did the Roman legions and the hordes of Genghis Khan.

There is no place in the entire world more steeped in history, more complex in its politics, more charged in its religious fervor than the Tigris-Euphrates river basin. For the US to take control of this region at America's moment of vulnerability and power is utterly profound. America reacted to a blow and demonstrated world dominion by seizing the most sacred and fought-over soil in the history of the world.

What disturbed the world most about the US-led invasion of Iraq was the manner in which it was done. There was none of the finesse with which President Bush Sr. mobilized an entire international coalition and utilized the resources and legitimacy of the UN during Operation Desert Storm in 1991. George W. Bush went into Iraq belligerently, threatening and then marginalizing the UN, and invading essentially alone with the British against pervasive international public opposition and in violation of international law.

The vindictive and highly militarized response of President Bush to 9/11 provided the world with an experience of America that was aggressive, ruthless, cynical and dogmatic. Prior to 9/11, Clinton focused his entire administration on the economy: balancing the budget, eliminating the deficit, forging trade agreements and presiding over robust economic growth. The US economy was better tended during his watch than perhaps at any time in modern American history. Americans were generally positive about the future and content with the multilateral framework of international relations whereby the US operated.

In the aftermath of 9/11, however, America experienced a fundamental reversal of emotions and perceptions. Almost overnight, the 'Jacksonian' impulse gripped the president, and under his leadership, the American public. What had been a world-centric orientation was radically replaced by nation-centric tribalism. Multilateralism was replaced by unilateralism, global diplomacy by military force, and congeniality with confrontation.

While the starkness of this transformation startled the world, it was actually a very natural response. Under the impact of trauma, psychologists have long observed that people and groups can experience a radical reversal of values. There is something about trauma, especially among large groups of people, that activates our altruistic as well as our aggressive impulses. If one considers the magnitude of the trauma inflicted on the American psyche by the attack of 9/11, coupled with the fact that it was in essence a military attack against the US, it is both normal and predictable that the initial response was to come together behind a heightened sense of community, as well as to respond with belligerence.

The US proceeded to break out of the norms of international law and procedures, and conduct its own retribution. President Bush often referred to himself as the sheriff heading up a posse. At some level, it felt good for Americans to brush the UN aside and go into the Arab world and 'kick ass'. In this sense, Saddam Hussein was the occasion, not the reason for the invasion of Iraq. This point was noted by Thomas Friedman in his column in the *New York Times*. He observed that the attack on 11 September was the 'real reason' the US invaded. As Friedman put it, removing the Taliban from Afghanistan was not enough. America needed to go into the Arab world and clobber somebody else, and Saddam was it. 'Smashing Saudi Arabia or Syria would have been fine. But we hit Saddam for one simple reason: because we could, and because he deserved it, and because he was right in the heart of that world' (Friedman, 2003). All other reasons were of secondary importance, including the issue of weapons of mass destruction and the alleged link between Iraq and Al-Qaeda.

What came together in the aftermath of 9/11 was the psycho-emotional need for vengeance with the geostrategic opportunity to demonstrate to the world the overwhelming military might of the US. The effects of this attitude and this action reverberated around the world. At one level, there was mimicry. The Russians renewed their efforts to crush Chechnya, the Indonesians invaded Acheh, Israel increased military pressure on the Palestinians, and India mobilized against Pakistan, all of them citing the US war on terrorism as a legitimizing model for their own behaviour. At another level, world public opinion reacted sharply to the aggressiveness of the Bush administration and dramatically questioned the integrity of America's leadership. The invasion of Iraq in defiance of overwhelming opposition indicated to many that America the global leader had become America the rogue imperium. Since the war, anti-American sentiment continues to rise virtually all over the world, including in Europe, traditionally America's strongest ally.

Questions of empire

At the core of the current dialectic between America and the world is the issue of where the centre of gravity should be for international affairs: the United States or the United Nations. This presents the US and the world with a fundamental choice: should the world be ruled by an empire or by the community of nations?

At the end of World War II, the US established the UN out of self-interest. Today, the US disregards the UN out of a very different notion of self-interest. The US founded the UN to help prevent war among the nations. The US now considers the UN to be weak, corrupt, inefficient and bureaucratic, unable to exert leadership in critical issues pertaining to international security and rogue states. The US has thus marginalized the UN and has assumed the role of arbiter and enforcer in the international security domain.

At the same time, the UN represents to most people, including most Americans, the desire for a community of nations, governed by the sanctity of international law and cooperating through dialogue and consensus. Whatever its flaws, it is the carrier of the deep human aspiration for peace. US disparagement of the UN and its willingness to act alone in spite of the UN are of deep concern to the international public.

But the challenge that now confronts the UN and the larger world community is the reality that the US is no longer a nation among nations. It is an empire among nations, an absolutely key concept in understanding why America is acting the way it is and why the international community is so concerned. America has emerged as an unchallenged superpower, controlling countries and institutions all around the world. As such, it can and will assume certain imperial prerogatives, particularly in the immediate aftermath of 9/11 and because there is now no countervailing power to challenge it.

Both Americans and the world must understand this new reality, whatever the desire of the international community for consensus through the UN or for everyone to work together according to the legalities of international law. Empires invariably reserve the right to act in their own interests, precisely because, from an imperial point of view, might makes right. In assessing American actions, the world must remember that military power is the beginning and the end of empire and that empires seek to weaken international law and multilateral institutions in order to maximize manoeuverability and maintain dominion. The master strategy of empire is to divide and conquer.

Part of the confusion and resentment expressed about the US is due to the fact that many in the secular world were lulled into believing, with Francis Fukyama, that when the Cold War ended we had somehow reached the 'end of history', and empires and other nasty things would no longer occur. But with the highly militarized foreign policy formation of the Bush administration, to say nothing about the general crisis of the world situation, we have been shocked to discover that here history is again, and it has been our lack of preparedness for this that constitutes a major part of our predicament.

This is another reason why the US should be considered an empire: it is a continuation of history as we have known it. Through its own sheer force and through mediating institutions such as the World Bank and International Monetary Fund (IMF), along with numerous other bilateral and multilateral institutions, the US now controls more nations in more ways than any nation in history.

Paradoxically, while the American empire is a continuation of history, history itself is moving beyond empire. It is actually in the penultimate stage of development before full global integration. This is the key concept in understanding why the US needs to consider itself as a *transitional empire*. It will be the *final empire* by choice or as victim. What history demands, even empires must address, or they are consumed.

The world is rapidly becoming an integrated system under the impact of economic globalization and the technology of instantaneous communication. In an integrating world, leadership must change from domination to stewardship. Cultural nuances and social disparities matter far more than military might, and issues of ethnicity and religion go far deeper than the power of the state. Governance cannot be exercised successfully simply by the application of precision warfare. Brute force does not make friends and cannot change a person's mind.

There is increasingly a *civilizational* context for governance that needs to be taken into account. The international community requires leadership that is sensitive to societal and cultural differences as well as to political and economic conditions. It needs leadership that will foster the integrating institutions necessary to bring these complex factors together for the equitable management of the global system. Integrating diversity can only be achieved through patience and compromise. It requires honouring all the voices and building consensus within the context of mutual respect and international norms and procedures. Leadership in this context is successful more through influence than by coercion, more through empowerment of others than by exerting power over others.

This interplay between American power – unsurpassed and currently militarily oriented and unilaterally directed – and the needs of an integrating world – highly diverse, culturally conditioned, and requiring a spirit of stewardship in order to govern effectively – is the framework within which the American empire will play out its unique and special destiny during the 21st century. Both America and the world, for better or for worse, will be shaped by how this is done.

The final empire

Leadership during periods of historical turbulence and change is supremely challenging. It must enable people to abandon what they hold as secure, but which is actually insufficient, and embrace what seems insecure but is potentially sufficient. This can only be done through a vision of the future that instills hope in human possibility. Above all, the US must articulate a vision of greatness for the 21st century. Simply fighting terrorism is not enough. It is the product of fear, not leadership, and thus serves merely an occasion to exercise military power abroad and erode democracy at home. What is needed is a combination of vision and practical politics that can lift the world again, and in so doing, create a new world order. This is the real challenge ahead. What must be seized is the historical moment of a world in transition from a disjointed amalgamation of nation states to an integrated global system. What must be confronted are challenges that are global in scope that can only be addressed through a new sense of community and democracy.

The re-election of George Bush does not bode well for the relationship between the US and the world community, for President Bush is single-handedly turning what was *pax Americana*, the American peace, into *pox Americana*, the American plague. The almost universal antipathy against him during his first administration, now that the majority of the American electorate has cast its lot with him, will lead to rampant anti-Americanism. And justly so. This means that the major question of the 21st century will not be the nature of American leadership in a world that supports that leadership, which largely characterized the 20th century, but how the international community will organize itself to counter an empire that has forsaken its founding vision for the sake of the repressive and rapacious exercise of power.

What the US needs is the next Wilson, the next Roosevelt, the next Truman. In the spirit of these leaders, the US should now provide global leadership. It must do so through the three pillars of its greatness: economic power, democratic idealism, and military strength. All three, taken together, brought it to world supremacy. All three, taken separately, must now be reworked and applied in new ways, appropriate to an integrating world.

The challenge ahead: Establishing effective global governance

Looking to the future, the US must lead in providing for the global security of the international community. This includes taking seriously the challenges presented by failed or failing states and the need to solve international threats by creating new cooperative structures. As it exercises its dominion, the US must recognize that there is in fact another superpower: world public opinion, which it must respect and deal with creatively. The US must work at the global level to ensure that private gain is regulated within the context of the common good. It must support network democracy and global issue networks as the key ingredients to establishing democracy at a global level. And, above all, the US must ensure that an effective global governance regime is established before, not after, the global catastrophe that will inevitably ensue if we do not solve the problems at hand.

Today, what seems impossible is, in fact, imperative. The current crises are overwhelming, but they must be solved. The system of sovereign nation states seems eternal but must be transformed. The world is crippled by ineffective government, but it can be delivered by network governance. The world community is critical of the US, but it requires American leadership.

If the US would affirm rather than oppose these kinds of measures, it would find the better part of the world ready to begin collaborating, just as Wilson and Roosevelt did. The world is weary of conflict. It is ready for inspirational leadership and audacious action. The international community is ready to eliminate HIV/AIDS, it is ready to take action on global warming, and it is ready to eliminate poverty. People are yearning for somebody from somewhere to bring about a more equitable and effective management of the global system. For America to simply chase the shadows of terrorists and consolidate military hegemony in the face of the totality of our global challenges is to completely miss the point of world affairs in this first decade of the new millennium.

The opportunity before America is this: the League of Nations was established in the ashes of World War I, the United Nations in the ashes of World War II. The challenge now is for the US to build on these achievements and lead in the building of the next iteration of global governance. Can the US be so inspirational in its leadership of the world that is prevents the kind of catastrophe that produced the other two advances in global governance? Can it prevent the repetition of the most ancient pattern in human history: that real change never actually comes until *after* a crisis? Can the human community break out of this chain of cause and effect?

The next catastrophe, whenever and wherever it arises, will, again, be global. World War I and World War II were both global conflagrations. They affected the whole world. This could happen again, only the next time with more virulence and destructive effect. It is up to the people of the earth to think consciously for the first time in our history, to engage collectively in the pursuit of light Bacon hoped for, and to become what more recently the theologian Pierre Teilhard de Chardin and the physicist Niels Bohr called '*Homo noeticus*': a new species of humanity that can use its intuition to lead its intelligence, with a heart filled with commitment to light.

American leadership at this time in history is crucial, provided that the US combines its light with its power in such a way that the integrating institutions and mechanisms needed for effective management of the global system are infused with the same kind of radical democracy with which America itself was founded. A global system of governance, based on inclusive democratic principles, would make impossible the emergence of any other nation state with imperial ambitions, for the planet will have united as a single matrix of collaborative, self-regulating connections. America's great contribution to history, as the first global democratic empire, could be to make obsolete the necessity for empire.

The challenge to America is whether it can rise to the occasion and provide the kind of global leadership that will seize the opportunities buried in our crises. Midwifing a democratic global system, before going through a global cataclysm, will not be an easy task. If it succeeds, America will gain the accolade of greatness. If it fails, America will be consigned the opprobrium of tragedy.

How America exercises its strength on the global stage during the next several decades will shape the drama of the 21st century and the legacy that the US will leave in the annals of history. America will be the first empire graced with the consciousness to choose its imperial pathway. Given what is at stake for its own people and for the whole world, may it make its choices guided by the wisdom of its past and with the intention of exercising its power in service of the light by which it was founded. What is at stake is nothing less than the foundations of the first planetary civilization.

Notes

1   Compiled with extracts from *America as Empire: Global Leader or Rogue Power?* by Jim Garrison. Reprinted with permission of the publisher. Copyright © 2004, Berrett-Koehler Publishers, Inc, San Francisco, CA. All rights reserved. www.bkconnection.com

References

Doyle, M. (1986) *Empires*, Cornell University Press, Ithaca, New York, p4

Friedman, T. (2003) *The New York Times*, New York, 4 June, op-ed page

Ignatieff, M. (2003) 'American empire', *New York Times Sunday Magazine, New York Times*, New York, 1 May, p22

16

The Emergence and Role of Regional Governance

Sabin Intxaurraga

We consider regional governments, from the point of view of proximity, efficiency and spatial dimension, to be strategically located as a necessary and crucial sphere of government for the development of policy for and implementation of sustainable development. By reason of scale, we are in many circumstances best placed to address specific sustainability issues and in other circumstances we are essential partners in solidarity with other spheres of government and civil society for integrated and co-coordinated policy and implementation. In co-operative relationships with other spheres of government, the principle of subsidiary should be applied.

nrg4SD, 2002

Introduction

One of the great successes of the Johannesburg World Summit on Sustainable Development (WSSD) was the creation of the Network of Regional Governments for Sustainable Development (nrg4SD) launched in Gauteng Province, South Africa, in August 2002. Although there had been a network for local government at the global level active on sustainable development issues since the United Nations Conference on Environment and Development (UNCED) held in Rio in 1992, none existed for regional government. The Gauteng Declaration, the founding document of the nrg4SD, was our attempt as regional governments in a globalized world to take up our responsibility and play a key role in delivering the Rio, Johannesburg and Millennium Development Goals (MDGs).

Of particular interest to me as a minister for the environment in a regional government fully committed to sustainable development – at a local Basque level and at the global level through the nrg4SD – is the role of regional governments in favour of peace and sustainable development and, in particular, their important work in the fight against climate change, which I believe to be the greatest threat to a sustainable planet.

Regional governments facing the pressures of globalization play a critical role for people between national and local levels in protecting and strengthening distinctiveness and diversity, so that peoples' values, cultures, identities and traditions are respected and honoured. Regional governments can and do play a role in ensuring the benefits of globalization can be brought to all parts of the globe and ensuring that they can be made democratically accountable.

The nrg4SD plans to play an increasing role over the next 10 years in delivering sustainable development and strengthening democracy. It can work to help the intergovernmental system give the right policy drivers for regional government. As important, it can act as one of the most appropriate levels of government to enable capacity building, technology transfer and additional funding. It was no coincidence that we held our first global Congress on North Sumatra in Indonesia in March 2005: the summit provided an excellent occasion to hear from the regions affected by the Indian Ocean tsunami, from other regional governments, from academia, business and other stakeholders, on the issue of global partnership on rehabilitation and reconstruction of post-disaster settlements, as well as on sustainable development as a whole (nrg4SD, 2005). We see ourselves as a network that puts international cooperation at the heart of our sustainable development, an emphasis at the heart of the Gauteng Declaration:

> *Democracy, the rule of law, the establishment of peace and security, the recognition of human rights and freedoms, the opportunity for people to participate in decisions that affect them, the eradication of poverty and the promotion of sustainable consumption and production are all essential for the full achievement of sustainable development. They are themselves strengthened by the active promotion of sustainable development. In giving our full commitment to sustainable development for our societies we commit ourselves at the regional government sphere to play our part in striving for a world that is free from conflict, in which democracy and respect for human rights are supported everywhere, and whose people are free from want and all forms of unjust discrimination.*

> *nrg4SD, 2002*

There is no question that 2005 will play a critical role in creating the landscape that will determine the actions of stakeholders, governments (at all levels) and intergovernmental bodies for the foreseeable future. United Nations (UN) Secretary-General Kofi Annan's March 2005 Report, 'In Larger Freedom', maps out the challenges ahead and makes explicit the links between security, democracy and sustainable development (UN, 2005). The report recognizes the need for country strategies that draw together poverty reduction and sustainable development strategies into one. I agree with the Secretary-General that the implementation of the MDGs needs a strategic framework for all governments at all levels. I also believe that this applies strongly in our own regional spheres. In fact, I would argue that a sustainable development strategy is, in effect, one that addresses poverty and other aspects of the MDGs and so should be the framework by which all work is done at all levels. The September 2005 Millennium Review Summit, which will discuss the recommendations put forward by Kofi Annan, has a huge agenda to address. Its success will be measured on the ability of member states to endorse these recommendations and make subsequent and tangible progress on the implementation of their global agreements.

Regional governments need sustainable development strategies as central frameworks for linking all their other strategies, ensuring that each is sustainable and that they are mutually supportive of each other. An effective regional sustainable development strategy should also recognize the importance of those features that distinguish the identities of regions as well as those features that help bind the broader society together.

Although the regional reality can be very different from one continent to another, and even within the same continent, it is a fact that in many parts of the world regional governments have considerable powers in all areas related to sustainable development – economic, social and environmental – to the extent that they play a critical role in utilizing the political instruments at hand to contribute to the economic development of their respective countries. They are also critical actors in creating more cohesive and balanced societies, from a perspective that respects the environment and the need for social cohesion and economic development. I would add that many people see themselves more through the regional lens than the national. Reflecting this outlook, there has been a growing move to devolve power over the last 20 years from central government to regional and local government. Now, in many cases, regional governments have executive responsibilities in matters concerned with agriculture, industry, energy, transport, consumption, education, health, housing, social welfare, the environment, and so on. In Belgium for instance, the government has gone as far as to abolish the central environment ministry and devolve all responsibilities to the regions.

What role for regional governments?

The policy work undertaken by the nrg4SD since its inception in 2002 demonstrates the wide range of areas in which regional governments can have an important impact. We have produced policy documents on water, sustainable tourism, sustainable energy and renewables, and on developing the added value of regional action for international cooperation. (nrg4SD, 2004)

One aspect of the Report of the Secretary-General's High Level Panel on Threats, Challenges and Change I would briefly like to touch on – coming as I do from a region that has a very strong identity of language, tradition and culture – is that of combating terrorism. As I mentioned, regional governments can play a vital role in stabilizing democracy and in promoting the rights of all. The report rightly identifies the need for 'discussion working to reverse the causes or facilitators of terrorism, including through promoting social and political rights, the rule of law and democratic reform; working to end occupations and addressing major political grievances' (UN, 2004).

Terrorism finds a breeding ground in those who are poor and marginalized in society. The report quotes from the excellent work of Macartan Humphries of Columbia University, who emphasizes the link between poverty and civil war, which are reduced by half when people have at least US$1 a day to live on. The MDG target of halving those on less than US$1 a day is something that must be reached and surpassed (UN, 2000). The Basque Government is committed to this goal and we give 0.7 per cent of our operating budget for development aid. I am not aware of any other regional government replicating our approach, but I strongly believe this should be investigated as a potential new financial mechanism. In many cases, this will require national agreement or regional referendums to enable regional governments to change their constitutions.

Equally important is the recognition of social and political rights. Spain, like many countries, is new to democracy, and the threat of terrorism must not be used as an opportunity to erode those rights or create an atmosphere where dialogue within a state becomes impossible. In our most recent election, the electorate sent a clear message to the politicians that they expect us to work together to find a solution to our issue of Basque identity.

Regional governments and the fight against climate change

To focus my discussion on the role of regional governments, I want to use the key issue of climate change and, by extension, comment on the Basque Strategy for Sustainable Development.

Regional governments have a significant and under-recognized role to play in tackling climate change. In my view, it is fundamental that having powers and responsibilities for the environment as regional governments – or auto-nomous communities, nations without state, Länder, federated states, regions or provinces, as referred to elsewhere in the world – we come down firmly in favour of a policy against climate change based firmly on protecting all human-ity, building sustainable, democratic and secure communities, and developing strategies to implement that policy urgently.

Regional governments have a critical role to play in delivering the targets of the Kyoto Protocol – or as some non-governmental organizations (NGOs) are now calling for, 'Kyoto plus'. Perhaps one of the most important places where regional government could play the leadership role is in the United States (US). If President Bush or the US Congress is unable to act on climate change, then I believe that the US states will.

Already they are showing leadership in this area. In 2001, the New England Governors and Eastern Canadian Premiers (NEG/ECP) produced an historic

Climate Change Action Plan, calling for reduction of the greenhouse gas emissions that cause global warming. The governors of every state in New England agreed to develop a plan with specific policies to reduce greenhouse gas emissions. The governors' short-term goal is to reduce greenhouse gas emissions to 1990 levels by 2010 (NEG/ECP, 2001). Likewise, California has been instrumental in defying the Bush administration's official policy on Kyoto, its republican governor adopting an Action Plan for the Environment described by former Vice President Al Gore as 'an extremely important national precedent providing the kind of leadership that the federal government in Washington has, for the time being, abdicated' (Bush Greenwatch, 2005; Join Arnold, 2003). As these examples suggest, to deliver Kyoto, the American people don't need Congress: they can do it themselves through their regional governments.

The Basque environmental strategy for sustainable development

Based on the premise that regional governments are crucial to the strategic implementation of sustainable development, thanks to their relative scale and responsibilities, the Gauteng Declaration committed all members of the nrg4SD to prepare sustainable development strategies for their regions. The Basque Environmental Strategy for Sustainable Development sets out five goals and five conditions to achieve a better quality of life and comply with commitments taken at international forums: Kyoto, Europe and within the Spanish state.

The fifth goal of our strategy in fact proposes curtailing the negative influence of climate change in the Basque Country with two concrete actions: limiting the emissions of Greenhouse Gas Emissions (GGE) into the atmosphere and increasing the number of carbon sinks. These objectives are to be realized by means of specific commitments in the medium term for 2006 and in the long term for 2020, targeting energy generation and transformation sectors (industry, transport, construction) and the primary sector, especially this last sector with regard to carbon sinks (Basque Government, 2002).

It would be too much to describe all that would be needed in order to comply with the requirements in the fight against climate change, but emphasis should be placed on the necessity of using alternative, renewable energies to substitute for the traditional, fossil fuel-burning (coal and fuel oil) power stations, as well as the need for energy efficiency in industry and the construction of sustainable buildings.

Today, it is reasonable to revise and even extend many of those commitments made in the Basque Environmental Strategy for Sustainable Development 2002–2020. Both at an international and regional level, new situations have arisen, changing the current discourse on climate change: the ratification by Russia of the Kyoto Protocol, which came into effect 16 February 2005; the internalization of the European Union Emissions Trading Directive; the Spanish Assignation Plan (of emission rights); and the challenges arising from the Basque Environmental Strategy for Sustainable Development itself.

The new situation that has arisen requires us to take action that is more co-coordinated vertically between international, state and regional bodies, as well as horizontally between regional governments, national governments and other stakeholders. In the case of the Basque Country, we should take full advantage of the specific measures complementing those of the Spanish state through the regional programmes to fight against climate change, though it is not an essential requisite. We should also share our experiences with other regional governments and expect them to learn from us as well. As regions we can undertake a number of initiatives:

- promote renewable energies;
- reduce GGE in transport, industry, housing and the energy sector;
- promote energy efficiency;
- promote sustainable forest management;
- promote change through international cooperation;
- reduce tax incentives and grants which run contrary to the fight against climate change (where responsibilities and powers exist).

The Basque approach

Before starting the active fight against climate change at a regional level, it is necessary to carry out a detailed diagnosis of the situation and, to this end, a sector inventory is essential. For the past four years in the Basque Country, we have been carrying out a GGE sector inventory, in line with the methodology of the Intergovernmental Panel on Climate Change (IPCC). This inventory is based on a number of detailed energy balances drawn up since 1982 by the Basque Energy Authority. Regarding the three gases considered in our inventory – carbon dioxide (CO_2), methane (CH_4) and nitrous oxide (N_2O), making up about 98 per cent of the total greenhouse gases emitted – in 2003 we registered 19.4 million tonnes equivalent to CO_2, a 28 per cent increase on the 1990 figure.

Over recent years, the Basque Country has been taking action in four important sectors: energy, industry, transport and the construction industry, these last two within a joint vision with the tertiary and residential sector. Much of what we have done and are doing is transferable, and we are developing with the nrg4SD ways to share our experiences in addressing climate change.

In the energy sector, the Environmental Strategy for 2010 in the Basque Country set the goal, for this date, of not surpassing by 111 per cent the 1990 figure for GGE in the Basque Country Autonomous Community and, more-over, of taking on board sustainable energy development policies and intro-ducing a range of new aspects:

- emphasizing energy saving and efficiency in consumer sectors in order to reduce energy consumption and energy intensity;
- improving the wise use of our own resources and in particular of renewable energies;

- enhancing safety in the supply and quality of the energy system;
- progressively replacing fossil fuels with bio-fuels;
- boosting technological research and development, basically into renewable energies and energy efficiency.

In the industrial sector too, we have a range of instruments aimed at enhancing eco-efficiency:

- programmes of energy efficiency in industry;
- gradual phasing out of less efficient fuels and fuel consumption systems;
- sector agreements;
- signing of voluntary agreements between the government and sectors having greatest environmental impact, with a view to setting additional objectives for the reduction of GGE.

In the Basque Country, we have signed six agreements with the following sectors: cement, paper pulp, steel, chemicals, ferrous and non-ferrous casting and waste management, involving a total of 129 companies; with the target for this year being 250 through 10 agreements being currently negotiated:

- emissions trading between installations that are large emitters (in the Basque Country there are 71 such plants corresponding to 67 companies);
- application of mechanisms for flexibility recognized in the Kyoto Protocol;
- tax incentives for investment in clean technologies and for those that reduce GGE. This year in the Basque Country we have a series of 30 clean technologies that companies may incorporate and thus reduce their corporation tax by up to 30 per cent.

We have approached the tertiary and domestic sector through action aimed at rationalizing energy consumption in what is a fragmented and dispersed sector, through sustainable construction that takes into account the concepts of energy savings and optimization of the consumption of materials – from the urban planning stage to the end of a building's useful life, starting with publicly owned housing and buildings.

Three departments within the Basque Government (Industry, Housing and Environment) are drawing up technical guidelines and an evaluation code for the construction of sustainable buildings. Likewise, in collaboration with the Department of Education, we are designing and building a sustainable school centre wherein the following criteria of sustainability are integrated in a practical and educational manner:

- The management of demand through information and training that favours rational consumption and also includes the application of economic instruments (for example, tax incentives for the incorporation and use of renewable energies, and the Sustainable Consumption Plan, shortly to be approved)

- The design at a regional level of means of transport and transport networks and infrastructure, always in coordination with territorial models and urban planning, that are coherent with sustainability criteria. This theme, taken up in the overall Basque Country Transport Plan, implies a new Basque rail infrastructure (known as the 'Y'), as a mixed transport (passengers and goods) means
- The plans for waste that we are drawing up in the Basque Country are aimed at reducing methane emissions as much as possible by means of incineration of waste and using biogas from dumping sites to the optimum
- Plans for environmental education, training and information in order to encourage the change to more sustainable behaviour patterns, at an individual and collective level.

In addition to our strategies and responsibilities as regional governments, the importance of working with local governments – closest as they are to the public – must not be overlooked, as they play a key role in the management of channels of participation and public awareness campaigns. Individual local authorities working alone can play an important role, but working within a strategic plan developed with their regional government partners can amplify enormously their impact. In the Basque Country, working with our local governments, we envisage making progress in the fight against climate change through a number of measures. These include incorporation of *Local Agenda 21* (LA21), which streamlines the channelling of public participation and provides for integrated and transparent management at the municipal level. This involves the development of municipal plans of action in energy efficiency, the encouragement of renewable energies and the mobility and treatment of waste. There are currently over 5000 LA21s worldwide and the International Council for Local Environmental Initiatives (ICLEI) has played a critical role in this.

The Basque Environmental Strategy for Sustainable Development 2002–2020 sets 141 specific commitments for 2006 and 223 by 2020, most of them quantitative. The strategy also sets out five conditions for making progress towards sustainability in the Basque Country:

1   the integration of environmental factors into other sector policies;
2   the improvement of current legislation and its application;
3   the encouragement of the market to favour the environment when using resources, improving competition, innovation, learning and eco-efficiency;
4   enabling and empowering the public, government bodies and the business community in such a way that behaviour is modified to achieve greater sustainability;
5   conducting research, enabling technological development and innovation in environmental matters.

Working together in our communities, regions and states, we can make significant progress in addressing the challenges that climate change presents. It is

Box 16.1 Environmental goals of the strategy for 2002–2020

Goal 1: To ensure clean, healthy air, water and soil

Attaining standards in these areas of the environment such that levels of pollutants of human origin (including radiation of all kinds) pose no significant risk to human health, ecosystems or our natural and cultural heritage:

- Objective 1: Reduce emissions and discharges of hazardous substances and contaminants into the environment
- Objective 2: Improve the quality of environmental resources

Goal 2: Responsible management of natural resources and waste

This goal is intended to establish sustainable use of natural resources (materials, energy, water and land) – that is, to ensure that their use and the consequences thereof do not exceed the capability of the environment to tolerate them. This means de-linking the consumption of resources and the generation of waste from economic growth by producing more efficiently, thus dematerializing the economy, and preventing the production of waste:

- Objective 1: To ensure that the consumption of resources and its consequences do not exceed the capability of the environment to tolerate them and regenerate itself, and to de-link economic growth from the use of resources
- Objective 2: To cut the amount of final or ultimate waste produced and avoid waste at source so as to de-link economic growth from the production of waste
- Objective 3: To manage final waste safely and locally

Goal 3: Protection of nature and biodiversity: a unique value to be fostered

To consolidate the biological diversity and sustainable use of natural systems and the variety of landscape, understanding these to be fundamental elements of the human environment and the expression of the diverse common natural and cultural heritage of a region and therefore important identifying features of that region

- Objective 1: To conserve and protect ecosystems, species and landscapes
- Objective 2: To restore ecosystems, species and landscapes in their natural environment
- Objective 3: To investigate and heighten awareness of biodiversity

Goal 4: Balance between territories and mobility: a common approach

To consolidate a more balanced, more accessible territory where social and economic activities of general interest are viable, while at the same time conserving the heritage, variety, richness and attractiveness in terms of nature and culture of our rural, urban and coastal areas:

- Objective 1: To achieve sustainable use of the whole territory
- Objective 2: To achieve a level of accessibility which will allow sustainable development in the various land uses and activities (residential, economic activities and leisure)
- Objective 3: To de-link economic development from the generalized increase in demand for motorized transport

Goal 5: Limiting effects on climate change

To reach levels of greenhouse gases in the atmosphere that will not result in non-natural variations in the earth's climate, thus contributing from the Basque Country to the application of the Kyoto agreement:

- Objective 1: To limit GGE into the atmosphere by 2020
- Objective 2: To increase carbon sinks

Source: Basque Government (2002)

fundamental that, from the regions, we come down clearly and firmly in favour of policies advocating urgent action on climate change that achieves the aims of the Kyoto Protocol in each of our spheres of responsibility, and begins to map out targets beyond Kyoto. To this end, the Basque Country is actively working towards the creation of a specific working group on climate change at the nrg4SD and we are examining new mechanisms that would make both our participation in and compliance with international objectives increasingly viable.

Where next for the Basque Country and the nrg4SD?

With the launching of the nrg4SD in Johannesburg and through the Gauteng Declaration, regional governments decided to initiate the search for new solutions so that development in our regions can be sustainable. The formulation of Regional Strategies for Sustainable Development as frameworks for the promotion of sustainable production and consumption stand out as essential elements for this achievement of Sustainable Development.

In the declaration of the third conference of the nrg4SD, held in Western Australia in September 2003, and in the working programme drawn up for the forthcoming years, we decided to contribute actively to international forums (nrg4SD, 2003). In particular, these included the Ninth Conference on the Parties to the UN Framework Agreement, held in Milan in December 2003, the conference on renewable energies in Bonn in 2004, and the Tenth Conference on the Parties to the United Nations Framework Agreement, Buenos Aires, in December 2004. The nrg4SD also agreed to develop and interchange good working practices, at a regional level, in the field of renewable energies and climate change.

Given that the Basque Government is determined to continue working for compliance with the Kyoto Protocol, we are currently immersed in a study aimed at clarifying the position of the Basque Government regarding flexible mechanisms in order to provide access to small and medium-sized Basque companies (90 per cent of Basque industry). To this end, and in view of the predictable deficit in CO_2 emission rights, the Basque Government intends to manage all these rights through collaboration with our industrial sector and through interchanges with the other regional governments making up the nrg4SD. In addition, we will work out how to design and develop the corresponding Clean Development Mechanisms (CDMs), even with the possibility of the creation of a Basque Carbon Fund, a fund which would undoubtedly enjoy the support and collaboration of Basque and international banks.

Building on this series of initiatives, the longer-term objective of the Basque Government is to create an Office for Climate Change that will develop inter-departmental policy and actively collaborate with any Centre for Climate Change created at national, state or international level.

Conclusion

The problems facing the world – notably that of climate change – at times seem enormous and the obstacles insurmountable. The hope of the Basque Country, working principally with the nrg4SD, is that we can face them together as a world community of equals, a point emphasized in the Gauteng Declaration:

> *Regional governments both want and need to work with all other spheres of government and with other stakeholders in promoting sustainable development. We call upon the heads of government and other world leaders assembled in Johannesburg and the United Nations itself to recognize and support the necessary and essential role of the regional governments in the promotion of sustainable development and in the achievement of Agenda 21 and the Millennium Development Targets. We also recognize that our shared work in this field must develop in a spirit of close collaboration and partnership in-*

cluding fostering and supporting community-based sustainability initiatives. Similarly we invite international organizations, local government and all other stakeholder groups to work with us in the development of their work as equal and essential partners on sustainable development.

nrg4SD, 2002

For this to happen, developed countries must carry the burden – after all, it was we who created many of the problems. If there is to be a sustainable world, and a reversal in the negative impacts of climate change, then it will only come about if we work together as regional governments, local governments, national governments and international stakeholders. In this, the 50th anniversary year of Albert Einstein's death, perhaps his words provide a fitting direction for the future: 'setting an example is not the main means of influencing others; it is the only means.'

References

Basque Government (2002) 'The Basque environmental strategy for sustainable development', The Basque Government, www.ingurumena.net/English/Doc/Estrategia/Index.htm

Bush Greenwatch (2005) 'Gore claims Bush has "Crisis" analysis all wrong', *Greenwatch Today*, 16 February, www.bushgreenwatch.org/mt_archives/000241.php

Join Arnold (2003) 'Schwarzenegger details specifics of environmental action plan', Californians for Schwarzenegger, 21 September, www.joinarnold.com

NEG/ECP (2001) 'Climate Change Action Plan 2001', New England Governors/Eastern Canadian Premiers, www.negc.org

nrg4SD (2002) Gauteng Declaration, www.nrg4sd.net/ENG/Network/Documents/Index.htm

nrg4SD (2003) Perth Declaration, Third Conference of the nrg4SD, Western Australia, 16–19 September, www.nrg4sd.net/Download/Events/Perth/Perth-Declaration-EN.pdf

nrg4SD (2004) Policy Papers, March, www.nrg4sd.net/ENG/Network/Documents/Policy.htm

nrg4SD (2005) Lake Toba Summit and First General Assembly, Medan and Lake Toba, North Sumatra, 10–12 March 2005; www.nrg4sd.net/ENG/Events/News/detalle.asp?Id=255

UN (2000) *Millennium Declaration*, General Assembly, 54th session, document A/RES/55/2, 18 September

UN (2004) *A more secure world: Our shared responsibility*, Report of the Secretary-General's High Level Panel on Threats, Challenges and Change, document A/59/565, 2 December, United Nations, New York

UN (2005) *In Larger Freedom: Towards development, security and human rights for all*, Report of the Secretary-General, document A/59/2005, 21 March, www.un.org/largerfreedom

17

Human and Environmental Rights: The Need for Corporate Accountability

Hannah Griffiths

Introduction

The case for collective security today rests on three basic pillars. Today's threats recognize no national boundaries, are connected, and must be addressed at the global and regional as well as national levels.

UN, 2005

The quote above could apply to the actions of transnational companies (TNCs). Unfortunately, however, unlike the rules developed under the Security Council for the actions of countries, there are none that deal with the actions of companies. Yet, of the 100 largest economies in the world, 51 are corporations and 49 are countries. And of these 51 corporations, 47 are American, making US companies the dominant economic power (Garrison, 2004). The top 500 corporations now control almost two-thirds of world trade.

At the same time as this unprecedented global corporate growth, social and economic development is proceeding slowly, the gap between rich and poor is widening and environmental destruction and natural resource depletion is increasing. For example, 54 countries are poorer now than in 1990. The income of the richest 1 per cent of the world's population, about 60 million people, is equal to the income of the poorest 57 per cent, about 3.4 billion people (UNDP, 2003). About one-third of the world's population lives in countries suffering from moderate to high water stress, and 80 countries, constituting 40 per cent of the world's population were suffering from serious water shortages by the mid-1990s (UNEP, 2002).

As companies become increasingly large and powerful, they wield considerable influence over politics, society, human development and our natural resources. For example, the energy sector is often cited as the driving force within the modern global economy. In this sector corporate profits are unquestionably a priority above human and environmental security. Climate change looks set to exacerbate the problems of poverty and environmental injustice, with impacts likely to be felt most harshly in developing countries, which are least able to adapt. Yet oil and gas companies are putting unprecedented levels of investment into finding yet more fossil fuels to extract from the ground. At the same time, for many, the Iraq (and many other) wars were at least in part wars for oil, intended to secure oil companies' business in Iraq.

The growth of corporate power has not happened unopposed. Demonstrations in Seattle at the World Trade Organization (WTO) meeting, at meetings of the G8, of the World Bank and the International Monetary Fund (IMF) are centred on the need to create a fair international economic and trade system. TNCs often lie at the centre of campaigns for human rights, environmental justice, fair access to resources and an end to poverty – all crucial elements for achieving human and environmental security. One of the challenges facing us in creating a secure world is ensuring that multinational companies and their impact are controlled as part of a fair global economic system.

This chapter looks at some responses to this challenge. Consumers have responded by demanding ethically produced products. TNCs have by developing their own environmental and human rights policies and increasingly through the adoption of the concept of corporate social responsibility (CSR). This response has largely been supported by governments which have championed the role of voluntary agreements in raising environmental and social standards. But such a response, the chapter argues using examples of corporate activities, is failing people and the planet and doing little to improve our security. The chapter ends with suggestions for increasing corporate accountability – the idea that communities affected by a corporation should exercise some control over that corporation's activities and should be able to hold that company accountable for its impacts.

Cherry picking bad corporate behaviour

Over the years, non-governmental organizations (NGOs) – including Friends of the Earth (FOE) – have fought countless campaigns against companies over specific issues. We have criticized British Nuclear Fuels (BNFL) for pushing nuclear power as a secure, safe solution to carbon emissions and climate change. We have exposed Tesco for using its market power to achieve the lowest possible supply costs, squeezing out farmers. We have campaigned against Bayer's and Monsanto's genetically modified (GM) products, highlighting the environmental threat they pose.

We have forced companies such as Balfour Beatty to abandon plans to build controversial and destructive projects, such as the Ilisu Dam in Turkey. We persuaded high street banks such as Barclays into developing some expertise in environmental matters after we exposed how investors were financing rainforest clearance, human rights abuses and polluting industries. We put pressure on the oil giant Shell to withdraw from the Global Climate Coalition, a lobby group set up specifically to stop governments from taking action on climate change.

But other damaging and destructive projects have gone ahead despite our efforts. BP is building the controversial Baku-Tiblisi-Ceyhan pipeline, taking oil from the Caspian Sea to the West, and contravening human rights in the process. Shell is still polluting communities and the environment around the world from Nigeria to Texas, from Sakhalin to Brazil.

Even where projects have gone ahead, campaigning efforts have had some impact. Corporations do not like their activities to be under the spotlight or the subject of public criticism. One response to this has been the development of CSR – the idea that companies should recognize their impact on society and the environment and voluntarily take steps to negate them, frequently by promoting to the public the positive measures they are taking to reduce negative impacts.

The rise of CSR: Ethical business?

Is CSR a genuine attempt to change behaviour, as some commentators and most companies would claim? Political leaders have trumpeted the 'huge uptake' in CSR. In the UK, the government sees 'CSR as the business contribution to sustainable development' (Timms, 2004). Nigel Griffiths MP, the UK's Minister for CSR, recently noted that '2,000 international companies regularly report on their environmental and social impacts' (Griffiths, 2004). Business leaders often also promote CSR. Digby Jones, Director-General of the Confederation of British Industry (CBI) has commented that:'...business today understands fully that its responsibilities extend beyond maximizing profitability to include addressing the needs of its wider stakeholders' (Jones, 2001).

Individual companies, too, have embraced CSR as the way forward. Shell, for example, says, 'fundamental changes have occurred and continue to be made in the group. Sustainable development practices are gradually being integrated throughout the Shell business. These, and a commitment to people, the planet and profits will help Shell retain a competitive advantage' (Shell, 2005a). And Kofi Annan, Secretary-General of the United Nations (UN), has noted how nearly 1500 companies from 70 countries participate in the UN Global Compact, a voluntary initiative based on 10 principles of human rights, core labour standards, environmental protection goals and anti-corruption measures (Annan, 2004).

What does this widespread commitment mean in practice? Is CSR delivering increased environmental security, ensuring human rights are upheld, making development more sustainable and helping to end poverty? Is it delivering ethical business? Evidence in three main areas points to the answers being a resounding 'no'.

Firstly, little is said by the CSR advocates about companies that blatantly ignore CSR or are openly aggressive to it. What about companies that choose not to abide by their human rights responsibilities? Until an international boycott put the US oil giant Exxon under pressure, it virtually denied the existence of climate change. Instead it has been at the forefront of lobbying the US Government against signing the Kyoto Protocol.

And yet, a large number of corporations have so far failed to embrace CSR. In 2000, UK Prime Minister Tony Blair challenged the Financial Times Stock Exchange's (FTSE's) 350 largest firms to produce environmental reports by the end of 2001. Only 79 did so (Murray, 2003). Two thousand international companies may produce reports on their environmental and social impacts, but there are an estimated 61,000 transnational corporations in business and over 900,000 foreign affiliates (UNCTAD, 2004), implying that only 3.2 per cent are reporting on their social and environmental impacts. Similarly, only 2.5 per cent have signed up to the UN's Global Compact initiative. Can we really consider a 2–3 per cent take-up rate as a success? These low figures imply that the vast majority of the corporate world is failing to volunteer to be part of the voluntary approach.

Secondly, an analysis of the success of CSR must consider how changes to companies' social and environmental policies actually impact on the ground. A company can produce glossy reports, write laudable environmental and human rights policies and sign up to voluntary codes of conduct but this is only meaningful if it translates into action on the ground.

Take Barclays, for example, which, in June 2003, was one of the first UK banks to sign up to the Equator Principles, a set of voluntary social and environmental guidelines for private banks. Barclays and other banks received a cautious welcome from many NGOs and some publicity in UK and other newspapers as a result of their positive step.

In December of the same year, Barclays provided a loan to the National Hydropower Power Corporation (NHPC), the Indian company building the part of the Narmada dam in Central India. In 2004, Barclays helped advise on the project finance for the Omkareshwar dam, which is part of the Narmada dam project. This is one of the most controversial dam projects in the world, involving building over 30 major dams and resulting in the resettlement of two million people. No independent environmental impact assessment (EIA) has been carried out for the project, there has been no informed participation of local communities, it breaches Indian federal and state laws, and violates policies on natural habitats, cultural property and involuntary resettlement (Friends of the Earth, 2005). Not surprisingly then, funding the project is in breach of the Equator Principles. But as the principles are voluntary, Barclays, it seems, can sign up, enjoy the publicity, and yet continue with business as usual.

In January 2003, the UK diamond industry made commitments to the Kimberley Process, an international certification scheme aimed at preventing the trade in conflict diamonds. In October 2004, a report by Amnesty International and Global Witness concluded that, 'Only a minority of diamond jewellery retailers have demonstrated they have effective measures in place to implement the self-regulation and combat the trade in conflict diamonds and have made efforts to be transparent about these efforts' (Amnesty, 2004).

BAE Systems (BAE), the world's largest arms producer, also makes much of its corporate responsibility principles, with policies on the environment, supply chain and the workplace and the production of sustainability reports. In 2004, BAE Systems won commendation for its CSR status and was listed in the Dow Jones Sustainability Index, (DJSI, 2004): 'global indexes tracking the financial performance of the leading sustainability-driven companies worldwide', which provide 'asset managers with reliable and objective benchmarks to manage sustainability portfolios' (DJSI, 2005). But its policies have not prevented BAE from exporting Hawk ground attack aircraft to Indonesia where over 200,000 people were killed in East Timor; or from selling 60 Hawk jets to India at a time when, owing to India's dispute with Pakistan over Kashmir, the region was very unstable; or from exporting to Saudia Arabia whose governmental regime has been described by Amnesty International as having a 'persistent pattern of gross human rights abuses'.

The Anglo-Dutch oil company Shell embraced CSR in 1995 following negative publicity surrounding the disposal of one of its oil platforms, the Brent Spa, and the execution by the Nigerian dictatorship of Ken Saro-Wiwa and eight others in Nigeria, who were campaigning against the devastating environmental impacts of oil corporations, particularly Shell. Policies on Shell's impact on the environment and human rights were developed and, over the 10 years since, have constantly been refined. These days, Shell's slogan is 'Principles and Profits'.

Despite this, Shell is still involved in fundamental environmental destruction and in violation of human rights across the world. Shell's 'fenceline' communities – those living right next door to the company's plants and operations and experiencing the direct impacts of Shell's business operations – have come together to expose the impact Shell is having on their communities and to fight for justice from Shell. In Brazil, Shell has polluted an entire community's supply of drinking water by industrial waste. In Nigeria, Shell breaches Nigerian law by continuing to flare gas, spewing flames and acrid plumes of smoke over farms and homes, damaging people's health and destroying their livelihoods. As a result of leaks, emissions, and accidents releasing tonnes of toxic chemicals on people in Texas, Shell is accused of contributing to serious and fatal health problems in a community with high rates of infant mortality and early death (FOE, 2004).

In a Shell advert, an employee claims: 'I want to fight climate change, that's why I work for Shell.' Yet, Shell continues to pursue an aggressive rate of increase of fossil fuel extraction year on year, putting its projected expenditure for 2005 on 'new energies' of up to US$500 million (Shell, 2005b) into perspective.

Shell's practice flags up a third shortcoming with CSR. While a company may embrace social and environmental values in its policies, it may still not be opposed to lobbying against such policies being enforced. Lobbying is big business, with lobbyists employed by most businesses to maximize corporate influence over government policy, ensuring a corporate agenda is pursued in the public sphere. Corporations are not the only lobbyists of course, but they are by far the most powerful. For example, 70 per cent of Brussels lobbyists work for corporate interests, 20 per cent represent NGOs, trade unions and similar organizations and 10 per cent represent cities, regions and international institutions (Corporate Europe Observatory, 2004a).

Corporate lobbyists may be direct employees of the company, may work for a consultancy, or may represent companies through trade associations or corporate lobby groups. Being largely out of the public's sight, lobbyists and lobby groups represent a behind-closed-doors side of company policy compared to the very public CSR side of the same company's policy, potentially allowing a company to say one thing with one face and a different thing with another face.

Shell, the self-proclaimed CSR leader, was instrumental in lobbying against the UN Human Rights Norms for Business. The norms make the human rights obligations of companies explicit, and by compelling companies to abide by them, moves a step beyond pure voluntarism, taking us closer to upholding human rights across the world. But an international campaign against the norms was led by the International Chamber of Commerce (ICC), the 'world business organization' representing hundreds of multinational companies from around the world. Leading the ICC's campaign was Robin Aram, Vice President of External Affairs at Shell (CEO, 2004b).

The ICC's main concerns about the norms are centred around the fact that the Norms 'clearly seek to move away from the realm of voluntary initiatives'[1]. While Shell has largely remained silent on the issue, Aram was reported to say that the norms were 'undermining voluntary initiatives like the Global Compact' (CEO, 2004b). In response to an article on the issue, Shell has said, 'it is wrong... to imply that because we express our concerns about the draft norms that in some way undermines or puts into question our commitment to support human rights'[2] But this is exactly the implication intended here – the message from Shell and the ICC is clear: leave us to decide how and if we implement our human rights responsibilities.

It is these and many more similar examples that have led organizations like Friends of the Earth to believe that the voluntary approach to CSR simply isn't working. Worse, it may well have largely been a smokescreen, a diversion from the real issue of making concrete changes, a public relations and marketing exercise, a greenwash. It is obvious to Friends of the Earth and many others that the voluntary approach to CSR simply isn't enough.

Ethical consumerism?

Another response to the problems of human rights abuses, unfair trade and environmental destruction caused by companies has been the rise of ethical consumerism including fair trade, green consumerism and socially responsible investment. The development of this ethical business sector offers consumers the chance to choose between products produced in an environmentally and socially responsible way and those that are not.

Ethical consumerism fits into a supply and demand based market logic: if consumers demand ethical products, suppliers will respond by producing these products, thereby reducing the volume of production of unethical or destructive products. This logic has worked to a degree, with some successful schemes.

The international fair trade mark, Fairtrade, is widely known, and most supermarkets now stock a range of Fairtrade products, which ensure farmers and producers are given a fair price for their goods, helping to give them a secure income and stable livelihoods. Most supermarkets also stock a range of organic products so that consumers can be happy in the knowledge that production of their food is causing minimal damage to the environment. Farmers' markets, where farmers sell their (often organic) produce directly to the public, have sprung up all over the UK. Ethical investment, in which fund managers screen out some damaging companies from their portfolios, and socially responsible investment, where fund managers engage with the companies in which they invest to persuade them to improve their social and environmental performance, continue to grow.

Ethical consumerism overall will probably also continue to grow. The Co-operative Bank's Ethical Consumerism Report (2003) estimated the value of ethical consumption at £19.9 billion, an increase of 44 per cent in the period from 1999 to 2002. This sounds impressive, until it is considered that overall ethical goods and services account for just 1–2 per cent of the total market share.

This hints at the limits of ethical consumerism. Ethical and green products are for the most part more expensive and often represent a niche, middle class market. At present, demand for cheap products in our consumption fuelled society far outweighs demand for ethical and green products.

Another limit is that even the most ardent, caring and affluent consumer can never possess all the information needed to buy ethically all the time. Social and environmental issues are ever more complex and dynamic. Consumers cannot possible keep abreast of all the latest developments and then have the time to work out for themselves what this means for their shopping basket. How can an ethical consumer boycott a company – such as a mining company whose products end up in soap, talcum powder, washing powder, electrical goods and more – that may be involved in the supply chain of thousands of products but have their brand on none of these?

Ethical consumers may also face a situation where producers of unethical products attempt to obscure or block information that would make their products less attractive. Unfortunately, the trade system is rigged in a way that can help companies to do this. For example, food labelling is a big concern for the GM industry. Consumers in the European Union (EU) have made it abundantly clear that they don't want to buy GM foods, and current EU legislation requires labelling on GM foods. Yet such labelling could be illegal under World Trade Organization (WTO) trade rules if it can be shown it discriminates against some products (in this case, those containing GM). The US, with the assistance of the American Soybean Association, is preparing for a potential WTO dispute on such labelling. This could be just the tip of the iceberg. It looks likely that other labelling on organic and fair-trade products could also be included in the dispute.

The example of GM also shows how the corporate sector can use the current trade system to tackle democratic legal mechanisms that help consumers make choices. The EU's approvals mechanism for GM crops is based on the Precautionary Principle and requires a more rigorous level of assurance against harmful effects of GM products than the US system. After lobbying from the American GM industry, the US lodged a formal complaint at the WTO against this 'discriminatory' treatment of US GM products. This dispute is a test case for the international trade system – it will show whether we will be able to approach trade in ways that meet our own needs and basic safety requirements or if the world will be forced to accept the lowest common denominator anyone can devise.

A further, deeper limit to ethical consumerism is that it goes no distance towards addressing the potentially fundamental problem of our consumption-driven society. It does not ask if we can afford (in an environmental, equity and long-term security sense) to continue with the current levels of consumption that we enjoy in the West. It doesn't ask us to reduce the footprint we leave on the planet; it doesn't ask us to question whether we have a fair share of the earth's resources, or whether some of the things we demand as consumers we simply could not have in a fair and equal world.

Despite these limits to ethical consumerism, it has undoubtedly made a difference to the lives of thousands, giving them a fairer deal and leaving them with a less degraded, better protected environment. On a more general level, perhaps the key strength of ethical consumerism is that it demonstrates what can be done where there is a will. And it gives consumers a sense of empowerment – a feeling that they can make a difference.

Corporate accountability

The response of governments to corporate abuse has largely been to champion voluntary CSR. From the viewpoint of Friends of the Earth and others, such a position echoes the words of TNCs, demonstrating the power of the big business lobby. Friends of the Earth believes that instead of bowing to corporate interests, governments should be acting in the interests of society as a whole to maximize human and environmental security. Governments, as our representatives, should be forcing our companies to act in the best interests of all their stakeholders.

Definitions and concepts of corporate accountability range from imposing minimum environmental and human rights standards on companies, to transforming them radically beyond recognition from today's TNC. The common ground between these two extremes lies in the end of voluntary self-regulation of companies' social and environmental impacts. A good working definition of corporate accountability, which can house much of the spectrum, is provided by Jem Bendell as 'the ability of those affected by a corporation to regulate the activities of that corporation' (Bendell, 2004 p19).

Over the past few years, there have been a variety of proposals for mechanisms to help deliver corporate accountability. Some of these, such as the Framework Convention on Tobacco Control, focus on specific sectors. Some, such as the International Right to Know Campaign's call for disclosure and transparency, focus on particular elements of corporate accountability. All these are helpful in dealing with specifics and moving the debate and situation forward. Achieving the radical transformation needed in the corporate sector will require mechanisms for all sectors at all levels. Corporate accountability will not be attained through one mechanism or one new set of regulations.

International corporate accountability legislation

Friends of the Earth International (FOEI) has developed proposals for an international legally binding convention on corporate accountability and liability (FOEI, 2002). The proposals seek to address problems common to the corporate sector as a whole; to provoke debate around the possible solutions to corporate wrongdoing; to promote a southern agenda around community rights, as opposed to a northern corporate agenda on voluntary codes of conduct; and to reverse the pendulum swing away from corporate voluntarism towards corporate accountability. It is based on the following principles:

Duties
Impose duties on publicly traded companies, their directors and board level officers to:

- report fully on their social and environmental impacts, on significant risks and on breaches of relevant standards (such reports to be independently verified);
- ensure effective prior consultations with affected communities, including the preparation of Environmental Impact Assessments (EIA) for significant activities and full public access to all relevant documentation;
- take the negative social and environmental impacts of their activities fully into account in their corporate decision making.

Liability
Extend legal liability to directors for corporate breaches of national social and environmental laws, and to directors and corporations of corporate breaches of international laws or agreements.

Rights of redress
Guarantee legal rights of redress for citizens and communities adversely affected by corporate activities, including:

- access for affected people anywhere in the world to pursue litigation where parent corporations claim a 'home', are domiciled, or listed;
- provision for legal challenge to company decisions by those with an interest;
- a legal aid mechanism to provide public funds to support such challenges.

Rights to resources

Establish human and community rights of access to and control over the resources needed to enjoy a healthy and sustainable life, including rights:

- over common property resources and global commons such as forests, water, fisheries, genetic resources and minerals for indigenous peoples and local communities;
- to prior consultation and veto over corporate projects, against displacement;
- to compensation or reparation for resources expropriated by or for corporations.

Standards

Establish (and enforce) high minimum social, environmental, labour and human rights standards for corporate activities based, for example, on existing international agreements, and reflecting the desirability of special and differential treatment for developing countries.

Introduce sanctions

Establish national legal provision for suitable sanctions for companies in breach of these new duties, rights and liabilities (wherever breaches occur) such as:

- suspending national stock exchange listing;
- withholding access for such companies to public subsidies, guarantees, loans or procurement contracts;
- in extreme cases the withdrawal of limited liability status.

Extend the role of the International Criminal Court (ICC) to try directors and corporations for social, environmental and human rights crimes, perhaps involving a special tribunal for environmental abuses.

Improve international monopoly controls over mergers and monopolistic behaviour by corporations.

Implementation mechanism: Establish a continuing structure and process to monitor and review the implementation and effectiveness of the convention.

A comprehensive international framework such as this represents an important part of the solution – one that many campaign groups are working towards. But of course, one international agreement will not form the entire solution. We need regulation and control at many levels – international, regional, national and sectoral – before we will see the emergence of meaningful corporate accountability.

National legislation

In the UK, over 100 groups have come together to form the Corporate Responsibility Coalition (CORE) stating that, 'The starting point of our Coalition is that we believe the voluntary approach to corporate responsibility has failed' (CORE, 2002). CORE is campaigning for changes to UK company law that would start to implement some of the principles of FOEI's international convention at a national level. These include three main pillars:

* mandatory reporting and access to information – a requirement for companies to report annually on the significant negative social and environmental impacts of their business operations, policies, products and procedures;
* new legal duties on company directors – new statutory duties requiring directors to take reasonable steps to reduce the significant negative social and environmental impacts of their business operations, products, policies and procedures, which have been identified through the mandatory reporting requirements. This new duty could be referred to as a 'duty of care' to people and the environment.
* new provisions for liability, including Foreign Direct Liability – individuals or communities who suffer significant negative impacts because of the failure of UK companies (and directors) to have proper regard to these new duties, would have the legal right to seek redress in a UK court, with legal aid. This would include negative impacts such as human rights and environmental abuses resulting directly from the operations, policies, products and procurement practices of UK companies or their overseas subsidiaries.

Similar campaigns are growing, and are due to be launched soon in other European countries such as France and The Netherlands. As with other international mechanisms, we are a long way away from any of these initiatives seeing the light of day. CORE's campaign in 2004 for the first and least radical or controversial pillar of their proposed legislation – the requirement for companies to produce annual social and environmental reports – was met with animosity from government and business alike.

Trade

This chapter has only briefly touched on some problems with the world trade system – one of the key frameworks that govern corporate behaviour across the world. In addition to re-establishing public and community control over corporations, to move completely towards businesses contributing to improved security rather than hampering it, changes are needed to the world trade system.

There is a need to challenge the principles of free trade and to recognize that it is not delivering human and environmental security. Rather, it is associated with increasing levels of inequality, both between and within countries; the concentration of resources and power in fewer and fewer hands, resulting in an erosion of democracy, and in social, political and economic exclusion and economic instability. The 'global North', using the resources of the 'global South' at rock bottom prices, has incurred an ecological debt to the South, yet in order to pay off their financial debts, those impoverished countries in the South find themselves compelled to play the neoliberal game by exporting more and more to the North. Thus we see spiralling rates of natural resource exploitation and a loss of biological and cultural diversity (FOEI 2003).

Free trade has led to weaker international agreements in other key areas, including on the environment and development. For example, multilateral environmental agreements such as the Kyoto and Biosafety protocols continue to play second fiddle to the WTO. Multilateral treaties on the environment, human rights, labour rights, development and health should take precedence over agreements on trade, be they WTO rules or bilateral agreements.

We need to rebalance trade, deprioritizing international trade, giving a higher priority to local self-reliance. We need to create transparency and democracy in our international trading system so that it is no longer rigged to serve solely financial interests of rich northern countries and TNCs.

International financial institutions (IFIs)

Trade is just one area where the government-business relationship needs to be overhauled. Governments must also stop handing multinational companies subsidies and other incentives to continue operating in an unsustainable manner. Through IFIs such as the World Bank and European Bank for Reconstruction and Development, and export credit agencies (ECAs) such as the UK's Export Credits Guarantee Department, governments give the corporate sector public money to support them in their operations.

Conclusion

TNCs and our current neo-liberal approach to economics and globalization are driving biodiversity loss, natural resource depletion, environmental injustice, increased poverty, human rights abuses and hence human and environmental insecurity. We need to act to stop this situation by reforming the way we think about and do business. Tweaks in the corporate sector are nowhere near enough: radical widespread change is needed and, in the face of irreversible damage, is needed urgently if we are to work towards a secure future.

The voluntary approach to CSR is proven not to be working as it doesn't address key issues such as what to do with those companies that refuse to participate, how to stop companies saying one thing and doing another or how to stop governments from putting big business interests before social and environmental justice.

Communities and citizens should have control over the sorts of business that take place in their area. Gaining this control will require widespread change at all levels and in all sectors. It will require a fundamental change in the world trade system and in the laws that govern the activities of TNCs to enable us to put human and environmental rights and our long term security before corporate profit.

Notes

1   Bertasi, S. (2004) Quoted in 'CSR Europe background note: United Nations Norms on the Responsibilities of Transnational Companies', www.csreurope.org
2   Shell (2004) Comment from Shell International on CEO's Article '*Shell Leads International Business Campaign Against UN Human Rights Norms*'

References

Amnesty International (2004), 'Déjà vu: The Diamond Industry still failing to deliver on Promises', Amnesty International and Global Witness, www.amnesty.org

Annan, K. (2004) 'The Global Compact Report 2004, The tenth principle', www. thepolitician.org

Bendell, J. (2004) *Barricades and Boardrooms: A Contemporary History of the Corporate Accountability Movement*. P19 UNRISD Paper PP-TBS-13, 6 June 2004, United Nations Research Institute for social Development(UNRISD), Switzerland

CEO (2004a), *Lobby Planet: Brussels, the EU quarter* Corporate Europe Observatory, Amsterdam, p12

CEO (2004b) *Shell Leads International Business Campaign Against UN Human Rights Norms,* CEO Info Brief, March 2004, www.corporateeurope.org/norms.pdf

CORE (2002) *The CORE Approach,* About CORE, www.corporate-responsibility.org

CORE (2005) CORE website, www.corporate-responsibility.org

DJSI (2004) *Sustainability Index,* Dow Jones Sustainability Index website, DJSI World www.sustainability-index.com

DJSI (2005) Dow Jones Sustainability Index website, , www.sustainability-index.com/

FOE (2004) *Behind the Shine: The Other Shell Report 2003,* Friends of the Earth, www. foe.co.uk/resource/reports/behind_shine.pdf

FOE (2005) *Barclays and the financing of the Narmada Dams,* Friends of the Earth, www.foe.co.uk/campaigns/corporates/resource/investors.html

FOEI (2002) *Towards binding corporate accountability,* Friends of the Earth International, www.foei.org/publications/corporates/accountability.html#

FOEI (2003) *Towards Sustainable Economies: challenging neoliberal economic globalisation,* Friends of the Earth International, www.foei.org/publications/pdfs/sustain-e.pdf

Garrison, J. (2004) *America as Empire,* Berrett-Koehler Publishers Inc, San Francisco

Griffiths, N. (2004) *International Strategic Framework on Corporate and Social Responsibility,* speech at Department of Trade and Industry (DTI) Conference Centre, 7 October, www.societyandbusiness.gov.uk/pdf/International_Strategic_Framework_ CSR_7_October.pdf

Jones, D. (2001) 'A realistic perspective of the balance of power between business, government and society', speech at The Guardian and Observer Conference, 9 July, CBI, www.cbi.org.uk/pdf/csrdigby090701.pdf

Murray, A. (2003) *Corporate Social Responsibility in the EU*, Centre for European Reform, London

Shell (2005a) *The History Of Shell:* Who We Are, Shell,www.shell.com

Shell (2005b), *Shell's approach to new energies*, Environment and Society, Shell, www. shell.com/home

Timms, S. (2004) Business Commitment to the Environment Awards, speech, 20 April, www.dti.gov.uk/ministers/speeches/timms200404.html

UN (2004) '*A more secure world: Our shared responsibility*', Report of the Secretary-General's High Level Panel on Threats, Challenges and Change, document A/59/565, 2 December, United Nations, New York

UNCTAD (2004) *World Investment Report: The Shift Towards Services*, United Nations, New York and Geneva, p17, www.unctad.org/en/docs/wir2004_en.pdf

UNDP (2003) *Millennium Development Goals: A Compact Among Nations to End Human Poverty*, Human Development Report 2003, Oxford University Press, Oxford, http://hdr.undp.org/reports/global/2003/pdf/hdr03_complete.pdf

UNEP (2002) *Global Environmental Outlook 3: Past, present and future perspectives*, UN Environment Programme, Nairobi, http://geo.unep-wcmc.org/geo3/pdfs/overview. pdf

18

Reforming Environmental Governance

Serge Lepeltier

Si nous allons sur le chemin que nous avons, le défaut est notre avarice et si nous ne sommes pas disposés à changer, nous disparaîtrons du visage du globe, pour être remplacés par l'insecte.[1]

Jacques Cousteau

Introduction

In his March 2005 report, 'In Larger Freedom: Towards development, security and human rights for all', United Nations (UN) Secretary-General Kofi Annan recommended the setting up of an integrated structure for environmental standard-setting to be built on existing institutions such as the United Nations Environment Programme (UNEP) and the treaty bodies (UN, 2005). This call for reform reflected the growing recognition of the need to integrate in a single structure all environmental standard-setting issues.

Towards an international framework for environmental governance

French President Jacques Chirac has made reform of environmental governance a major cornerstone of French environmental diplomacy, first conveying this ambition when he addressed the UN General Assembly in September 2003:

> *Against the chaos of a world shaken by ecological disaster, let us call for a sharing of responsibility, around a United Nations Environment Organization.*
>
> *Chirac, 2003a*

More broadly, the international community has, for a long time now, noted the inadequacies of the international framework for intervention in the environmental field, namely: the system's fragmentation, which causes duplication and ineffectiveness; partial scientific expertise too loosely connected to policy-making processes and not linked with collective alert mechanisms; inadequately addressed specific requirements of developing countries, in terms also of their capabilities to implement their obligations under agreements; and over-fragmented and, above all, volatile sources of funding.

In December 2004, the High Level Panel on Threats, Challenges and Change – established by the Secretary-General to report to him on security threats facing the world in the 21st century and how to respond to them – noted in its report that environmental degradation was one of the biggest threats to collective security. In particular, regarding governance, the panel concluded that rarely are environmental concerns factored into security, development or humanitarian strategies:

> *Nor is there coherence in environmental protection efforts at the global level. Most attempts to create governance structures to tackle the problems of global environmental degradation have not effectively addressed climate change, deforestation and desertification. Regional and global multilateral treaties on the environment are undermined by inadequate implementation and enforcement by the Member States.*

> *UN, 2004*

Their assessment has lent emphasis to the growing call for strengthening and giving coherence to international environmental governance (IEG).

Informal intergovernmental working group on environmental governance

To initiate a concrete discussion on the reform of environmental governance, France convened an informal working group bringing together 26 countries[2] from the world over, as well as the European Commission, to undertake a collective debate in order to better identify desirable developments and possible reforms, and to consider the transforming of United Nations Environment Programme (UNEP) into a United Nations Environment Organization (UNEO). This initiative was based on the following observations:

• The degradation of the environment has been recognized as one of the most serious threats, not just for the future of the planet and its natural resources, but also for the survival of human kind. Climate change, the loss of biodiversity, desertification, and an ever-increasing number of natural disasters affect all countries and all peoples – in particular, those that are most vulnerable. This observation, already included in the Millennium Declaration (UN, 2000), gained weight in the January 2005 UN Millennium

Project Report, *Investing in Development: A Practical Plan to Achieve the Millennium Development Goals*, which recommended structural changes in order to be able to reach Millennium Development Goal (MDG) 7, including the strengthening of governance and of competent agencies[3]
* Since the creation of UNEP in 1972, there have been attempts to strengthen environmental governance – and, in particular, following the Earth Summit in Rio de Janeiro in 1992 (where the UN Commission on Sustainable Development (CSD) was formed) and the Johannesburg Summit in 2002. These important efforts have been made at an international level. At Johannesburg, the heads of state and government stressed the importance of the institutional framework for sustainable development, and asked that the concrete recommendations adopted at the UNEP Governing Council in Cartagena in February 2002 be fully implemented. The goal of these recommendations is to strengthen UNEP so that it can fulfil its mandate as the principal agency for international environmental governance. UNEP duly initiated a process for the strengthening of environmental governance, when it decided in February 2002 to 'consider further measures for the strengthening of the United Nations Environment Programme in light of the outcome of the World Summit on Sustainable Development at its twenty-second session'. (UNEP, 2002). However, this crucial move does not go far enough
* At the present time, the international community is having difficulty in adequately responding to global phenomena that threaten or degrade the environment, as well as in providing sufficient support to countries that need it. This situation is made even more worrying by the fact that these challenges will only increase in the coming years.

Given this analysis, the French president proposed in September 2003 that a UNEO be put in place, based on the transformation of the present UNEP. A UNEO would strengthen the effectiveness, efficiency and coherence of international environmental governance by pursuing three objectives: giving more political weight to international environmental action, making this action more coherent, and allowing developing countries to devise and implement their national environment policies. In light of these objectives, the French proposal is grounded on three main guidelines:

1 the preservation of the environment as a key issue in the collective security of our planet;
2 the degradation of the environment as a threat to development;
3 the need for a multilateral response and a central role for the UN in this respect.

Numerous meetings of the working group have been held since its formation in February 2004. A meeting of foreign affairs ministers was held in New York on 22 September 2004. Several meetings of environment ministers were held during international meetings and, in particular, on 30 April, in the margin of CSD 12. Technical meetings were also held in Nairobi. The active participation by group members at all levels showed an interest in the future of IEG. The initial phase of the group's work (first half of 2004) was devoted to an analysis of the strengths, weaknesses, threats, and opportunities related to current IEG, and a report of these reflections was presented to the foreign affairs ministers on 22 September. The second phase (second half of 2004 and early 2005) was devoted to an initial analysis of concrete options for addressing the weaknesses that were identified in various areas. The group examined the added value that transforming UNEP into a UNEO could bring (French Government, 2005).

It became quickly apparent during these sessions that not all participating states supported the idea of questioning current IEG modalities; nevertheless, all accepted to discuss the issue. Some of those states proved to be ardent supporters of a UNEO. Others adopted a more wait-and-see, even sceptical, attitude. This diversity of viewpoints proved very useful because questions and objections helped fuel a debate that led to initial results, presented to foreign ministers in September 2004. The group made four observations of the present inadequacies of IEG, which corroborated, to a large extent, with diagnoses made by other bodies, and with the analysis I outlined at the beginning of this chapter:

- that there are problems of coherence and efficiency because of the increasing number of multilateral environmental agencies, resulting in fragmentation of effort;
- that there are significant gaps in scientific expertise, early warning systems and information provision;
- that the specific needs of developing countries are not adequately taken into account;
- that financing for the environment at the international level is marked by instability.

Having reached these conclusions, the group determined several key principles for building the future. Firstly, it was crucial to recognize that the current process for strengthening UNEP, and the prospect of transforming it into a UNEO, must be viewed as complementary in the long run. Secondly, in order to ensure coherence and continuity, the UNEO, like UNEP, should be headquartered in Nairobi. This would have the added attraction that the UNEO would become the first UN specialized agency to have its headquarters in a developing country. Thirdly, the legal autonomy of multilateral environmental agreements (MEAs) must be respected. And finally, the rationalization made possible by creating a UNEO should serve to mobilize additional resources for action – namely, for achieving the MDGs, which will be reviewed for the first time in September of this year.

The work conducted during the first phase also underscored two requirements relating to methodology:

- the need to analyse existing resources even more finely, in order to identify more accurately the shortcomings and inadequacies of the present network, and to highlight its positive aspects;
- the need to think in terms of value added by a UNEO so as to determine the more relevant solutions.

These rules of methodology are, in fact, going to be applied immediately: at the January 2005 Paris International Scientific Conference, 'Biodiversity: Science and Governance', the scientific community issued an appeal to governments, asking them to study the implementation of an international mechanism for strengthening scientific expertise in the field of biodiversity. How is one to organize all the competencies that can be marshalled to serve the scientific expertise useful to policy makers? This is one of the fundamental questions we are trying to answer by proposing the creation of a UNEO. To put it plainly, good governance needs to rely on knowledge.

In this respect, one point deserves particular emphasis: our efforts to encourage the creation of a UNEO is one aimed at giving coherence to expertise and to be carried out by the countries of the North and the South. Developing countries sometimes lack the resources to develop scientific expertise. In the countries of the South, moreover, environmental problems have specific features that deserve specific solutions. At its core, good governance calls for an effort at solidarity between the North and the South.

What is the next stage?

The objective behind the setting up of the informal working group on a UNEO was a clear one, namely putting the issue of International Environmental Governance on the UN's agenda. No doubt this objective has, in itself, been successful, given the prominence afforded the subject in the UN Secretary-General's March 2005 report, 'In Larger Freedom', in which he sets out the challenge for environmental governance:

> *It is now high time to consider a more integrated structure for environmental standard-setting, scientific discussion and monitoring treaty compliance. This should be built on existing institutions, such as the United Nations Environment Programme, as well as the treaty bodies and specialized agencies. Meanwhile, environmental activities at the country level should benefit from improved synergies, on both normative and operational aspects, between United Nations agencies, making optimal use of their comparative advantages, so that we have an integrated approach to sustainable development, in which both halves of that term are given their due weight.*

> *UN, 2005*

But while 'In Larger Freedom' is an important and welcomed step in keeping the issue on the international agenda, it should be clear from the perspective advanced by the Secretary-General that the idea of creating a UNEO does not currently enjoy universal support. As such, there is still much work to be done by the September summit to convince states of the merits of the French proposal. This can be achieved, at least in part, I believe, by advertising as widely as possible the results of the informal working group's conclusions, which should reflect as objectively as possible the positions of each of the 26 countries, and indicate the points of agreement and the options studied. But beyond diplomatic action, support from civil society is essential. International non-governmental organizations (NGOs) recently expressed their support for creating a UNEO. We must build on this support in mobilizing public opinion.

At the Davos World Economic Forum (2005), the French president suggested the holding in Paris of an international conference on corporate social and environmental responsibility. Corporations will certainly seize this opportunity to make their point of view heard on this important issue. Beyond this specific theme, we will have to take the opportunity to make them aware of this project, and even to convince them of its importance, a task recently lent prominence by President Chirac:

> *Support from the corporate world is crucial. I suggest to the Secretary-General of the United Nations that a meeting of the Global Compact be organized in Paris, in order to include as many companies as possible in this morally necessary struggle on which the very future of globalization depends...We want the peoples and the youth of the world to see a project for hope and progress in the globalized economy. For this to be the case, we must simultaneously set up, on a planetary scale, new forms of political governance and rules for the global market, as our predecessors did in the nineteenth and twentieth centuries on a national or continental scale.*
>
> *The history of Europe and the United States shows that there is a dynamic link between economic progress, supported by market rules secured by public authorities, social progress and democracy.*
>
> *It is up to us to strengthen global governance. This, together with development, will be the goal of the United Nations Summit in September.*

Chirac, 2005

What might the UNEO look like?

I am convinced that our first task is to communicate widely the viewpoint of the working group and place emphasis on requirements UNEO would be expected to meet. For my part, I have identified four such requirements:

First of all, it is essential for the steering authorities to be clearly identified. At the present time, UNEP and the Conference of Parties to the major environmental agreements are sharing power; no single body, however, is invested with the role of arbiter that is crucial for ensuring overall coherence, the first requirement to be met by UNEO.

Secondly, because financial resources, in particular, are scarce, it has become vital to rationalize and pool their use. The challenges we have to meet are so varied and great in number that they require significant resources. We should bear in mind the large number of multilateral agreements governing environmental issues, and that their areas of application sometimes overlap. In view of this, it should be possible to list those of their functions that may be pooled together. As all agreements would benefit from such a move, so would the environmental issues addressed by them. But who could implement such a rationalization, other than an 'authority' invested with the required legitimacy?

Thirdly, both the international community and public opinion need to get their bearings: given the complexity of the issues we are dealing with, in terms of the international environment, it is difficult for us to make the great majority of people understand their crucial importance; it is no easier to clarify who does what and how and for what purpose. Yet the environment is everyone's concern. Given the power of the media in a world such as ours, it is surprising that the environment should be denied institutional representation, like health (through the World Health Organization, WHO), culture (through the United Nations Educational, Scientific and Cultural Organization (UNESCO)), trade (through the World Trade Organization, WTO), and even intellectual property (through the World Intellectual Property Organization, WIPO).

Finally, with a view to sustainable development, it is important to build more balanced relations with the major international institutions. I am well aware that this is of particularly sensitive concern to some of our major partners. I think it would nonetheless be unrealistic to examine the issue of international environmental governance while disregarding the institutional context within which it is to be implemented. The principal institutions I mentioned – including the WTO, the WHO, and UNESCO – address, for their own specific purposes, issues relating closely to the environment. Yet what weight does the executive secretariat of a multilateral agreement truly carry when faced with these organizations? A UNEO would very likely help to establish more balanced relations and ensure that the voice of the environment was heard and noted.

Conclusion

The UNEO I hope to see emerge could be established in the form of an umbrella organization like the WIPO and offer existing or yet-to-be-negotiated MEAs a common reference point and action framework, while preserving their legal autonomy. A UNEO could hence perform certain cross-cutting functions with respect to the MEAs in question, such as the provision of conference services, early warning, communication, implementation monitoring, capacity-building, and so on. It could draw up a strategic work programme based on cross-cutting priorities common to the different conventions. Global-scope missions could be carried out by the UNEO Secretariat in consultation with the secretariats of the

MEAs concerned and in partnership with the competent UN bodies. Regional-scope missions could be implemented in a decentralized way.

The new agency would fulfil other missions in addition to those conducted today by UNEP. It would be in charge of coordinating implementation at the global and regional levels. It would define the strategic orientations discussed with the MEAs and presented to the Council of the Global Environment Facility (GEF). It would have the resources to monitor commitments made by states. It would establish a genuine capacity for scientific and technical expertise, and be responsible for systematically collecting information intended for an early-warning mechanism. It would be competent in areas such as that of renewable energies, which are inadequately addressed internationally.

Lastly, and above all, a UNEO should be provided with adequate and predictable resources. It should be desirable for it to be financed according to a system combining assessed contributions and unallocated voluntary contributions.

The reality is that the UNEO already exists, albeit at this stage merely as pieces of a jigsaw puzzle that is today incomplete. What needs to be done is to put the pieces together in order to provide its scattered bodies with a solid and durable architecture. President Chirac's remarks at the Eleventh Ambassadors' Conference in Paris in August 2003 perhaps provide the best incentive for this continuation of effort:

> *Given the looming threats, we want globalization to respect the environment. We need a world authority able to carry out a global ecological diagnosis, guarantee compliance with environmental protection principles and treaties and assist the developing countries. This mission should be vested in a United Nations environment agency.*

> *Chirac, 2003b*

Notes

1   'If we go on the way we have, the fault is our greed, and if we are not willing to change, we will disappear from the face of the globe, to be replaced by the insect'. Cousteau, J, quoted in *The Guardian* (2005) 'What a Dive'; http://film.guardian.co.uk/features/featurepages/0,4120,1411202,00.html

2   The countries involved in the informal intergovernmental working group are: Belgium, Brazil, Burkina Faso, Canada, China, Colombia, Czech Republic, France, Germany, India, Indonesia, Italy, Japan, Kenya, Luxembourg, Mexico, Morocco, Nicaragua, Nigeria, Norway, Senegal, South Africa, Sweden, Switzerland, United Kingdom, Vietnam, and the European Commission.

3   United Nations Millennium Project (2005) *Investing in Development: A Practical Plan to Achieve the Millennium Development Goals*, United Nations publication, Sales No. 05.III.B.4; see section of the report dealing with environmental sustainability; www.unmillenniumproject.org

References

Chirac, J. (2003a) Opening of the Fifty-eighth session of the United Nations General Assembly, speech by M. Jacques Chirac, President Of The Republic of France, 23 September, United Nations, New York

Chirac, J. (2003b) Address, by Jacques Chirac, President of the Frence Republic, on the occasion of the Eleventh Abbassadors' Conference, 29 August, www.info-france-usa.org/news/statmnts/2003/ambassadors_conference082903.asp

Chirac, J. (2005) Special Message at the World Economic Forum, Davos, Switzerland, by Jacques Chirac, President of the Republic of France, 26 January, www.weforum.org

French Government (2005) 'Concept of a UNEO' Ministry of Foreign Affairs, www.diplomatie.gouv.fr/frmonde/onue-en/onue66.html

UN (2000) *Millennium Declaration*, General assembly, 54th session, document A/RES/55/2, 18 September

UN (2004) *A more secure world: Our shared responsibility*, Report of the Secretary-General's High Lev-el Panel on Threats, Challenges and Change, document A/59/565, 2 December, United Nations, New York

UN (2005) *In Larger Freedom: Towards development, security and human rights for all*, Report of the Secretary-General, document A/59/2005, 21 March, United Nations, New York

UNEP (2002) Decision SS.VII/1 of the UNEP Governing Council adopted at its seventh special session in Cartagena, Colombia, on 15 February 2002, www.unep.org/dpdl/IEG/docs/IEG_decisionSS_VII_1.doc

19

Democracy in an Uncertain World

Felix Dodds

We are seeing the emergence of a new, much less formal structure of global governance, where governments and partners in civil society, private sector and others are forming functional coalitions across geographical boarders and traditional political lines to move public policy in ways that meet the aspirations of a global citizenry... These coalitions use the convening power and the consensus building, standard setting and implementation roles of the United Nations, the Bretton Woods Institutions and international organizations, but their key strength is that they are bigger than any of us and give new expression to the UN Charters 'We the people'.

Mark Malloch Brown, 1999

Introduction

It is striking just how much our map of the world has changed in the 15 years since the end of the Cold War. In 1990, the United Nations (UN) had as members 159 states; now, in 2005, it has 191, roughly a 20 per cent increase. So many new nations have come into existence, and even the older ones have undergone significant changes. Indeed, according to the *Hoover Digest*, in 1890, there was no country that would qualify as a democracy by today's standards, while as of January 2000, there were 120 democracies – the largest number in history (Diamond, 2000).

During the same period, two seemingly competing agendas have come into tension with one another – that of enriching society through sustainable human development, and that of the security agenda – exposing the very different nature of the threats and challenges the world now faces, compared with those prevalent at the time the UN was founded. Among these is the need for states to come to grips with the emergence and continuing dominance of the United States (US) as the sole superpower, which accounts for something like 40 per cent of the world's total military spending and currently displays a distressing ambivalence toward multilateralism in its international relations. But this is by no means the only or over-riding challenge, as the report of the Panel of Eminent Persons on UN-Civil Society Relations ('the Cardoso Report') makes clear:

> *Nations are no longer as unified by the imperatives of preventing future world wars, rebuilding devastated states and making colonies independent. Now the challenges range from terrorism to unilateralism and war, from pandemics and climate change to economic crisis and debt, from ethnic or sectarian tensions to international crime, from the universality of rights to respect for diverse cultures.*

> *UN, 2004a*

This changing geo-political landscape of the world coincided with the impacts of globalization, bringing with it new information technologies, low cost forms of communication, and an inevitable interconnection of global affairs. An obvious by-product of this development has been the rapid growth of global civil society, which has had a profound impact on the mechanisms of global governance and democratic practices. This point was recently emphasized by UN Secretary-General Kofi Annan:

> *The UN once dealt only with governments. But now we know that peace and prosperity cannot be achieved without partnerships involving governments, international organizations, the business community and civil society. In today's world, we depend on each other.*

> *Annan, 1999*

Despite the increasing acceptance of democracy on a state level, and the recognition of a multitude of actors on the international scene, the role of civil society – encompassing trade unions, professional associations, social movements, indigenous peoples' organizations, religious and spiritual organizations, academia and non-governmental organizations (NGOs) – remains somewhat ill-defined. The reality is that the combination of factors outlined above has ensured that we are living in an uncertain world in which our participatory, stakeholder democracy faces numerous challenges. The precise nature of these challenges, and the state of our democracy in the first decade of the 21st century, is the topic of discussion in this chapter.

Stakeholder democracy

Present-day global civil society perhaps materialized in 1992 with the UN Conference on Environment and Development (the Earth Summit, UNCED), where over 50,000 people from around the world descended on Rio de Janeiro to the Global Forum around Hotel Gloria and Flamenco Park. For the world community, it was reminiscent of Paris 1968, with teach-ins, lectures, workshops and conferences on the key global issues concerning sustainable development. It took place at a time of great hope and expectation, as perestroika (economic restructuring) and glasnost (openness) had seen the bipolar world of two competing superpowers give way to a great swell of people power and a firm belief that a new Utopia could be created. Such a desire for change was unsurprising and has in fact been apparent throughout history, as Oscar Wilde once reflected:

> *A map of the world that does not include Utopia is not worth even glancing at,*
> *for it leaves out the one country at which Humanity is always landing. And*
> *when Humanity lands there, it looks out, and always seeing a better country, sets*
> *sail. Progress is the realization of Utopias.*
>
> *Wilde, 1891*

But Rio was something of a high point of political achievement, and according to the Global Forum's organizer, Chip Lindner, 'it became the first international experiment in democratizing intergovernmental decision making'. It produced two legally binding conventions on climate change and biodiversity; agreement on these helped initiate four others negotiated after Rio, on desertification, straddling fish stocks, persistent organic pollutants and prior informed consent (PIC). The Rio Declaration also provided two sets of principles: the Forestry Principles and, of course, Agenda 21 – a 40-chapter 'blueprint for the Twenty First Century' on sustainable development.

Hidden and integrated in the text was a commitment to stakeholders. Indeed, the Rio Declaration became the first UN document to recognize explicitly that governments alone could not deliver the agreements, and identified roles and responsibilities for nine stakeholder groups in society. These were the first steps towards what I would call stakeholder democracy, and the first signs of what Chip Lindner determined as a move towards global democracy:

> *Given the problems that confront us as a community of nations and peoples, we*
> *are now more than ever bound together by a common destiny. And solutions to*
> *those problems will have to be found both nationally and internationally. That*
> *means that international institutions and national governments must become*
> *increasingly more accountable and responsive to the views and expectations of*
> *the world's peoples as a whole. Indeed, it means that as we approach the next*
> *century we must move even further in the direction of global democracy*
>
> *Lindner, 1993*

Of course, civil society is not homogeneous. Some use protest to put muchneeded pressure on governments to live up to their commitments and responsibilities, vividly expressed by the demonstrations at the G8, World Trade Organization (WTO) and World Bank meetings each year. Examples of more positive expressions might include through the Social Forum meetings in Port Alegre in Brazil, at Mumbai in India, and through a multitude of community and local solution-oriented approaches. But a good, albeit broad, definition of stakeholders might nonetheless be:

...those that have an interest in a particular decision, either as individuals or representatives of a group. This includes people who influence a decision, or can influence it, as well as those affected by it.

Dodds, 2002

It should also be remembered that, just as stakeholders reflect varying standpoints, political institutions evolve in response to dynamic processes and can therefore digress from original aims stated in documents, including Agenda 21, now over 12 years old. There is no question that the increasing involvement of stakeholders in the UN is in response to a need to change our form of democracy – people banding together in different forms to put forward their views is nothing new.

What is new, however, is the process of stakeholders pursuing their aims in an institutionalized fashion, a point seized on by Paul Hohnen, the former strategic Director of Greenpeace:

Multi-stakeholder processes (MSPs) are a new species in the political ecosystem. They will make mistakes. They will not solve all problems to everyone's satisfaction.

Hohnen, 2002

The idea that stakeholders basically use a space to be 'against something' – a government or an institution – is now redundant. Instead, we are seeing the evolution of a stakeholder space where stakeholders try to help governments and institutions make better decisions and then involve themselves in the implementation.

Box 19.1 Key principles and strategies of stakeholder democracy

Accountability: Employing agreed, transparent, democratic mechanisms of engagement, position finding, decision-making, implementation, monitoring, evaluation; making these mechanisms transparent to non-participating stakeholders and the general public.

Effectiveness: Providing a tool for addressing urgent sustainability issues; promoting better decisions by means of wider input; generating recommendations that have broad support; creating commitment through participants identifying with the outcome and thus increasing the likelihood of successful implementation.

Equity: Leveling the playing-field between all relevant stakeholder groups by creating dialogue (and consensus-building) based on equally valued contributions from all; providing support for meaningful participation; applying principles of gender, regional, ethnic and other balance; providing equitable access to information.

Flexibility: Covering a wide spectrum of structures and levels of engagement, depending on issues, participants, linkage into decision making, time-frame, and so on; remaining flexible over time while agreed issues and agenda provide for foreseeable engagement.

Good governance: Further developing the role of stakeholder participation and collaboration in (inter-) governmental systems as supplementary and complementary vis-à-vis the roles and responsibilities of governments, based on clear norms and standards; providing space for stakeholders to act independently where appropriate.

Inclusiveness: Providing for all views to be represented, thus increasing the legitimacy and credibility of a participatory process.

Learning: Requiring participants to learn from each other; taking a learning approach throughout the process and its design.

Legitimacy: Requiring democratic, transparent, accountable, equitable processes in their design; requiring participants to adhere to those principles.

Ownership: People-centred processes of meaningful participation, allowing ownership for decisions and thus increasing the chances of successful implementation.

Participation and engagement: Bringing together the principal actors; supporting and challenging all stakeholders to be actively engaged.

Partnership cooperative management: Developing partnerships and strengthening the networks between stakeholders; addressing conflictual issues; integrating diverse views; creating mutual benefits (win–win rather than win–lose situations); developing shared power and responsibilities; creating feedback loops between local, national or international levels and into decision making.

Societal gains: Creating trust through honouring each participant as contributing a necessary component of the bigger picture; helping participants to overcome stereotypical perceptions and prejudice.

Strengthening of intergovernmental institutions: Developing advanced mechanisms of (transparent, equitable, and legitimate) stakeholder participation strengthens institutions in terms of democratic governance and increased ability to address global challenges.

Transparency: Bringing all relevant stakeholders together in one forum and within an agreed process; publicizing activities in an understandable manner to non-participating stakeholders and the general public.

Voices, not votes: Making voices of various stakeholders effectively heard, without dis-empowering democratically elected bodies.

Source: Hemmati (2002)

The emergence of a stakeholder space

Dick Morris, an adviser to former US President Bill Clinton, in his book *The New Prince*, argues that we are moving from Madisonian democracy (representative) to Jeffersonian democracy (participatory) (Morris 1999). Although I support this broad direction, I would assert that we are in a phase of stakeholder democracy and that we are trying at various levels in society to develop the structures, vocabulary and institutions to embed this phase (see Box 19.1). I firmly believe that such developments will strengthen our democracy. The drop in voter turnout in many countries clearly demonstrates that people are no longer happy to just elect a politician for four or five years, trusting they will have the knowledge, the judgment and the foresight to take difficult decisions in a complicated world. The emergence of the stakeholder approach, in effect, is grounded on the realization that our present institutions – at all levels – are inadequate and have to change.

For stakeholders, a basic requirement is the assurance of checks and balances on governmental institutions. To this end, a new and important development in the last decade has been the cultivation of the stakeholder space. By this I mean the creative involvement of stakeholders working together with governments at all levels – local, provisional, national and international – to make better informed decisions and to develop and implement agreements.

At the international level, this debate on global governance and the role of stakeholders developed initially in an unstructured way. The first international body to recognize the role of relevant stakeholders was, in fact, the International Labour Organization (ILO), which, in 1919, set a model for tripartite representation from governments, employers and unions. In many ways, the stakeholder engagement we are currently experiencing therefore has a rich root in the oldest intergovernmental body. Several decades later, building on the momentum of Rio, the Commission on Global Governance in 1995 outlined that:

> *Global governance, once viewed primarily as concerned with intergovernmental relationships, now involves not only governments and intergovernmental institutions, but also NGOs, citizens' movements, transnational corporations, academia, and the mass media. The emergence of a global civil society, with many movements reinforcing a sense of human security, reflects a large increase in the capacity and will of people to take control of their own lives.*
>
> *Commission on Global Governance, 1995, p335*

Gradually though, this new approach gained a foothold in government circles. Political leaders, such as former President Clinton and UK Prime Minister Tony Blair, have flirted with the stakeholder approach. Clinton frequently referred to governments as 'the great facilitators' in speeches, recognizing a reduced role for governments. Taking a slightly different tack, Tony Blair's vision, outlined in a speech in Singapore in 1996, was of what he defined as a 'stakeholder economy':

> *The creation of an economy where we are inventing and producing goods and services of quality needs the engagement of the whole country. It must become a matter of national purpose and national pride. We need to build a relationship of trust, not just within a firm, but within a society. By trust I mean the recognition of mutual purpose for which we work together, and in which we all benefit. It is a stakeholder economy in which opportunity is available to all, advancement is through merit and from which no group or class is set apart or excluded. This is the economic justification for social cohesion, for a fair and strong society.*
>
> *Blair, 1996*

Although this was a vision outlined prior to Tony Blair's election in 1997, it resoundingly articulated New Labour's desire at that time for a new component to complement social democracy – part of defining the 'Third Way'. Like many social democratic parties in the post-Berlin Wall period, Blair and the Labour Party required a new approach. The weakness of the stakeholder concept, however, was that, in its infancy, it was not robust enough to survive a general election.

Had the stakeholder space been limited solely to the sustainable development discourse, then it might merely have been confined to the status of a footnote in history in the development of democracy. Fortunately, as John Pender points out in his book, *A Stake in the Future*, stakeholder democracy has a much broader appeal: 'the stakeholder solution provides an opportunity to tame the harsher aspects of capitalism' (Plender, 1997).

In effect, as demonstrated in Rio, we are witnessing the recognition that governments no longer – if they ever did – have the ability, on their own, to implement fully agreements to which they sign up. Society is made up of interacting forces – some economic, some institutional, some stakeholder focused, and some citizen based. This recognition of the stakeholder space can be a liberating one. But at the same time, it can be an unsettling one for politicians who, forced to accept that governments might not always know best, find themselves operating in an insecure and thus more frightening world of decision making.

Nevertheless, politicians at the highest level are conveying an acceptance of an emerging new role for stakeholders. What has become clear, however, is that the diplomacy of stakeholders is of a starkly different nature to that of governments. On the one hand, government diplomacy is based principally on the projection of national interest. By contrast, stakeholders are not restricted to national boundaries, and invariably adopt a broader view. Multi-stakeholder processes can therefore make decision-making processes more accountable and less frightening. At the same time, they boost the likelihood that agreements will be implemented, since the stakeholders themselves have been involved in the creation of the agreements. This is noticeably true in the area of the environment and development – issues that require common global responses – and in the drive for a global system of corporate social responsibility (CSR).

Stakeholder pressure for corporate social responsibility

Multinational companies have become a focus for criticism by many in civil society, often for good reason. Although governments negotiate international laws relevant to multinationals, as yet they are subject to only limited and ineffective global regulation in many spheres, including the environment. Non-governmental organizations (NGOs) have long been calling for a global UN Convention on CSR. Despite the recent spate of corruption scandals in large US-based companies – resulting in tougher national legislation in a number of countries – the current US administration seems uninterested in addressing the issue of global corporate regulation, which in any case would take many years to develop.

There are many creative initiatives designed to encourage adherence to common human rights, social and labour standards such as the UN Global Compact. That said, one of the new and exciting areas being reviewed at present is a multi-stakeholder approach to hard law. There is a need for effective implementation of present environmental law and sustainable development principles, a process that necessitates an independent body. An existing example of this is the International Court of Environmental Arbitration in San Sebastian, which is inviting corporations and other stakeholders to engage in developing a multi-stakeholder hard law instrument. The court would offer a hard law option for companies and stakeholders that were serious about CSR and international law. It would concurrently put pressure on those that chose not to sign up and perhaps create the first international stakeholder convention. The obvious advantage to this approach would be an independent international court outside national jurisdiction that could be trusted by all parties. Although it is too early to assess realistically the merits of this approach, some stakeholders, including multinational companies, are seriously considering the attributes of such a court.

Post-11 September challenges to democracy

The Cardoso Report of 2004 called for a system-wide change to UN-civil society relations based on the increasing desire of stakeholders for democratic accountability:

> *Concerning democracy, a clear paradox is emerging: while the substance of politics is fast globalizing (in the areas of trade, economics, environment, pandemics, terrorism, and so on), the process of politics is not; its principal institutions (elections, political parties and parliaments) remain firmly rooted at the national or local level. The weak influence of traditional democracy in matters of global governance is one reason why citizens in much of the world are urging greater democratic accountability of international organizations...Today it is increasingly likely that a civil society movement and a crescendo of public opinion will bring a new issue to global attention, and that initial action on new issues will be taken through multi-constituency coalitions of governments,*

civil society and others. Increasingly, multilateralism includes ongoing processes of public debate, policy dialogue and pioneering action to tackle emerging challenges.

UN, 2004a

In reality, however, the chances of such a wholesale reform of stakeholder engagement is limited given the post 11 September, 2001 climate. In truth, the real or perceived threats of the post-9/11 world have seen governments clamour to tighten their grip on national security, a move with dangerous implications for human rights, civil liberties, and democratic practices. Put at its most basic: when the world is dominated by a sole superpower, the way that it responds to threats and challenges, and the way it projects its authority, reverberates not only at home, but throughout the rest of the world.

Across the world the response in the weeks and months following 9/11 was an outpouring of enormous sympathy and support for the American people, and at home an increased sense of unity and national pride, encapsulated by Tim Robbins in his 2003 speech to the National Press Club:

> *For all the ugliness and tragedy of 9/11, there was a brief period afterwards where I held a great hope. In the midst of the tears and shocked faces of New Yorkers, in the midst of the lethal air we breathed as we worked at Ground Zero, in the midst of my children's terror at being so close to this crime against humanity, in the midst of all of this, I held onto a glimmer of hope in the naïve assumption that something good could come out of all this. I imagined our leaders seizing upon this moment of unity in America, this moment when no one wanted to talk about Democrat versus Republican, white versus black, or any of the other ridiculous divisions that dominate our public discourse.*

Robbins, 2003

Just a few days after 9/11, the European preparatory meeting in Geneva was held for the Johannesburg World Summit on Sustainable Development (WSSD). Stakeholders invited the US delegation to discuss the agenda. Time after time, stakeholders, before beginning their questions, first expressed words of sympathy for the families who had lost loved ones and to the American people more broadly.

Not too long afterwards, however, this unity of purpose crumbled, and as the war on terror gained momentum, President Bush offered a stark choice for governments around the world when he declared 'You are either with us or against us' (Bush 2001). As the months passed, governments started to introduce legislation to restrict the liberties of people and organizations. In Russia for instance, President Putin declared that the US and Russia have a common foe because 'Bin Laden's people are connected with the events currently taking place in Chechnya' (Glasius and Kaldor, 2002). Meanwhile, in Zimbabwe, six journalists were arrested because of their reporting on the political violence taking place there. A government spokesman announced that the journalists would be treated as terrorists:

As for the correspondents, we would like them to know that we agree with US President Bush that anyone who, in any way, finances, harbours or defends terrorists is himself a terrorist. We, too, will not make any difference between terrorists and their friends and supporters.

Glasius and Kaldor, 2002

It should have been unsurprising to find the veil of the war on terrorism being used in this manner, given the nature of political sentiment emanating from the US itself. In December 2001, US Attorney General John Ashcroft had gone as far as to declare to the US Senate Judiciary Committee that any act of opposition to the antiterrorist measures would be considered an unpatriotic act. The previous month, President Bush had given the go-ahead to institute military commissions that can arrest, try, convict and even execute any foreign national designated by the president as a suspected terrorist, without access to a lawyer, without the presumption of innocence, and without the right to appeal except to the president himself (Glasius and Kaldor, 2002).

As the state justifies its increase in *security apparatchiks*, we see the institution of surveillance devices to monitor the internet, email and telephone conversations, as well as the expanded use of closed-circuit cameras and iris scanning and finger printing as we arrive in the US. In the UK, however, a first attempt to introduce identity cards met with virulent resistance sufficient to force a shelving of the issue.

The report of the High Level Panel on Threats, Challenges and Change calls for the negotiation of a comprehensive convention on terrorism (UN, 2004b). I would urge governments to err on the side of caution in respect of this recommendation. Not too long ago, people such as Michael Collins (the first president of Ireland), Nelson Mandela, Menachem Begin, Vladimir Lenin and George Washington were considered terrorists in some quarters. The age-old difficulty in deciding whether someone is a terrorist or a freedom fighter is very much one to bear in mind as this recommendation is taken forward for debate. Remember, it was Barry Goldwater, the Republican presidential nominee, in his acceptance speech, July 16, 1964, who said:

I would remind you that extremism in the defense of liberty is no vice. And let me also remind you that moderation in the pursuit of justice is no virtue.

Goldwater, 1964

For stakeholders, the events of 9/11 have ushered in a feeling of uncertainty, but with it an immense air of responsibility. Stakeholder Forum with the Heinrich Boll Foundation conducted an online debate on the implications of 9/11 for the WSSD. In the afterword of the resulting publication, Kurt Klotzle said:

Yet, despite the apparent monumentality of events on and pursuant to that day, civil society actors must not lose sight of the fact that they can and must influence policy making decisions at the local, national, regional and global levels.

> *One crucial component of civil society efforts is the promotion of an open and democratic international public debate that encourages both the free expression of ideas as well as increased international exchange and understanding.*
>
> Klotzle, 2001

In a democratic society, how much intrusion from the state will we accept? Maybe developing a society based on more advanced forms of democracy will prove an effective counterbalance that helps to build trust and overcome fear.

Tomorrow's agenda

The *threats* facing the world today are very real, and need addressing both directly and at their roots causes. Our *challenge* – a challenge relevant to governments and stakeholders – must be to create the political will to deal with both. Realizing and achieving the Millennium Development Goals (MDGs) will go a long way to addressing the root causes. The Millennium Development Summit in 2000 tried to bring together the lessons of the 1990s and to focus on a critical agenda that governments, the UN and stakeholders could work together to deliver. Underlying all of this is the attack on poverty. The link between poverty and civil war – expressed so competently in the research of Macartan Humphreys of Columbia University – showed that the predictability of civil war was about 12 per cent where income was less than US$1 a day; this figure fell to under 6 per cent if people had at least US$1 a day (UN, 2004a). The report identified that the impact of 9/11 alone increased the number of people in poverty by 10 million.

The five-year review of the MDGs in September 2005 will be of critical importance in bringing together decision makers and providing the stakeholder space for action in response to today's challenges. The review summit will focus, in particular, on the recommendations of the UN Secretary-General's report 'In Larger Freedom', which sets out with authority the human and environmental security agenda we as stakeholders must address.

But looking beyond September 2005, it is crucial that as we seek ways to reinvent our democracy and address the challenges of the post-9/11 world, the advances in stakeholder democracy of the 1990s and early 21st century must to be built on. Institutions that have yet to embrace stakeholder participation at the global level – such the World Bank, International Monetary Fund (IMF) and WTO – should be persuaded to do so.

These *changes* demand an opening up, not a closing down, of our societies. The creation of a strong democracy is one that needs an ever vigilant and vibrant civil society. The world will always have many different visions of the societies we want to create, as the human imagination has immense capability. The involvement of all stakeholders is one way of harnessing this capability, a vision best summed up by Robert Kennedy:

Each time a person stands up for an ideal, or acts to improve the lot of others, or strikes out against injustice, they send forth a tiny ripple of hope, and crossing each other from a million different centers of energy and daring, those ripples build a current that can sweep down the mightiest walls of oppression and resistance.

Kennedy, 1966

References

Annan, K. (1999) Address to the World Economic Forum, Davos, Switzerland, www.globalpolicy.net/UNandGPP.htm

Blair, T. (1996) Speech to the Singapore Business Community, January, www.psa.org.nz

Bush, G. (2001) Address to a Joint Session of Congress and the American People, 20 September, www.whitehouse.gov/news/releases/2001/09/20010920-8.html

Commission on Global Governance (1995) *Our Global Neighbourhood*, Commission on Global Governance, Oxford University Press, Oxford

Diamond, L. (2000) 'A report card on democracy', *Hoover Digest 2000*, No 3, Hoover Institution, www.hooverdigest.org/003/diamond.html

Dodds, F. (2002) 'The context: Multi-stakeholder processes and global governance', in Hemmati, M., *Multi-Stakeholder processes for Governance and Sustainability: Beyong Deadlock and Conflict*, Earthscan, London, pp26–38

Glasius, M. and Kaldor, M. (2002) *The State of Global Civil Society 2002*, Oxford University Press, Oxford

Goldwater, B. (1964) Acceptance Speech, 1964, Republican National Convention, Cow Palace, San Francisco, www.nationalcenter.org/Goldwater.html

Hemmati, M. (2002) *Multi-Stakeholder Processes for Governance and Sustainability: Beyond Deadlock and Conflict*, Earthscan, London

Hohnen, P. (2002) 'One step beyond multi-stakeholder processes', in Hemmati, M., *Multi-Stakeholder Processes for Governance and Sustainability: Beyond Deadlockand Conflict*, Earthscan, London

Kennedy, R. (1966) 'A tiny ripple of hope' a speech in Cape Town, South Africa, in MacArthur, B., *The Penguin Book of Twentieth Century Speeches*, Penguin, London

Klotzle, K. (2001) *Road to Johannesburg after September 11*, Heinrich Boll Foundation, Berlin

Lindner, C. (1993) *The Earth Summit's Agenda for Change*, Centre for Our Common Future, Geneva (reprinted 2005 in *The Plain Language Guide to theWorld Summit on Sustainable Development*, Earthscan, London, pviii)

Malloch Brown, M. (1999) *UNDP Human Development Report*, Oxford University Press, New York

Morris, D. (1999) *The New Prince*, Renaissance Books, Los Angeles

Plender, J. (1997) *Stake in the Future: The Stakeholding Solution*, Nicholas Brealey Publishing, London

Robbins, T. (2002) 'A Chill Wind is Blowing in This Nation', Speech to National Press Club, Washington DC, April 15 2002, www.referralblast.com/cs/com/co1.asp

UN (1992) *Agenda 21* UN, New York, Chapters 24–32)

UN (2004a) *Report of the Panel of Eminent Persons on United Nations–Civil Society Relations*, United Nations, New York

UN (2004b) *A more secure world: Our shared responsibility*, Report of the Secretary-General's High Level Panel on Threats, Challenges and Change, document A/59/565, United Nations, New York

Wilde, O. (1891) *The Soul of Man Under Socialism in Selected Essays and Poems*, Penguin, London (republished in 1954)

Appendix

Stakeholder Forum

Stakeholder Forum is a multi-stakeholder organization, which has been working to further the implementation of the sustainable development agenda since 1992. The organization operates at the national, regional and international levels, involving local government, trade unions, industry, NGOs, women's groups, youth, academics and regional governments. Within its remit, Stakeholder Forum engages in a range of activities: providing space for dialogue and policy development between stakeholders; researching and influencing policy development; providing and spreading information on the intergovernmental agenda; and training and capacity building. In addition, we work closely with UN agencies addressing environment and development issues by facilitating access to their processes and raising awareness of their work with civil society. These agencies include the UN Commission on Sustainable Development, the UN Environment Programme and the World Health Organization.

Stakeholder Forum has played a significant role in the development of a number of multi-stakeholder dialogues and processes at the UN and at intergovernmental meetings, including:

- the UN Commission on Sustainable Development
- the Second World Water Forum
- the Informal Environmental Ministers Meeting
- the WHO London European Health and Environmental Conference
- the Bonn International Freshwaters Conference
- the Bonn International Renewable Energy Conference.

To promote the work of sustainable development Stakeholder Forum has two publications: a monthly online newsletter 'Network 2005'; and 'Outreach 2005', a daily news bulletin released at UN meetings.

In its partnership with Earthscan, Stakeholder Forum has brought out eight other books:

1997 *The Way Forward: Beyond Agenda 21*
1998 *Earth Summit II: Outcomes and Analysis*

1999 *Poverty in Plenty: A UK Human Development Report*
2000 *Earth Summit 2002: A New Deal*
2002 Multistakeholder Processes on Governance and Sustainability Beyond Deadlock and Conflict
2004 *How to Lobby at Intergovernmental Meetings: Mine is a Café Latte*
2005 *Plain Language Guide to World Summit on Sustainable Development*
2005 *Governance for Sustainable Development*

Stakeholder Forum for a Sustainable Future
3 Bloomsbury Place
London WC1A 2QL
UK
Tel: +44 (0) 207 580 6912
Email: info@stakeholderforum.org
Website: www.stakeholderforum.org

Index